BUSINESS MODELS

Investing In Companies And Sectors With Strong Competitive Advantage

By DAVID WATSON

Produced in Association with The Serious Investor Groups network

HARRIMAN HOUSE LTD

43 Chapel Street
Petersfield
Hampshire
GU32 3DY
GREAT BRITAIN

Tel: +44 (0)1730 233870
Fax: +44 (0)1730 233880
email: enquiries@harriman-house.com
web site: www.harriman-house.com

First published in Great Britain in 2005

ISBN 1-897-59758-4

British Library Cataloguing in Publication Data

A CIP catalogue record for this book can be obtained from the British Library.

Printed and bound in the United Kingdom by Ashford Overload Services, Southampton.

Contents

Index of tables

About the author

David Watson read a bachelor's and master's degree in economics and finance at Manchester University. He is a Fellow of the Institute of Chartered Accountants, qualifying with Price Waterhouse in London. He has extensive UK and international business experience, principally in financial services and media, and was Deputy Editor of *Investing for Growth*, an investment newsletter devised by Jim Slater, author of *The Zulu Principle*. He welcomes comment and feedback and can be e-mailed at businessmodels@gmail.com.

Internet access

Extracts from this book can be accessed on the internet at:

The Serious Investor Groups network's website: www.signet.org.uk

The Harriman House website: www.harriman-house.com/businessmodels

Acknowledgements

I would like to thank Stephen Beesley, Caroline Churton, Dean Collins, Ann Corrigan, Dr. John Dilworth, Bill Erasmus, Malcolm Green, Gerry Faulds, Bill Hughes, Ravi Jesubatham, John Lander, Jeff Perrin, Peter Phillips, Christopher Pratt, Evangeline Rahming, John Read, Jim Steel and David Wash for their valuable help and advice in editing and contributing to this book. Thank you, too, to everybody at Harriman House who helped on the book, especially to Stephen Eckett, Myles Hunt, Nick Read, Laura Barker and Claire Wright. I would also like to acknowledge the work carried out with Nigel Milton, the Editor of *Investing for Growth*, on various business models used in this book.

Foreword

I am delighted as Chairman of The Serious Investor Groups network (SIGnet) to contribute a foreword to Business Models as I believe this book fills an important gap. Hitherto, investors have employed various traditional methods in deciding which shares to buy and sell. These methods include fundamental and technical analysis and relying on press recommendations. What has been missing has been an assessment of business models of companies and sectors to ascertain their competitive advantage. This is crucial as the latter will be reflected in their profitability and share prices in due course.

In previous literature, references to business models have been non-existent, at worst, or superficial, at best. Not any more, as this book comprehensively analyses business models, enabling an investor to understand the business and help to see the future. Not only that, but it contains three tables that enable a company or sector to be scored very quickly.

The author analyses 64 company business models and 65 sector business models according to six yardsticks: competitors, customers, economics, management, products and suppliers. The business models are ranked in importance and include first-mover advantage, bolt-on acquisitions, owning the standard, size, and 'make once, sell many times'. Usefully, there are hundreds of examples of companies and sectors.

He stresses that competitive advantage can only be achieved with low cost activities and/or doing something different from the competition. This difference must add value to the customer who then pays a premium price. Companies lacking competitive advantage because they have the same costs and/or do the same as the competition are best avoided.

Of particular value, in my view, is an assessment of the economic cycle and when sectors should be bought or sold. Being aware of these macro forces is often the key to successful investing.

Business Models offers a complete set of investment tools, as it also covers share valuations, technical analysis, scuttlebutting and 'accounting for growth'. An investor's worst enemy is often the person he sees in the mirror and the chapter on investment axioms is a useful reminder of the 'do's and don'ts' learnt the hard way by gurus. These robust tools are brought together in a succinct conclusion.

I am now confident that investors will be able to find companies and sectors with excellent business models that are anticipated to prosper. With its wealth of content, this is a book that should be kept at hand for regular reference, especially as the economic cycle unfolds.

Business Models is the first book to have been produced in association with SIGnet and several of its members have been contributors. We wish it well as it is a new and valuable addition to the font of investors' knowledge.

John Lander, Fellow of the Institute of Directors,

SIGnet Chairman.

Glossary

Beta

Beta measures how much a share price movement correlates with a movement in the stock market. A high beta share has a value over 1.0 and its price has historically increased or decreased more than that of the market. A low beta share has a value under 1.0 and its price has historically increased or decreased less than the market. Betas are shown in Yahoo Finance under each company's details, as well as in REFS (Really Essential Financial Statistics).

Business model of a company

A business model describes a company's operations, including all of its components, functions and processes, which result in costs for itself and value for the customer. Its goal is to achieve low cost and differentiate itself from the competition. This depends on having good economics, management and products, plus power over customers, competitors and suppliers, which result in strong competitive advantage.

Business model of a sector

A business model describes a sector's competitive advantage and is derived from a set of factors or capabilities that allows consistent outperformance. This depends on having good economics, management and products plus power over customers, competitors and suppliers, which result in strong competitive advantage.

CEO

Chief Executive Officer.

Commodity product

Commodity products, such as sugar and steel, lack differentiation. Price is the single most important factor determining a purchase and competition is intense. The low-cost producer triumphs and the quality of management is crucial.

Contrarian

An investor who does the opposite of what most investors are doing at any particular time.

Dead cat bounce

A quick, moderate rise in the price of a share following a precipitous decline.

Defensive

A defensive company has inelastic demand and is recession resistant.

Differentiation

One of the two ways to achieve competitive advantage is for the company to do something different from the competition that adds value to the customer and can take place anywhere in its value chain. It is most obvious in the end product but could be in logistics, management, quality of inputs, delivery times, etc.

EPS

Earnings per share, after tax, are the amount attributable to the shareholder to pay as dividends or retained in the company.

Factors of production

The four factors of production are land, labour, capital and enterprise, and contribute to the production of a product or service.

Gearing

Debt financing, and is another word for leverage.

Goodwill

Goodwill is an intangible asset that cannot be touched or counted. It may provide a competitive advantage, such as a strong brand, reputation and expertise. Purchased goodwill is the difference between the cost of buying a company and the book value of its net assets.

Gorilla

A gorilla is a dominant company, usually a blue chip, and is typically overvalued with modest growth prospects.

He

For purposes of brevity, 'he' includes 'she'.

KISS

Keep It Simple, Stupid.

Leverage

Debt financing, and is another word for gearing.

Long

Being long means investing in a share or market. The opposite is being short, as explained below.

Low-cost activities

One of the two ways of achieving competitive advantage is for the company to have low-cost activities in its value chain. Differentiation is the other way.

Low-ticket items

Low-ticket items are products or services that sell at a low price.

PER

Price earnings ratio.

Player

A player is a company in a sector.

Product

A product is not just a physical good but can also include a service.

Reach

Reach is the ability of a company or sector to operate nationally or globally.

Scalable

A scalable business can easily and quickly expand to meet increased demand.

Scuttlebutt

Scuttlebutt means assessing a product or company by testing it for yourself through empirical observation.

Short

Short means selling shares that an investor, or 'shorter', does not own. The expectation is that the share price will have fallen below the investor's agreed selling price when the contract is settled. He can then buy the shares to cover the contract and make a profit.

Sticky customer

A sticky customer tends to continue to buy from a company because of factors such as habits, inertia, switching cost or lack of knowledge.

Stop loss

An order to a broker to sell when the price of a security falls to a designated level. This locks in a profit or stops further losses being incurred.

Transactional

Transactional customers are one-off, as compared to repeat customers.

TMT mania

TMT was the technology, media and telecommunications mania that ended in 2000.

Value added

Value added means that the company has combined its inputs in a way that creates demand from the customer and results in profit. It can be created anywhere in its value chain.

Value chain

The value chain is all the activities and costs of a firm in the entire production process from the initial receipt of inputs, then processing and resulting in the final output.

Introduction

129 business models

'Between every individual and his tomorrow a veil is drawn. There are ways by which this veil can be penetrated to some extent.'

Laurence Sloan, author of *Everyman and his Common Stocks*.

Mankind has three main goals in life: seeing the future, amassing wealth and living forever. They are recurring themes in novels and films, as well as in people's private lives and thoughts. This book occupies the space of the first two of these, as it should enable an investor to see the future performance of a company and, in doing so, increase his wealth. Living forever is left to others.

This book is different from other investment books because it breaks new ground by assessing the business models of companies and sectors. It provides critical tools that enable an investor to assess whether a company's business model leads to strong competitive advantage and if it is in a sector that, in turn, also has strong competitive advantage. It casts a keen eye on the economic cycle, the ultimate arbiter of an investor's success or failure. Other important tools are growth at a reasonable price, technical analysis, scuttlebutting, accounting for growth and investment axioms. The 129 business models are used to analyse companies and sectors. For example, a company may be in a favourable sector but has frittered away this tailwind through incompetence. Likewise, it may be superbly run and very profitable in spite of being in a dreary sector. These tools are designed to unearth the very best companies to outperform in a bull market. They should also thrive in a bear market and minimise the chance of a profit warning. Thus, the investor has a real advantage over those who lack this knowledge.

Summary of this book

The first four chapters are the most important.

Chapter 1. Business models: investing in companies with strong competitive advantage

This chapter is the core of the book and examines 64 business models. The aim is to choose companies that have sound business models. This is achieved by having low costs and/or doing something different that adds value to the customer. The result is strong competitive advantage, leading to superior profits.

Chapter 2. Business models: investing in sectors with strong competitive advantage

Having selected companies with sound business models, the next step is to ensure that they are in attractive sectors by examining 65 business models leading to strong competitive advantage. Both the company and the sector should have the ability to mould the economic world their way rather than being under the power of others. We also examine companies and sectors that should be avoided. If a company does not have a sound business model in a sector with strong competitive advantage then it can be readily dismissed. If it does pass the test, then further consideration can be justified, as discussed in the remaining chapters.

Chapter 3. Shifting deck chairs on The Titanic

The company's attractions are further strengthened by being in a favourable place in the economic cycle. Buying and selling at the right stage of the cycle and moving between different asset classes is a prime determinant of investment success. Ignoring the economic cycle is like pointlessly shifting deck chairs on The Titanic to obtain a better position, oblivious of the iceberg ahead.

Chapter 4. Which sectors to buy and sell during the economic cycle

Each of the sectors is scored according to its recession resistance and competitive advantage. Having identified those that offer the greatest investment opportunity, they are then assessed according to when they should be bought and sold during the economic cycle.

Chapter 5. Growth at a reasonable price

The share must offer growth at a reasonable price. Seek to invest in established companies that have a reasonable PER combined with profits growing strongly and at a sustainable rate.

Chapter 6. Technical analysis of the company and sector

The trend in the price graph is your friend, so aim to buy shares that are rising and sell those that are falling. The relative strength of the share is a proxy for technical analysis and is a very important tool.

Chapter 7. First-hand experience of the product or scuttlebutting

First-hand experience of the product or 'scuttlebutting' can be very useful in detecting early warning or success signs that the City has not spotted.

Chapter 8. Accounting for growth

In a world of spin and declining financial morality, it is important to understand what the financial results really mean and how to avoid companies which 'account for growth' in order to mislead the unwary.

Chapter 9. Investment axioms

The investment axioms, or rules, summarise a total of 1,000 years of trading experience from 35 of the greatest investment gurus. These valuable lessons should enable you to avoid pitfalls and enhance your gains.

Conclusion

This book sets out six tools to help investors choose shares that outperform. These tools are wrapped up in a simple table to rate a company's attractiveness overall.

Summary

This methodology may seem a tall order in choosing to buy and sell shares but a familiarity with these tools is invaluable in asking the right sort of questions. For example, if you rely on a professional advisor, such as a broker, ask him the next time he recommends a share: what is the business model of the company and sector and do they have strong competitive advantage? Is this share well positioned in the economic cycle? Does it offer growth at a reasonable price? Is the share price in an up trend? Is there any accounting for growth? Do not be surprised if there is deathly silence at the other end of the phone, in which case you should go elsewhere.

A moderate grasp of this methodology should enable the private or professional investor to correctly evaluate a company in 15 minutes and dismiss the vast majority in much less time. This is how long an evaluation can take Warren Buffett, who uses business model analysis to avoid commodity businesses and invest in companies with strong competitive advantage.

CHAPTER 1

Business models: investing in companies with strong competitive advantage

What is a business model?

'Competitive advantage is based not on doing what others already do well but on doing what others cannot do as well.'
John Kay, economist.

A business model describes a company's operations, including all of its components, functions and processes, which result in costs for itself and value for the customer. Therefore, it is how the engine of the business actually works. The objective is to have low cost and high value and thus maximise profit. All attractive business models will have some magical secret or 'pixie dust' and the investor's task is to find it. More importantly, it is to discover the pixie dust that others cannot see. A company's strategy of combining the four factors of production, namely land, labour, capital and enterprise, will determine its unique business model, the superiority of which over the competition is a crucial determinant of sustainable, competitive advantage. The ability of a company to achieve this is largely determined by the competitive advantage of the sector, which is discussed in chapters 2 and 4.

Business models are not a new phenomenon. They have existed since time immemorial, whether it was the success of the Roman Empire, Christopher Columbus' discovery of the New World or the advent of the industrial revolution. For example, an excellent and simple business model was the monasteries in Britain. They usually received a free grant of land from a pious king and set up shop. The land was expanded by gifts from local landowners, such as knights, who had an eye on the afterlife. It was grazed by sheep that added great value just by eating what nature provided free. All that was needed was to cut white gold off their backs. This enabled fabulous monasteries to be built and furthered their expansion and power. This virtuous circle continued for centuries until eventually these tycoons owned two million acres or a fifth of all cultivated land. There were 600 establishments with 40,000 people, enjoying a mouth-watering income, given their strong competitive advantage. Then Henry VIII and rapacious politicians decided to confiscate them and sell the assets to private individuals in an early form of privatisation.

Why are business models so important?

An attractive business model (also called a franchise by some people, like Warren Buffett) is of crucial importance in choosing winners. It can only be achieved in two ways, both of which management must comprehend and sustain:

a. Low cost

If a company has the same costs as competitors, then it will have the same profits. Superior profits will, however, be earned if costs are lower and bite less into revenues. Therefore, the strategy is to have the lowest-cost business model compared to the competition. This can be done in a variety of different ways, such as by being number one in the sector, having excellent management, a modest head office, power over suppliers, and superior raw materials, buying skills, technology and quality control. There are trade-offs, so, for example, cost savings on quality of inputs may lead to more product rejects, thus increasing overall cost. Value is added to the customer if his costs are lowered and this can be achieved through a variety of means, such as increased reliability, being easier to use and therefore needing less training, an extended free warranty or insurance, cheap financing and just-in-time delivery.

b. Different

A company should strive to do something different from the competitors in its 'value chain', which is all the activities and costs in the entire production process from the initial receipt of inputs, then processing and resulting in the final output. If it does the same as competitors, then customers have no reason to prefer it and it will earn the same, rather than superior, profits. The value the company captures from differentiation depends on the price charged and profit margin earned, rather than the cost borne by the customer. Thus, if a company succeeds in erecting high barriers to entry then it could charge a premium price and earn a high profit margin. However, the cost borne by the customer would be higher than if the barriers did not exist.

Companies often focus on creating differentiation in their product, but it can be done anywhere in the value chain, which encompasses competitors, customers, economics, management and suppliers. However, product differentiation is singled out because of its prime importance to the customer. It must be valuable to him, either by lowering his cost and/or increasing the utility of the product. Either way, if it offers better value it will be bought instead of the competition's product. The differentiation must be both real and understood by the customer. For example, there could be a wonderful product but the customer may be oblivious of its benefits. There are trade-offs, so, for example, a firm may focus on improving reliability but also cut back on the length of the guarantee. Consequently, the product is better but the customer may be unaware of this and choose a substitute with a longer guarantee.

Sources of product differentiation include advertising, customer care, management, delivery time, guarantee, quality, reliability, reputation and service. One example of a differentiated product is the BBC. It does not have irritating advertisements and has two terrestrial channels so it can readily cater for minority audiences.

Companies that do something different in their value chain are attractive investments and are contrasted with commodity products and commodity-type businesses. Commodity products, such as sugar and steel, are indistinguishable from one another and so lack differentiation. Price is the single most important factor determining a purchase and competition is intense. The low-cost producer triumphs and the quality of management is crucial. Companies can have commodity-type businesses where little value is added and price competition is paramount, such as box-shifting distributors. Such activities are unattractive and should be avoided as they have poor competitive advantage. The future belongs to those companies that have products containing less material and more thought. This combination is often difficult but it frustrates the competition and is more highly prized by customers.

The holy grail

'When I was young I used to think that wealth and power would bring me happiness. I was right.'
Gahan Wilson, cartoonist.

Competitive advantage stems from low cost and/or differentiation. The holy grail is for the extra cost of being different to be less than the premium price charged to customers. If the extra cost is higher than the premium price, then profits will be less than those of competitors. For example, a restaurant chef may want to use top quality ingredients to produce superb food but the extra cost may exceed the higher price charged, thus leading to lower profits.

There can be trade-offs between lower costs and being different. A bar may serve cheap, unbranded drinks to lower costs but customers might reject the taste or image, thus reducing the ability of the firm to differentiate itself. Firms should concentrate on finding out what really matters to customers and satisfy those wants that cost little or nothing to provide. Thus, a software company may discover that customers really want technical support and this could be satisfied by a trouble-shooting page on the internet at minimal cost, rather than a telephone support centre.

All-weather shares not share price killers

The combination of low cost and motivated customers choosing to buy from a company, rather than a competitor, and at a premium price means it will have strong competitive advantage. This results in superior, sustainable and growing profits. The operating risk of the company will also tend to be low and the predictability of profits should be greatly enhanced. The strong control over revenues means that the share should be resilient throughout the economic cycle and, as such, will be more suitable for 'all-weather' not just 'fair-weather' stock markets. This minimises the chance of profit warnings, which are share price killers. Companies with no competitive advantage are hammered in a bear market, whereas those with strong competitive advantage tend to be de-rated much less and are quick to recover. Note that competitive advantage stems from what companies do, rather than from such 'advantages' as being a 'gorilla' (blue chip company) or having a leading market share. This is a common misconception, although these advantages could be important if the companies had a low-cost or differentiated business model.

A strong business model also means that if the share price weakens then an investor should be confident that the setback is likely to be temporary because the company is sound. He will be less worried about selling at the first whiff of a falling share price. This is because buyers will be tempted back and thus push up the low share price. It is also a buying opportunity for contrarians, who are investors that do the opposite of what most investors are doing at any particular time. Some companies have better business models than others within a sector, just as some sectors have greater competitive advantage than others. Both are subject to constant change and this can happen swiftly. The mission is to find companies with excellent business models in the best sectors, which are likely to be comprised of many profitable companies that have low costs and/or different activities that add value to the customer. However, there can be profitable companies in unattractive sectors and vice versa.

64 company business models

Sixty-four company business models are now examined in detail and, although this list is not exhaustive, it is designed to cover the main points. Six factors determine the strength of a business model that gives a company its competitive advantage, which is achieved through low cost or differentiation. These factors are: having good economics, management and products, plus power over customers, competitors and suppliers. This format is also used to analyse the competitive advantage of sectors in the next chapter. A summary is provided in the table below, for ease of reference, that can be a useful checklist for investors to evaluate any company. Some companies feature several times and the aim is for candidates to score well in numerous business models, not just one or two. A worked example, Radstone Technology, illustrates this point in appendix 1.

Business models, prices and valuations are in a constant state of change, given the fluctuations in the economy and unfolding events. Therefore, examples of companies and sectors given are illustrations of the points being made and are not recommendations. Indeed, it is the test of a company that its business model does change over the medium term, which is about five years. This ensures it moves to where the profit zone has shifted. Otherwise, it will become marooned in a profitless zone as competitors encroach. For example, it may be necessary to enter a new sector, as South Staffordshire did when it moved from the water to the support services sector.

All business models are not equal

'Look for companies that have high returns on capital, strong balance sheets, sustainable competitive advantages and shareholder-oriented management.'
Joe Mansueto, founder of investment information provider Morningstar.

All business models are not equal, as some are more powerful than others. Consequently, the company business models table overleaf scores them on a rating of 1, being the highest, to 5, being the lowest. These ratings are inevitably subjective and some could arguably be moved up or down to an extent but a top rated business model would unlikely to be relegated to the bottom or vice versa.

Company business models table

Company business models	Competitive advantage (1 highest, 5 lowest)	Illustrations
1. Competitors		
1a. Barriers to entry and exit	2	Radstone Technology, Michael Page
1b. Being number one or two in the sector	2	Royal Bank of Scotland, Coca-Cola
1c. First and late mover advantage	2	Ford, McDonald's
1d. Lack of competition	2	BAA, British Airways
1e. Moats	1	Berkshire Hathaway, Ratner
1f. Threat of substitute products	2	Microsoft, ARM
2. Customers		
2a. Choosing customers	2	Chorion, Barclays Bank
2b. Cross-selling	2	Alliance & Leicester, Ford
2c. Global reach	3	Accounting firms, HSBC
2d. Long-term contracts	1	Umeco, McAlpine
2e. Niche player	2	Plasmon, Merchant Retail
2f. Not dependent on a few customers	2	Interlink Foods, CRC
2g. Owning the customer	2	Tesco, Telecom plus
2h. Payments in advance	4	Berkshire Hathaway, RAC
2i. Recurring contacts	3	Hit Entertainment, Belhaven
2j. Recurring revenues	1	Eurocopy, South Staffordshire
2k. Selling directly	3	Direct Line, Dell
2l. Stature of customers	3	KPMG, Watermark
3. Economics of the company		
3a. Appropriate gearing	4	Gallaher, British Sky Broadcasting
3b. Asset-backed shares	4	Hardys & Hansons, Lloyds TSB

3c. Bolt-on acquisitions	3	BAE Systems, Eurocopy
3d. Bull market acquisitions	4	Marconi, Vodafone
3e. Changing sector and FTSE index	5	South Staffordshire, AOL Time Warner
3f. Economies of scale	2	Stagecoach, Belhaven
3g. Feed off another's growth	2	Aero Inventory, Biotrace
3h. Good institutional and directors' shareholdings	4	Umeco, Merchant Retail
3i. Headroom to grow	2	JD Wetherspoon, Plasmon
3j. High dividends	2	Friends Provident, Broadcastle
3k. KISS principle	3	Mears, ICAP
3l. Low break-even point	2	Microsoft, General Motors
3m.One-off action provides revenue for years	2	RJR Nabisco, Albemarle & Bond
3n. Public perception	4	Shell, Virgin
3o. Recreate the company	2	General Electric, Hornby
3p. Strong cash flow	3	Barratt Developments, Telecom plus
4. Management		
4a. Auditors, opinions and policies	3	Lloyds TSB, Berkshire Hathaway
4b. Changes in professional advisors	4	BCCI, Arthur Andersen
4c. Conflicts of interest	2	Polly Peck, Versailles
4d. Corporate governance	2	Robert Maxwell, WorldCom
4e. Excellent, honest, well-motivated management	2	BP, Umeco
4f. Follow the man when a talented director moves on	4	Carpetright, Aero Inventory
4g. Modest head office	4	Boo.com, British Airways
4h. Past success	3	Morrisons Supermarkets, NSB Retail Systems
4i. Shareholder values	2	Racal, Hardys & Hansons
4j. Something new	2	Celsis, Stagecoach
5. Products		
5a. Brand loyalty rather than a well-known name	2	Nokia, Lastminute.com
5b. Dumbing down of products creates niche market	4	ITV, Tesco

5c. Focus on competitive advantage	1	Hanson, Scottish & Newcastle
5d. Growth in profits for a decade or more	3	Associated British Ports, Provident Financial
5e. Launching new products	2	Boeing, Diageo
5f. Lean manufacturing	3	Toyota, Hewlett Packard
5g. Like-for-like sales growth	3	Pizza Express, Tesco
5h. Low depreciation and amortisation	3	Tomkins, Telecom plus
5i. Maximising profit from different revenue streams	2	Dana Petroleum, Faroe Petroleum
5j. Moving up the value chain	2	Shell, General Electric
5k. Owning the standard	1	Microsoft, JVC
5l. Product differentiation	1	Halifax, Tesco
5m.Rolling out a consumer chain	3	JD Wetherspoon, Harry Ramsden's
5n. Secondary profit zones	3	Avesco, Chorion
5o. Superior product or service	2	GlaxoSmithKline, Sellotape
5p. Supported by a famous personality	5	Planet Hollywood, Pepsi
5q. Unique selling point	2	Gateway, Ford
6. Suppliers		
6a. Bargaining power over suppliers	1	Luminar, Premier Direct
6b. Buying opportunistically	4	Merchant Retail, Lastminute.com
6c. Not dependent on a few suppliers	2	De Beers, BOC

The competitive advantage points from 1 to 5 above are awarded according to the business model's power to achieve low cost and/or differentiate itself from the competition. Above all, it is crucial for a company to be able to control its revenue streams. Consequently, those that score the maximum 1 are: moats, long-term contracts, recurring revenues, focus on competitive advantage, owning the standard, product differentiation and bargaining power over suppliers. Medium scorers include selling directly and lean manufacturing. At the bottom of the pile are those that do not have a major impact on revenue streams or have limited applicability, such as supported by a famous personality and changing sector and index. This same scoring is used for the sector table in the next chapter and includes business models to avoid.

As noted above, a company should have multiple business models and be scoring well throughout to be highly-rated, as this strengthens their overall competitive advantage. For example, Radstone Technology has erected barriers to entry, put a moat around its business and does not have intense competition. JVC owns the VHS industry standard and is also a brand. Diageo is five times bigger than the number two gorilla in beverages, SABMiller, and thus dominates the sector, owns the customer and has some of the best brands in the world. Microsoft owns the standard, it piggybacks on the work and growth of others and is a brand.

1. Competitors

'I read the annual report of the company I'm looking at and I read the annual reports of competitors – that is the main source of material.'
Warren Buffett, CEO of Berkshire Hathaway.

Companies with sound business models will be able to compete. This section examines some ways that this can be achieved and is also a guide to analysing the threat from competitors.

1a. Barriers to entry and exit: competitive advantage rated 2

A company's business model is attractive if it has erected high barriers to entry. An example is Microsoft which has largely locked out the competition by owning the industry standard in computer operating systems with its Windows product. The barrier stops new companies entering the market, which would otherwise increase capacity and put pressure on prices. Avoid companies that seek to diversify into sectors where such barriers exist, as it is likely to be an uphill struggle. There are many forms of barriers to entry. A classic barrier is the pyramid, where companies have cheap and cheerful products at the base and high margin products at the top. The base is protected by a firewall of low prices and brands to stop competition from attacking it and working their way up the pyramid to the top where the pot of gold lies. Japanese car makers penetrated such a barrier in Western markets by starting with building British motorbikes and cars under licence and steadily moving up the value chain to compete in the luxury market with brands like Lexus. Sheer size can be an important barrier, such as in steel and mining which need large economies of scale to operate efficiently. Life insurance companies and banks need national coverage with the attendant branches and marketing organisation. The cost of complying with the formidable regulations is significant with HSBC, for example, having to contend with over 350 bodies worldwide. Establishing a brand name may be very difficult in a crowded market where consumers are reassured by an existing brand they trust.

Licences are effective in stopping new entrants. For instance, the number of black cabs in London or commercial television stations is controlled by the authorities. Know-how and proprietary products provide effective barriers, as in the case of Radstone Technology with its made-to-order, rugged computer boards. Large international professional firms, such as accountants and lawyers, win multinational accounts because they provide worldwide service, which is not feasible with smaller competitors who are locked out of the bidding. A professional recruitment company like Michael Page can often be the first port of call, as it has a leading database of candidates thus offering more choice. The barrier could be location, as is the case with the few available sites for supermarkets and airports.

The barriers to entry may be low, on the other hand, but the reaction of existing players may still be effective in preventing new entrants from establishing a foothold, for example, by threatening a price war. The existing players may dominate the available distribution channels, such as in newspapers, with the likes of John Menzies and WHSmith. Another illustration is the restriction on the location of dispensing pharmacies near doctors' surgeries, where the demand for fulfilling subscriptions is high. A new entrant is locked out by being unable to obtain a site. There are low barriers to entry in telecommunications, thanks to the regulator, and a myriad of both large and small resellers provide ferocious competition. Providing office plants has low barriers to entry but Rentokil Initial has been adept at winning new customers before some of the competition was even aware of the opportunity.

Conversely, an attractive company should have low exit barriers so it can easily leave the sector should the need arise. For example, a struggling holiday operator can easily leave that sector and cut its losses. By contrast, heavy industry, such as aluminium, coal or nuclear power, may face crippling exit costs and it may be cheaper to carry on. This creates a profitless zone for all players.

1b. Being number one or two in the sector: competitive advantage rated 2

'We are watching the dinosaurs die but we don't know what will take their place.'
Lester Thurow, MIT economist.

Being number one or two in the sector implies that the company has achieved competitive advantage to reach this position, examples being BP and Royal Bank of Scotland. It can be particularly attractive if the number one company is much bigger than the number two, say by a factor of five times, as it can then reign supreme in the sector. Coca-Cola, for example, has half of the world soft drink market whereas Pepsi has a fifth. The advantages of being the top dog include: economies of scale; tying up suppliers; dominating distribution channels; superior know-how; advertising; and brands. These can be important sources of low cost and differentiation, the two essential ingredients of competitive advantage. However, size is not everything, and gorillas are a list of yesterday's winners rather than of tomorrow's. Many with dominant market share face problems, such as intense competition and adding little value. Consequently, profits have been eroding, at the likes of Invensys, BT and ICI. Market share does not translate into a successful business model unless the company has competitive advantage, like Diageo and Tesco who add value and possess strong brands. The single-minded pursuit of market share is a dazzling but flawed strategy for many companies, such as Vodafone, which has been a key ingredient in curbing net profit. It is crucial to think of customers and profit first and then determine an appropriate business model, rather than have preset ideas and strategy and hope that customers and profits emerge at the end.

The problem with a gorilla is what to do next. Its big disadvantage is its very size, because it may not be able to grow by much more than that of the overall market. The recourse is often to grow via acquisitions, but studies have shown they generally destroy shareholder value. Blue chip companies' shares tend to be overpriced and bought because they are well known. Although they seem to offer the allure of stability, they can fall dramatically from grace, like British Energy, ICI, Invensys, Marks & Spencer, Railtrack and Royal & Sun Alliance, and are no panacea for protecting your wealth. Further, once they are troubled, they are like an oil tanker and take considerable time and money to turn around, with no guarantee of success. High exceptional costs can be expected during such restructurings and these destroy shareholders' wealth.

A gorilla can dominate the market by setting prices and standards, launching new products and controlling the entrance and exit of competitors. A second division player may be weak and takes what crumbs it can from the table if it lacks strong competitive advantage. It may have to accept the ruling price set by the gorilla if it is unable to lower its price to gain new customers, either for fear of retaliation by the gorilla or because production constraints inhibit increasing output. Examples of well-known companies that are gorillas include Microsoft, Vodafone, HSBC, Sony and Toyota. Second division companies include mmO2, Bradford & Bingley and Fiat. Buying shares in a company like Microsoft or Vodafone when they are small but have the tenacity and competitive advantage to become the gorilla can be one of the most rewarding plays in the stock market. A sensible strategy is to sell when growth tails off and look for the next upstart. One way to spot companies making this transition is to look at those quickly moving up through the ranks from one FTSE index to the next. These movers are published quarterly and this information is widely available. The main FTSE indices are AIM, Fledgling, Small Cap, mid 250 and 100.

Gorillas are able to attract the top talent, so the management is usually the best around but often excessively paid, judging by the wrath expressed by shareholders. Moreover, they are usually run by 'employee' directors on a salary rather than being run with an 'owner's eye' by founders with a substantial stake in the business. Employee directors can also damage the company by empire building using shareholders' money. They can have conflicts of interest due to share options, which encourage 'accounting for growth' and maximising profit in the short-term rather than the long-term.

1c. First and late mover advantage: competitive advantage rated 2

'If you gave me $100 billion and said take away the soft drink leadership from Coca-Cola, I'd give it back to you and say it can't be done.'
Warren Buffett

To be the first mover in a new sector can be a great advantage for a company because it can enjoy high, initial profits for the first few years due to its power over the choice of sites, personnel, partners, sector standards, quality of product, pricing, distribution channels, brands, etc. There have been many examples of this, such as railways, mining, shipping, canals and textiles in the past, and technology and telecommunications in the present. It is more difficult for new entrants to gain market share after first movers are established, whose steep learning curves can be a source of competitive advantage as experience often leads to lower costs.

If the market is growing rapidly then the first mover may not be able to keep up with demand and, for the sake of the health of the sector, may not be too perturbed by new entrants. Usually, however, it will fight to maintain its dominance. Coca-Cola, Ford and McDonald's are instances of companies with first mover advantage that are still dominant in their sectors. Microsoft was an early mover in operating systems and triumphed over IBM, which was largely the latter's own fault as it did not insist on owning the rights to the software. In the UK, first mover examples include Shell and Lloyds TSB.

First mover advantage may be from a new process in an established sector. An example is Telecom plus, with its one database controlling all the services sold to customers and presenting just one bill. This is very hard for the gorillas to replicate because they have separate and cumbersome computer systems. The Japanese have been keen to grab first mover advantage and rush out a rudimentary prototype of a new product, such as automatic cameras and video, and refine them with later versions, as has Microsoft.

However, there can be advantages in being a late mover. This tends to happen when the new sector is very risky and costly. Many mistakes can be made along the way and a late entrant can avoid them, benefiting from the efforts of the pioneers in establishing the work force, technology and infrastructure, and buying their assets in a fire sale. A classic example is the debris of TMT, which was the technology, media and telecommunications mania, after its collapse in 2000, with companies bombed out and billions wasted. For example, BT was forced to sell off some good businesses cheaply, such as its Yellow Pages, to prop up its battered balance sheet.

1d. Lack of competition: competitive advantage rated 2

Companies are more attractive if they lack competition, a position gained through low cost and/or differentiation. Radstone Technology makes rugged computer products for use in military hardware, such as planes, and does not have intense competition. When it comes to protecting high value assets and operators' lives, saving a few pounds on components is not high on the priority list. Quality and delivery are more important so customers are not price sensitive. Its competitive advantage is based on a strongly differentiated, 'must-have' product that is very cost effective. The sales contracts are long-term, which secures revenue for years, and helps to shut out the competition. Albemarle & Bond has a chain of 53 pawnshops with a strongly differentiated product. Almost all its customers live within two miles of each outlet, allowing it to dominate the area and achieve a high level of repeat business. Since physical goods are handed over the counter, competitors' other normal channels to market, such as post or phone, are not a threat. This controlled customer base is cross-sold ancillary products like unsecured loans and pay day advances.

Supermarkets and retailers have intense price competition. Their 'known value items', such as milk and bread, are largely commodity products and are easy for price-sensitive consumers to judge. The competition in media is intense, as people are usually short of time, inundated with supply and have many compelling, alternative claims on their disposable income, such as mobile phones and cars. This makes life hard for newspapers, books, television, music and cinemas. The fiercest competition may increasingly be from the internet, where price comparison is but a click away. Some products are free, such as music and films which are swopped by consumers on the internet, and it is difficult for companies to combat this threat to their revenues. Holiday companies regularly have to discount prices to tempt customers, as over-capacity is often prevalent and consumers wait for last minute bargains.

Swap an investment in a company facing strong competition for one that is shielded from it. Incumbent gorilla utility companies, like BT and British Gas, used to have an easy life. Then their sectors were opened to a multitude of competitors. They relied on customer inertia rather than keen pricing to stem the lost sales but it is a strategy of death by a thousand cuts. A nimble, fast growing company like Telecom plus is a more attractive prospect than BT. British Airways is a full cost carrier and is under tremendous pressure from fast growing, no frills airlines like Ryanair and easyJet. Their business models are similar to the very profitable Southwest Airlines that pioneered low-cost airlines in the US. Neither was British Airways successful in trying to emulate the competition by starting its own low-cost carrier. BAA, the national airport operator, may have competition from regional airports but they are small and in remote locations. It earns low risk landing fees and makes money from its monopoly retail outlets. BAA faces far less competition than British Airways and is more attractive on this score.

1e. Moats: competitive advantage rated 1

'Wonderful castles, surrounded by deep, dangerous moats where the leader inside is an honest and decent person. Preferably, the castle gets its strength from the genius inside; the moat is permanent and acts as a powerful deterrent to those considering an attack; and inside, the leader makes gold but doesn't keep it all for himself. We like great companies with dominant positions, whose franchise is hard to duplicate and has tremendous staying power.'
Warren Buffett

A company with a moat around the business can powerfully ward off competitors and has the highest competitive advantage rating of 1. Sometimes the moats are benign and filled with water, whereas others are infested with sharks. One example is Microsoft, which will leave players alone in some areas or collaborate with them, if it so chooses, but will fight fiercely if anyone tries to cross or even approach its moat. Evidence for this was its demolition of Netscape, which has been the subject of court action, as outlined in appendix 2. Warren Buffett's objective is to widen and deepen the moat round Berkshire Hathaway every year and he reports his progress, or otherwise, in achieving this goal. By any measure, he has been successful.

One classic way to build a moat is to take out the competition by various means, examples being: acquisition (banks and insurance companies); price wars (newspapers); and patents (pharmaceutical companies). Customers themselves can strengthen the company's moat by increasing their loyalty, turning them from being one-off, or 'transactional', into long-term customers. Also, they can shun the competitors, examples being the protests against Shell in Germany and fast food in France. Radstone Technology's moat is strengthened by sending its technicians to the customer's site to develop the rugged computer products. The technicians can then inform them of new products and are in pole position to make sales, compared to little known competitors who have to resort to banging on doors. Microsoft shares its computer codes with favoured partners, including Hewlett Packard, Intel and Logitech. This minimises compatibility problems, for example, and gives them an advantage over competitors.

Moats can be made by the ineptitude of competitors, such as that of British car manufacturers in their largely self-inflicted death throes in the 1970s, due to shoddy products and strikes. This handed success to the Japanese and Germans, whose differentiated cars were well made by a motivated workforce and offered value for money. Another example was British Airways' 'dirty tricks' campaign against Virgin. It was the height of foolishness to alienate its customers, given that British Airways did not compete on price but heavily relied on their loyalty. It compounded this error with its infamous decision to replace the union flag on its tail wings with what looked like graffiti, incurring the public ire of Margaret Thatcher. Gerald Ratner made a famous speech belittling the jewellery sold in his jewellery chain and said 'what we sell is crap'. It was a spectacular own goal that should have had its competitors rubbing their hands with glee.

1f. Threat of substitute products: competitive advantage rated 2

Companies have strong business models that suffer little from the threat of substitute products, one example being superior plastic corks supplanting wood corks in wine bottles. A substitute is a potential impediment to the quantity and quality of output and can cap the price a company can charge, given the fear that the customer can shop elsewhere. Remove that fear and the company can do pretty much what it likes. An extreme case was the East German Trabant car that remained unaltered in its appalling state for decades, as every one was sold for a high price and had a long waiting list. Microsoft's Windows operating system is routinely pre-installed in personal computers and has a 90% market share. There are operating system substitutes from the likes of IBM, Macintosh and Linux, but the consumer lacks knowledge and choice. He does know Microsoft, however, and is very wary about straying from the well-trodden path with such a complicated product. Consequently, Microsoft has an immensely powerful, monopolistic competitive advantage.

The threat of substitution can be low because of a company's superior product or control over the customer. For example, banks and stockbrokers control customers who are described as being 'sticky' because they wish to avoid the hassle or cost of changing the account to another provider, so accept the product on offer. Another reason may be due to customer ignorance. A tourist chooses a busy restaurant in a town square and is unaware of better alternatives in a back street or is unable to make a rational choice through lack of information. A company may have no wish to substitute since it may want return favours from the existing relationship. Examples include beverage companies that need the distribution channels provided by retail chains, such as pubs; investment funds that receive refund commissions from selected stockbrokers; and information technology companies that share information or technical specifications with each other. Substitution may be thwarted because there is ineffective competition at the point of sale. For instance, stores sell warranties when electrical products are sold and, similarly, travel agents sell insurance with holidays. These warranties can account for 30-50% of profits at retailers like Dixons. The Competition Commission has examined this area and aims to increase choice and reduce prices, thus generally increasing the threat to a company from substitute products.

Long-term contracts can be effective in stopping substitution because, when they are renewed, the incumbent has the relationship, inside knowledge and track record, so is in a prime position to win again. Examples of such contracts are in the support services activities of companies like McAlpine, Mears Group and MITIE Group. Generally, the threat of substitution diminishes if the price of the item is low because the potential cost savings from doing a bit of homework by the customer are much less. Thus, the threat is great when buying a car but very low for buying an ice cream. At the other end of the scale, commodity products are not differentiated and are easy to substitute, like food. When a company that was fairly immune from competition finds its products, like computer chips, are becoming easier to substitute it is undermined, as in the case of ARM, the once high-flying, information technology company. Surfcontrol is a world-leading, internet filtering company with a commanding position in controlling what content can be viewed but now faces substitute products from the US. Commercial terrestrial television enjoyed a loyal audience up to the 1980s but digital television has been a powerful substitute with hundreds of channels and unique content in some cases, like premier league football.

2. Customers

'The customer is the appreciating asset.'
Federal Express

Customers are the cornerstone of success and, whereas a company can automate the production of goods, it cannot automate the production of customers. Companies with the best business models will have customers glued to them who pay a premium price because their products add great value in a way that is not met by competitors. This section examines what the company can do to configure its value chain to try to achieve that objective. In a world awash with excess capacity, companies need to concentrate on customers rather than products. This turns the normal company on its head because, traditionally, the focus has been on making a product and then figure out how to sell it to customers. Instead, companies should think how they can satisfy a customer's wants and then determine how to deliver products which achieve that objective.

Focusing on customers tends to be easier in a small company rather than a large one. This can be partly because the former is entrepreneurial, closer to the customer and hungry for business, but also because the latter's world can seem to stop outside the career concerns of the employees and management, few of whom may have ever met a customer. Consequently, a gorilla is often an easier competitor to beat than an entrepreneurial firm. If you want to find what the customer wants then ask those who complain rather than those who are satisfied. Impressively, one CEO had his photograph and contact details in his retail outlets and asked customers to contact him directly, such was his keenness to obtain direct feedback. He had a print out of all complaints and held a weekly meeting with the directors to resolve them.

Successful smaller companies usually operate in a profitable niche. As they grow, they often and unwisely move out of this niche into areas where they do not have strong competitive advantage and where customers are best served by others. This dilution of the original sound business model undermines profits and the effect continues all the way up the growth path until the company becomes a moribund gorilla. The correct strategy is only to grow into associated business areas that can feed off the initial competitive advantage, such as the banks' move into mortgages and life insurance years ago. Diversifying, or 'diworseifying' as it is called by the guru Peter Lynch, into unrelated areas can be extremely risky, therefore, an example being banks and building societies moving into estate agencies in the late 1980s.

2a. Choosing customers: competitive advantage rated 2

'For all the money we spend on marketing, we know very little about our customers.'
Robert Thomas, CEO of Nissan USA.

Companies can improve their business model by choosing which customers they do and do not want, and this is a key to differentiation. It might be thought 'the more customers, the better, and who cares who they are, as long as they are buying'. The clue comes from looking at revenues, costs and market segmentation, with the overriding objective of maximising long-term profitability. Therefore, when analysing a company, consider who are its most profitable and highest growth customers.

Radstone Technology thought of customers and profit rather than market share and worked backwards to achieve this. It decided that it did not want to supply existing customers with its standard commodity computer boards. It spent a year re-engineering its business and launched value added, rugged computer products that would appeal to military customers. This enhanced its pricing power and control over the new customer base. GEC decided that it did not want its long established customers in aerospace and defence and sold the business, renamed itself Marconi and instead wanted customers for its telecommunications equipment. This strategy led to catastrophic failure. Publisher Chorion practises classic market segmentation because it caters to various age groups with different products, since it wants to cater to their needs when they change from children to teenagers and then adults. Saga Holidays wants customers over 50, while Club 18-30 caters for that younger age group. Advertising seeks to choose customers for products, like cars that are marketed to appeal to certain socio-economic groups.

Other companies have decided they do not want certain customers in order to deter undesirables or improve profits. Relinquishing unprofitable customers for the greater good of the company is one of the hardest decisions to make. Barclays Bank decided that it did not want marginal branches with few customers and preferred that the competition served them instead. It closed many rural outlets, causing much hostility. Its aim was to control costs and focus on main opportunities. Similarly, Lloyds bank shed many business accounts that had permanent overdrafts secured on property in the late 1980s by asking for repayment or transferring the account elsewhere. They thus avoided much of the bad debt that would have stemmed from these customers in the recession of the early 1990s. Banks have also weeded out nuisance customers with small transactions, which provides an opportunity for the pawnbroker Albemarle & Bond, who offers the sub-prime market rudimentary financial services, such as pay day advances. Many financial institutions, like brokers and private banks, choose not to serve low net worth individuals. Warren Buffett's Berkshire Hathaway shares have the highest quoted price in the world, at around $90,000 each. He did not want to split the shares and make them more affordable. However, funds were going to achieve this so reluctantly he allowed a split, although these B shares, which trade around $3,000, do not have voting rights. Personal Assets investment trust has a high quoted price of around £200 and the objective is to cater for long-term, serious investors, not the average person. McDonald's has decided that it no longer wanted certain countries as customers and announced limited withdrawal plans. Sometimes customers are not wanted because the size of the orders is too large or lumpy. Overheads may have to be increased to accommodate them and might make the company over reliant on a few important customers.

2b. Cross-selling: competitive advantage rated 2

'The essence of a megabrand is leveraging your brand into other product categories.'
Adelle Kirk, marketing consultant.

Cross-selling products and services to an installed customer base is a sound business model. The prospective customer is 'hot' and the chance of a successful sale is much higher than with 'cold' calling him, since he may have no knowledge of the company and even less interest in buying the product. The cost of marketing to hot prospects is low with account and personal details close to hand. The sales pitch can be included with regular statements and information that are sent to the customer routinely. A variation of this installed base model is selling follow-on products, such as paper for photocopiers, car hire for airline passengers, new heads for electric toothbrushes, refreshments on a train, insurance and warranties for physical goods and replacement parts in general.

An example of cross-selling is 'bancassurance' where a mortgage bank, like Alliance & Leicester, promotes other high margin financial services, such as pensions and life insurance. A banking customer wants a mortgage or house insurance and makes an enquiry the next time he is in the branch. Note that the threat of substitution by a competitor is low due to his loyalty, based on the existing relationship, and convenience, as he is in the branch anyway. Utility companies like Centrica use their installed base to sell household services, such as plumbing and servicing of appliances. Car breakdown organisations, such as the AA and RAC, cross-sell motor insurance for commission to their millions of customers. Microsoft can target its users to upgrade software by using the internet, which is virtually cost-free marketing.

Cross-selling is not practical for a one-product company. For example, ice cream maker Richmond Foods can sell further lines, such as one-litre tubs, to supermarkets but is a one-product company. Neither can this model be used where the customers are quite different. Defence company Chemring has two divisions, namely counter measures, such as flares, and marine products, but one set of customers would be uninterested in the products of the other division. Cross-selling can be successful, however, where a product is tangible and then a follow-on service can be bolted on, like Ford selling financing for its cars, electrical shops selling warranty insurance for televisions and clothing stores like Marks & Spencer selling financial services.

A trusted brand, like Marks & Spencer or Tesco, can be a powerful reassurance to customers when buying a product unrelated to its core retailing, especially if it is difficult to evaluate, like financial services with its small print. Further, Tesco has an extensive database obtained via loyalty cards that holds details of who shops where, plus when and what they buy. Thus, if a customer buys wine he could be targeted with offers or information that is likely to appeal, such as spirits. Life insurance companies and banks do the same. Flying Brands uses its database of two million customers who buy mail order flowers to cross-sell other products, like gardening. Thus, databases allow cross-selling to be targeted and cost effective.

2c. Global reach: competitive advantage rated 3

'If I could be master of The Channel for 12 hours, I would be master of the world.'
Napoleon

In some cases, it is important to achieve global operations, or 'reach', because multinational customers often require their suppliers to support them worldwide. This need has driven sector consolidation in many instances. It can be important to have a world product, like the Toyota Corolla, as this can lower costs, rather than have different products for various countries. However, this advantage needs to be weighed against local tastes and the need to differentiate. Global reach is easier to achieve by shipping products from a few locations so that factories do not have to be replicated. Services are harder to supply worldwide because that usually means personnel operating in many countries with all the attendant cost and complexity. A case in point is the accounting firms that have offices all over the world so that they can serve a client's operations wherever they may be. This has lead to consolidation from the 'big eight' down to the 'big four'. A competitor lacking such reach will not win this work and so size is a barrier to entry. Other examples are HSBC in banking, BP in oil, GlaxoSmithKline in pharmaceuticals, Lloyds in insurance and Honda in car manufacturing.

Some smaller companies can punch above their weight and achieve global reach, either in partnership or alone. Chemring, for example, is a world leader in decoy flares, which is a remarkable achievement for a small company. Global reach is not an issue for some companies because they might be operating in only one country, like perfume seller Merchant Retail, or it is not applicable, such as for a local water company like Severn Trent. Regional dominance can be more effective than being spread too thin on a national basis. Belhaven, for instance, has strong competitive advantage with its award-winning beer in Scotland due to its high quality and loyal following. Regional newspapers are another example.

2d. Long-term contracts: competitive advantage rated 1

A particularly advantageous business model is to have long-term contracts based on a differentiated product that adds value to the customer. This should lead to good margins and avoids transactional, or one-off, sales, based solely or mainly on price. Long-term contracts mean that revenue can be accurately predicted and, therefore, the quality of earnings is excellent. This minimises the chance of profit warnings since they are predominantly caused by falling revenue rather than cost increases. With one-off, or transactional, customers, tomorrow is always another day, bringing with it uncertain demand. Long-term revenue is especially valuable in an economic downturn, whereas competitors with transactional customers may be struggling for survival.

A long-term contract also engenders trust and a good working relationship that locks in the customer. This shuts the door on the competition during the course of the contract and also when it is renewed because the incumbent and customer know a great deal about each other. The tendency is for neither to want to go up the learning curve with new parties, with the attendant risk, cost and lack of efficiency. Cost is not, then, the only issue. It is also a vote of confidence in the company that the customer has chosen it, rather than any one else, to be a very important part of its operations and it can be more like a partner than a supplier. This success can be used as a selling point to other potential customers. This also gives competitive advantage because such a claim can squeeze out competitors who do not have such a seal of approval.

In aerospace, both Umeco and Aero Inventory have long-term contracts, providing components and servicing to customers like Rolls-Royce and Cathay Pacific. Private finance initiatives cover a wide gamut of activities and are the same concept. A supplier may build a facility, such as a school or road, and run it for a fee for 25 years, or provide housing services. Examples include McAlpine and Mears, with its order book representing three years' turnover. Life insurance companies have long-term pension and saving contracts whose revenues are highly predictable.

2e. Niche player: competitive advantage rated 2

Investment guru Jim Slater said, when describing big companies, that 'elephants don't gallop', unlike small companies which can react nimbly to a changing market and take advantage of short lines of communication, lack of bureaucracy and fast decision-making. They can compete by servicing a segment more effectively than a big company that may have to serve the whole market, lack focus and not be an expert in anything. The segment must be profitable and have different needs from the rest of the market, which can be satisfied with various strategies, including specialised products, pricing, quality and service. If the market is very broad, such as with commodities, then there may be no segment. A niche player can operate with the blessing, or not, of big companies, or 'gorillas'. For example, Plasmon has a niche in part of the hard disk drive market that was too small for the main players like IBM, which was content to see demand satisfied by a specialist. Other niche players like utility reseller Telecom plus are not welcomed by incumbent gorillas, like BT, but they can do little about it, except to try to stem the outflow of business.

There are many examples of focused small companies that are outmanoeuvring the gorillas by competing with low costs and/or by doing something different. One illustration is Merchant Retail's forte in selling a good range of discount perfume in a differentiated manner. Department stores sell at full price and the likes of supermarkets, like Asda, do discount but only offer a limited range. Premier Direct focuses on selling low-ticket goods, such as books and household accessories, directly in the workplace, using temporary displays and is a convenient, low-cost activity. Ask Central has been taken over but is a value-for-money restaurant operator, concentrating on its core pizza and pasta food. Urbium offers a different product in the bar/nightclub sector by combining dining, bars and dancing under one roof with its Tiger Tiger format, and caters to a wider market than competitors that offer just one of these services. The travel market has a host of niche operators, like Holidaybreak, that offer activities like walking, climbing, skiing, fishing, bird watching and exotic locations.

Generally, there will be better investment opportunities in good quality, smaller growth companies than cumbersome gorillas with sluggish prospects. They are also typically on a lower PER (price earnings ratio) with a higher growth rate.

2f. Not dependent on a few customers: competitive advantage rated 2

A company's control over its revenue is enhanced if it is not dependent on a few customers but instead has a good spread. The danger is that an important customer cancels a significant contract and the company can then be in dire straits. Pricing power follows this principle because a few dominant customers can strike a hard bargain, knowing that the supplier has little choice but accept or face the consequences of losing a major order. This has been the case with some unfortunate clothing chain and supermarket suppliers, for example, who have been totally or mainly reliant on one customer and have built dedicated plants for them. Interlink Foods, on the other hand, also sells to the supermarkets but no one customer accounts for more than 10% of turnover. CRC has a low risk 'picks and shovels' approach to riding on the back of growth in the new economy by repairing electronic and telecommunication products. The snag is that it was dependent on about 60% of sales from one customer, Nokia, and this risk became a reality when the latter carried out its own repairs instead.

Companies can also face this dependence problem if they sell big-ticket items. Examples include BAE Systems and VT, who sell military hardware to a few governments. Also, having a government as a customer increases the risk because politics can sometimes interfere with sound business sense. For example, governments are often very keen to support home industries rather than buying abroad, even if the home product is inferior. The law of large numbers benefits the reliability of revenues of many companies, an example being a utility like Scottish Power that has five million customers.

2g. Owning the customer: competitive advantage rated 2

'The first word she said was Coke. The second was mummy.'
Enthusiastic American consumer of Coca-Cola.

One of the most powerful business models is to 'own' the customer, as underlined in the Coca-Cola quote above. A company's objective is to glue the customer to it through power points so that he will not shop elsewhere. This can be achieved in a variety of ways and includes customer relationship management, brands, loyalty, reputation, convenience, status, reduction in hassle, value for money, industry standards, location and lack of choice. A company may have only one of these power points in its arsenal but the best business models have multiple points. For example, a supermarket like Tesco owns the customer due to its brand, loyalty, reputation, convenience, value for money and location. This ownership allows access points for selling follow-on products, like financial services, and it can segment the market and sell low-, medium- and high-priced products that meet the needs of different customers, according to their income. If a company is one step down the value chain and sells to the company that owns the customer, then it is in a far weaker position. Thus, a supplier to Tesco does not have the end customer relationship. It has to negotiate with this gorilla and has far less power because Tesco can take its business where it likes.

Many vertically integrated breweries decided that they wanted to concentrate on owning the customer by concentrating on the higher margin, retail business in their pubs and stop producing a commodity product like beer. They invested in premises, made them more family friendly and greatly expanded food to the extent that many are now more akin to restaurants that also sell drinks. Banks own customers who are reluctant to switch due to opaque pricing and the aggravation of moving. Tobacco companies excel at owning the customer through an addictive product and loyalty based on health, taste, price, familiarity and brand status. A utility re-seller, like Telecom plus, can own the customer because it is a one-stop shop, supplying gas, electricity and telecommunications on one bill. It beats the price of the gorillas and dealing with just one supplier, rather than three, makes life simpler for the customer.

At the other end of the scale are commodity-type businesses that add little value, like packaging, distributors, textiles, chemicals, metals and builders' merchants, which have to compete on price and have transactional, or one-off, customers who can easily go elsewhere. They do not own the customer and occupy a deeply unattractive space.

2h. Payments in advance: competitive advantage rated 4

Receiving payments in advance for a company's sales is very advantageous because this generates strong cash flow. In addition, the money is in the bank earning interest, rather than having debtors on the balance sheet, so the capital employed is minimised. It also eliminates the problem of bad debts. This is not a very common business model as customers like to pay when they receive their goods or settle in arrears on trade credit.

Subscriptions to publications are advance payments and can be for up to three years for titles such as the *Investors Chronicle* or *The Economist*. Holiday companies require a deposit when the booking is made and full payment weeks before the customer travels. General insurance premiums also are paid up-front and, in the case of Berkshire Hathaway, the use of this 'free float' has been invested in companies and is the root of Warren Buffett's success. Supermarkets sell food products in advance of having to pay for them. Other prepayments include: mobile phone calls; club memberships; roadside assistance, such the RAC; product warranties; household servicing for utilities; licence fees; and selling the future earnings of pop stars and Formula One motor racing.

The opposite is also true: companies that receive payment in arrears can have high levels of debtors, are less attractive and bad debts can be a problem, particularly in a recession when the customer goes bankrupt. Payment in arrears is a feature of manufacturing companies, although the problem is less if the product is made to order and up-front payment secured. The whole aim of banks, of course, is to be repaid over a number of years and they are notorious for bad debts in a recession. This greatly increases their operating risk and is an Achilles heel of their business model. Other financial service companies, like life assurers, do not have this drawback and are generally more tempting investments, depending on the stage of the economic cycle. This is covered in chapters 3 and 4.

2i. Recurring contacts: competitive advantage rated 3

Recurring contact with a product increases familiarity and reinforces its presence in a world of advertising that clamours for our attention. Each person is hit with an average of 3,000 advertising messages a day. High street shops, banks and supermarkets reinforce their presence because customers see the outlets on a daily basis. The cost of the outlets is high and, although the reinforcement is a free benefit, the outlet is there to conduct business and is not primarily there for advertising. Children's television contains 'must watch' programmes with popular characters like Bob the Builder, owned by Hit Entertainment. The programmes are a constant reminder of the brand that is instantly recognisable on merchandise, sales of which totalled $1 billion for Bob the Builder. The programmes are sold for a peppercorn because the profit zone is the merchandise. However, the programmes are cheap to make and are perfect for repeats, given that children grow up, and the audience changes every few years. Note that the television stations are only too happy to oblige by showing very cheap programming and so both parties are in a healthy 'win-win' situation. A sound business model is one where a customer, in this case a television station, pays a company, like Hit Entertainment, for the privilege of advertising its wares.

Recurring contact is evident in sports, like football and grand prix racing, where, again, spectators and television stations pay for the privilege of watching. The hard way is just to advertise constantly and is a feature of cars, where the manufacturer is trying to reassure potential customers about the quality of its products, given the consumer will own this big-ticket item for years. Sir Richard

Branson refreshes his Virgin brands frequently and very effectively using self-publicity. In the case of brewers, like Belhaven or Hardys & Hansons, the familiarity is with the pubs in the local community and their signs reinforce the message. In this way, a regional operator can become quite dominant, especially if the product is differentiated by quality, as it is in these two cases. Part of Richmond Foods' ice cream range is comprised of derivatives of famous chocolate brands, such as Rolo, owned by big brother Nestlé. The ice cream sales are enhanced by the expensive and recurring advertising of the chocolate. Again, this is a sound business model because the advertising cost is borne by the big brother and is not a direct expense of the beneficiary, Richmond Foods.

2j. Recurring revenues: competitive advantage rated 1

'Profit in business comes from repeat customers, customers that boast about your product, and that brings friends with them.'
Dr. W. Edwards Deming, management consultant.

One of the most important business models is recurring revenue. Conor McCarthy, the editor of the investment newsletter Techinvest, emphasised this point: 'Recurring revenue streams, the larger the better, are very attractive. Companies that change to a business model which steadily increases the recurring proportion of revenue are likely to undergo a market re-rating'. Recurring revenue means that a company can be reasonably confident that its budgeted revenue will materialise because its customers will not suddenly disappear or go to a competitor. Control over revenue is of the utmost importance because normally it is outside the company's control, whereas costs are ultimately under the company's control, depending on the time span involved. It is a failure on the income front that is behind the majority of profit warnings.

There are many companies with high recurring revenue, such as life insurers and mortgage banks. It is perhaps a sign of how valuable recurring revenue can be in a business model that both of the following companies have been bought out. Eurocopy had 95% recurring revenue from customers using its photocopiers. South Staffordshire had 85% renewals on its home service policies. These recurring revenues can be from long-term or short-term contracts. The contracts were for up to one and five years for Eurocopy and South Staffordshire, respectively. The percentage of recurring revenue may fall but it typically takes some time for this to make a material impact, so the operating risk of the company is low. Recurring revenues do not feature in companies that have transactional, or one-off, customers. They may well return due to loyalty, convenience, etc. but there is no contractual reason for them to do so once the current transaction has been completed. Illustrations include petrol, food and beverages.

2k. Selling directly: competitive advantage rated 3

Companies that sell directly to the customer cut out the middleman and capture that value themselves. Thus, they seek the competitive advantage of low costs. They are also more powerful because they have the relationship with the final consumer of the product and that can provide follow-on selling opportunities. This direct contact should improve the product offered as the company has first-hand knowledge of what the customer does and does not want. Feedback about problems should also be more streamlined and effective.

A good case in point is a soft drink company like Coca-Cola, selling direct via its vending machines. These limit choice at the point of sale and provide a service with fat margins, compared to being lined up as a commodity product amongst the competition on the supermarket shelf. Not only are the prices there much lower but also the supermarket is capturing much of the value instead. Direct Line pioneered selling insurance directly to the customer in the UK, which cut out brokers, and has been very successful. Call centres have grown rapidly as more goods and services are sold direct. This has been spurred on by the virtual world of electronic commerce, with the growth of the internet empowering customers, and is a great threat to the middlemen, such as high street retailers.

The computer manufacturers Dell and Gateway use this method of selling. The product is shipped directly from the factory to the home or office and is often made to order. Such companies typically have no shops displaying their wares. Selling direct is still quite rare for most manufacturers, however. In a world where the buzzword is focus, most prefer to concentrate on their core activity and leave the retailing to others.

2l. Stature of customers: competitive advantage rated 3

It is a powerful accolade for a company if the stature of its customers is high. Listing blue chip and respected clients in its marketing information can be very beneficial. The implication is that 'if it is good enough for them, then it is good enough for you'. For example, Peat Marwick (now KPMG) and Barings were accountants and bankers, respectively, to the Queen and, presumably, that royal association did their business nothing but good. Caribbean islands seeking their share of tourists use the same tactic to boost tourism by advertising that the rich and famous stayed there, such as Sir Winston Churchill, The Beatles and the Royal Family.

This enhanced standing through name association is less important for established, large players, as they are a name in themselves, but can be crucial for a small, niche company. Having blue chip customers can be a ringing endorsement that can influence other customer's perception of the company. One example is health company Celsis that, although small, nevertheless has blue chip customers like Unilever. Similarly, Watermark provides in-cabin services for the majority of airlines including Cathay Pacific. The advantage is particularly important in the service sector where quality and price are hard to assess, such as lawyers, advertisers and public relations companies. One way for a customer to choose is to be impressed by the client list and this is a fallback argument if it goes wrong, bearing in mind the old adage 'no one ever got fired for buying IBM'. However, what is not usually known is when the last service was sold to the blue chip customer or, indeed, whether it was a significant order or not. It might have been provided free or as a loss-leader just to achieve the kudos. Nevertheless, being able to demonstrate that respected players are doing business with a company is a competitive advantage and can be found in their advertising, websites and annual reports. Independent approval can be a significant reassurance for a customer and can include: BSI Registered Firm status; the ISO 9000 certificate; the Kitemark; the Royal Warrant; and the Investors in People standard. These awards can be withdrawn, so high standards need to be maintained.

3. Economics

Company success is heavily dependent on having favourable economics. This is broadly interpreted here and encompasses a wide variety of factors largely *within the company's control* that can affect the attractiveness of the shares, including, for example, the level of institutional shareholdings. It is difficult to separate the economics of the company from that of its sector, since they are so interlinked. However, sector economics encompass factors largely *outside the company's control* and this is discussed in the next chapter.

3a. Appropriate gearing: competitive advantage rated 4

'More than anything else, it's debt that determines which companies will survive and which will go bankrupt in a crisis.'
Peter Lynch, author of *One Up On Wall Street*.

Gearing is the amount borrowed by a company and is tax efficient because the interest payments are allowed against corporation tax, unlike dividends. It reduces the weighted average cost of capital, as debt is usually cheaper than share capital. The drawback is that the interest payments are a prior charge on profits and cannot be waived, unlike dividends. As pointed out by the economists Modigliani and Miller, the cost of capital increases as the level of gearing increases. This is because shareholders require a higher return to compensate for the increased risk of the company going bust, should it be unable to pay the interest on its borrowings. Therefore, some gearing can be beneficial but too much increases the overall cost of capital. The optimal point varies according to the type of company but gearing of up to 50% of capital can be reasonable. The appetite for gearing and thus risk also varies according to the country. Gearing tends to be very high in Japan, for example.

The amount of interest expense which is covered by profits is crucial. A good margin of safety would be an interest cover of more than five. It is essential that the company has a sound business model and control over its revenue streams so that the interest can be paid. Erratic cash flows can be a death knell. Also, be very wary of companies with over 50% gearing and entering a recession, since these have a higher risk of failure. Gearing is one of the prime reasons why companies collapse. Sectors that have high gearing but can be safely supported by tangible assets or solid revenue streams include property, retailers and tobacco companies, like Gallaher. Be suspicious of companies that embark on an acquisition spree using gearing and load up the balance sheet with goodwill, as this is a double risk. British Sky Broadcasting, for example, has very high gearing and goodwill plus negative net tangible assets. Goodwill is often a weak and unreliable asset, given that it is intangible. A write-down in its value reduces net assets and, if this breaks a banking covenant, the bank can call in the receivers. Please see chapter 8 for more details.

3b. Asset-backed shares: competitive advantage rated 4

There are many gurus, like Benjamin Graham and Sir John Templeton, who emphasise buying value. Buying a share that has significant net tangible assets is a good way of achieving this. If net tangible assets exceed the share price, the implication is that, if the worst came to the worst, then the assets could be sold and investors would be repaid. Hardys & Hansons, for example, is a regional brewer and pub operator. It has not revalued its properties for two decades and its share price has been estimated to be significantly less than its net tangible assets. Morrisons Supermarkets has £1.7 billion of land and buildings that have never been revalued. Having undervalued assets on the balance sheet is an admirably conservative accounting policy. In the TMT mania, concepts like tangible assets were discarded and replaced with valuations based on esoteric measures, such as counting eyeballs and website hits, with disastrous results.

Property companies have strong asset backing but can be risky since they are subject to asset write-downs in a recession. The quality of property assets is also important and realisation values depend on having an alternative use. There is not much of an alternative use for a coalmine or shipyard, for example, which undermines balance sheet values. Leisure operators, like bars and clubs, may have significant assets on paper but premises have been sold in fire sale conditions when overcapacity on the high street hit profitability.

Shares might be backed by intangible assets, such as purchased goodwill, but such value can be precarious and is a very 'soft' number in the balance sheet. There can be immense value in home-grown goodwill, although this is not in the balance sheet. The most obvious form is a brand name, like Coca-Cola that is regarded as the strongest in the world, but it can be an installed customer base, like Lloyds TSB, or superior technology in the case of Radstone Technology. It is not at all easy to value but an estimate can be made when there is a takeover elsewhere in the sector. Recall that Nestlé paid £2 billion for the brand names and operations of Rowntree chocolate bars. Thus, tangible and intangible assets can underpin the share price and increase an investor's margin of safety if the assets are valuable and not illusory.

3c. **Bolt-on acquisitions:** competitive advantage rated 3

'When a chief executive officer is encouraged by his advisors to make deals, he responds much as would a teenager boy who is encouraged by his father to have a normal sex life. It's not a push he needs.'
Warren Buffett

Bolt-on acquisitions are an attractive business model, in principle. They can lower cost and/or allow the company to be different, such as introducing customers, economies of scale, distribution channels, technology and extending geographic reach. However, the crucial requirement should be that they enhance earnings per share and not just increase turnover or pre-tax profit. The directors will usually assert that the acquisition will be earnings enhancing but reality can be very different. Generally, acquisitions that are lower risk are those that do not materially change the nature of the company and are bought cheaply. Acquisitions can be useful to allow a company to grow quickly and eliminate competition, particularly in highly fragmented industries that need consolidating. This growth can also increase the market capitalisation to a level that sparks interest from institutional shareholders, which typically starts in the £50 million to £100 million range. Examples of blue chips that have bolted on acquisitions are BAE Systems and HSBC. Eurocopy, which has now been taken private, was at the other end of the scale and acquired small photocopying firms that brought volume or increased the geographic coverage.

Beware of companies that make a string of acquisitions, issue significant amounts of highly-priced new shares or borrow excessively. Focus on the bottom line profit in the annual report that includes goodwill, exceptional costs and restructuring costs. Acquisitions, unfortunately, usually bring goodwill on to the balance sheet and this intangible asset can be perilous, as explained in chapter 8.

3d. Bull market acquisitions: competitive advantage rated 4

Shares are expensive in a bull market because the PER is propelled upwards. In the TMT mania, it was common to see companies with PERs of 50 to 100, if, indeed, that was a PER at all, given that so many were making losses. Nevertheless, such pricey paper is a form of currency that can be deployed to take over companies on lower PERs and thus boost profits. A raging bull market is the prime time for acquisitions and some CEOs lose the plot in the euphoria, paying ludicrous amounts for companies. The excessiveness is inevitably uncovered when PERs fall back to the norm in a bear market. The losers are shareholders who allowed their company to be taken over and held on to their new shares, which will now have fallen in price. Companies with poor economics tend to have low PERs and are thus restricted in using their shares for making bull market acquisitions. Indeed, they more likely to be takeover targets instead, since they are lowly priced.

One instance of a bull market acquisition was the $4.5 billion takeover by Marconi of Fore in the US. This resulted in huge amounts of worthless goodwill and a collapsing TMT market sealed Marconi's fate. Its cash mountain of £2 billion in the early 1990s was blown away. Another case was Vodafone, which grew using its expensive shares in the TMT mania. It embarked on an acquisition spree that cost over £100 billion. Therefore, be wary of companies that make too many acquisitions in boom times, especially if they are very material or fundamentally change the strategy of the company. There is likely to be little value acquired so new shares may be better issued for cash, which can then be hoarded to buy juicy pickings in the next market wash-out. Indeed, many TMT companies did just that and subsequently sat on piles of cash, pondering what to do with it.

3e. Changing sector and FTSE index: competitive advantage rated 5

Sectors have PERs too and if a company moves from a lowly valued sector to one that is more highly valued, then it can enjoy a re-rating and an increased share price. This does not happen often but this advantage is one factor to consider when analysing a share. If nothing else, it does imply that management are trying to increase shareholder value. One illustration is South Staffordshire, which has now been taken over and was in the lower rated water sector. It moved to the higher-rated support services sector, given that the majority of its income came to be derived from services rather than water. Demand for a share can also change if it moves into a different index. For example, if a company moves into the FTSE 100 then index tracker funds are obliged to buy and thus demand for the share usually increases. The opposite is true if it is demoted to the FTSE 250.

Sector PERs change continually and thus a re-rating from changing sector may not be permanent. In the TMT mania, some dull companies changed their name, but very little else, to be moved into this red-hot sector. After the mania, the reverse happened as companies tried to ditch TMT names and move out of the sector, since internet names tarnished, rather than added, value. An example is the move by AOL Time Warner to drop the AOL name, after their merger at the height of the TMT mania in 2000, when it was thought a good idea to marry the internet operation America Online with the publisher Time Warner. It is generally best to sell a company that has changed its name to move into a hot sector and buy a company that changes its name to move away from a bombed out sector. There will be little value in the former but it may be plentiful in the latter, which has become unfashionable.

3f. Economies of scale: competitive advantage rated 2

'If a company gets too large, break it into smaller parts.'
Sir Richard Branson, CEO of Virgin.

Economies of scale can be very important to lower costs and improve operations and products. A company that has reached a large size might afford television advertising for the first time, for example, and spread the overhead cost over a substantial revenue base, thus attracting more customers than a smaller competitor. It might be able to negotiate better terms from suppliers due to the larger volumes of business. Economies of scale could include opening overseas subsidiaries and employing superior management. A large scale is needed for some companies to achieve a break-even point, such as steel and car factories, which is not feasible for a small operator. The desire to achieve economies of scale is often the reason for acquisitions that bring benefits like attaining national or international reach and the need to service global customers. Examples include Stagecoach, Diageo, UK terrestrial television and the banking and life insurance sectors.

At some point, diseconomies of scale can arise, where cost increases rather than decreases as the output increases. This can be due to a number of factors. For example, large multinationals may grow so large and complex that management, employee motivation, communication, culture and decision-making are seriously impeded. One company wanted to sell a subsidiary to a Japanese car maker and just finding out who to contact in such an enormous empire was a major task. The media and transport group Virgin is keen to stop its subsidiaries becoming too large and splits them up to avoid them becoming unwieldy. Nimble, niche operators can have an advantage because they should not have diseconomies of scale. Examples of this include Broadcastle, a small finance company which, nevertheless, has its own low-cost bank and whose one branch is located in the head office. It has thus achieved economies of scale despite banks normally needing a huge size to be feasible. Albemarle & Bond is a niche operator that expanded through organic growth, partly to achieve economies of scale through national coverage for its pawnbroking activities. Belhaven is a regional brewer that makes beer under contract for gorillas and this helps it achieve the volumes to run the plant efficiently.

3g. Feed off another's growth: competitive advantage rated 2

Some companies feed off the growth of another company, sector, government, megatrend or the economy and is discussed further in the next chapter. This is an attractive business model, particularly if the company is shielded from the operating risk borne by the other company. Umeco, Aero Inventory and Watermark provide services to the airline sector. In the case of the first two, these include supplying components and services and, in the latter case, in-flight consumer items. This is a much less risky space to occupy than being in the high-risk, front line business of running airlines, the economics of which are very poor. Expro International is another example of feeding off another's growth, as it provides support services to oilfield operators and its fortunes depend on their prosperity.

Biotrace and Celsis ride the huge growth in the National Health Service (NHS) by providing sterilisation services. Unite Group benefits from the inexorable growth in university education by providing student accommodation, which has moved considerably up-market in the last few decades. Compass Group gains from the trend for companies to outsource non-core operations, like catering. Nightclub operators, such as Luminar and Ultimate Leisure, have the tailwind of increasing disposable incomes from a growing economy funnelled into activities like entertainment.

A variation of this model is a symbiotic relationship, whereby two businesses mutually benefit from growth. This co-dependence binds them and can make a more formidable duo. For example, Microsoft needs ever more powerful Intel chips to run its software and Intel needs Microsoft's new products to drive upgrades in personal computers to sell more of its chips. Mobile phone manufacturers need telecommunications companies to improve the capabilities, footprints, service, new products like 3G, reception quality and cost of calls and the telecommunications companies need ever smaller and more powerful handsets to drive demand. Other examples are cars and petrol or airplanes and airports, where growth in the former drives demand for the latter and both are indispensable to each other. Collaboration can be lost if one company steps into the other's space, as happened with Microsoft and Intel (see appendix 2). It can also be lost if a company moves up or down the value chain and upsets companies that were previously collaborating. An example is a vertically integrated company, such as oil or brewing, expanding into 'upstream' or 'downstream' activities.

3h. Good institutional and directors' shareholdings:
competitive advantage rated 4

'I like the directors to own a number of shares substantial enough to give the 'owner's eye', but not so many that they have control, can sit back and could at some future stage block a bid. I like to see a good cross-section of the directors with reasonable shareholdings and I always worry if the finance director is not among them.'

Jim Slater, author of *The Zulu Principle.*

Encouraging good institutional support is an advantage and blue chip companies are almost invariably majority-owned by institutions. A smaller shareholder's interest is likely to match that of the institutions and such big brothers can insist on remedial action, such as board changes and strategy. However, this mutuality of interest can fail if, for example, institutions want to accept a cheeky bid when the shares are going through a lean time, whereas smaller shareholders want to wait for recovery. The institutions are professionals and lack of their support can be a telling point. For instance, a 'colourful character' may run the company that the City knows about and are avoiding. Watch for reductions in their shareholdings. It is preferable to have good spread of institutions rather than a dominant one, which might want to pursue its own agenda regardless of the wishes of others. However, some institutions are failing to control boards properly, as evidenced by the debate over remuneration and share options, so their presence is not a panacea but it does provide at least some protection from mismanagement.

Institutional holdings may be scarce in smaller companies if their market value is below the typical minimum investment threshold of £50 million to £100 million. However, directors often have large stakes in smaller companies. This means that the company is likely to be 'owner' rather than 'employee' managed. A company that is employee managed may have directors who put personal gain above the interests of the shareholders. It is preferable for the board to have a material stake of up to, say, 20% and their stake should be less than that of the institutions. Directors' shareholdings should be well spread amongst themselves and include the finance director. One illustration is aerospace company Umeco, which is one third owned by numerous institutions. The board has a much smaller stake, which is well spread, largely paid for with their own money and includes the finance director. Likewise, perfume seller Merchant Retail is half owned by institutions and the directors' stake is 4%.

3i. **Headroom to grow:** competitive advantage rated 2

It is important that a company has the headroom to grow and is not hide-bound by the total market size or its share of that market. Gorillas dominate due to their size and, in effect, can only grow as fast as the overall market. Therefore, a small, nimble, niche player typically offers more potential because it will have the headroom to grow its modest share of a large market. This will be at the expense of the gorillas but may not attract predatory reaction if they are not materially threatened. Indeed, they may be unable to counter the threat.

There are many examples of growth companies with headroom. One instance is utility reseller Telecom plus whose market share is tiny and, even if it became a FTSE 100 company, there would still be headroom as the market is huge. JD Wetherspoon has been rolling out its pubs for years and still aims to open significantly more, although saturation must come at some point. Therefore, it is sensible to ensure that the overall market is large enough and growing so that a niche company has scope to increase its share. If the market is small then the ambition of the company is curtailed, such as Plasmon, which makes a hard disc product for a specialised and limited market.

3j. **High dividends:** competitive advantage rated 2

High dividends are attractive because they are a real cash return, so provide solace in a bear market, and are important because two-thirds of the total return from shares is due to dividends. They are paramount to certain investors, including retirees and institutions that need income. This is reinforced when the yield beats that of a bank account. Further, the bank interest rate may well remain the same but dividends should grow in line with the economy. However, a high dividend can be a trap because it often signifies that the company is in trouble and the market expects the dividend to be cut. A struggling company is a recipe for a falling share price and receiving an attractive dividend is futile if this is more than off-set by losing capital.

However, there are shares that are on low ratings, have a high dividend payout policy and a sound business model. If the dividend is 7% and the capital gain is 7%, then the investment will double in five years. In addition, dividends are cash in hand, whereas unrealised gains in a share price may vanish. The cash also provides funds for investing elsewhere, enabling diversification. They do, however, tend to be more highly taxed than capital gains and are best earned in a tax shelter, such as an ISA. Market wash-outs happen every four years or so and offer a good choice of companies, including blue chips, which have high dividends. By illustration, Lloyds TSB and Friends Provident at the bottom of the bear market in 2003 yielded 12%, which is four times the market norm, and such value offers an opportunity to lock in a high yield. It will also be a share price driver when recovery occurs because investors will want to buy such shares to secure the generous yield. This action will drive the yield back to the norm, resulting in a handsome gain in the share price. Examples of higher yielding shares are Broadcastle, a speciality finance company with a sound business model, and JZ Equity, a zero dividend preference share.

3k. KISS principle: competitive advantage rated 3

'In 1998 the markets learned a new reality of the post-cold war era – a nuclear power was allowed to default (Russia), but a hedge fund wasn't.'
Tom Gallagher, economic researcher, and his comment on Long Term Capital Management.

The KISS principle means 'keep it simple, stupid'. Simple businesses are easy to understand and evaluate. Indeed, if you cannot understand the business then do not invest. Simple businesses have a straightforward profit and loss account with no exceptional items and, preferably, immaterial goodwill. Sir Winston Churchill insisted that a report should be on one page so that it would be succinct and readily understood. Any subject can be simply explained and if an annual report, for example, is incomprehensible, that may be management's objective and the company should be avoided.

Simple businesses include: Richmond Foods (ice cream); Albemarle & Bond (pawnbroking); Belhaven and Hardys & Hansons (brewers, pubs); Morrisons Supermarkets; Mears (maintenance); and Telecom plus (utility re-seller). Banking and insurance are essentially simple businesses where customers entrust their cash, on which the company makes a turn, and it is repaid at some future date. Further examples include tobacco and retailing. This does not mean that some of these companies are necessarily easy to analyse, given their operations may be vast, diversified and worldwide, but their basic premise is simple.

Technology companies do not generally follow the KISS principle. They are typically very difficult to understand, not helped by frequent use of buzzwords and acronyms, like 'ERM'. ICAP provides a facility to trade in various securities but is a difficult business to assess adequately. Its actual activities are opaque and a shareholder just has to hope they carry on being successful. It is not practicable to assess the operating risks in detail. Do not forget the 'black box' operated by

Long Term Capital Management that worked its magic until it blew up in 1998 and threatened to undermine the financial system.

3l. Low break-even point: competitive advantage rated 2

Companies can achieve a quantum leap in profits if they have a low break-even point where fixed costs are quickly covered. Further sales are then able to improve profit directly rather than being swallowed up by costs. This is most effective when the marginal cost of the product is very small and the gross profit margin very large so the revenue falls unhindered to the bottom line. Information technology companies like Microsoft and Dicom have this cost structure, as do utility resellers, like Telecom plus, and financial services companies, such as Broadcastle. Casino gambling is another instance where the gross margins are good and increased volume can readily be handled with little marginal cost. A low break-even point is essential for cyclical companies in a recession, including engineering, construction and retailers, because sales can drop significantly. If the fixed costs are low then this can help to stave off losses.

Companies that have a high break-even point, like steel making and airlines, are riskier because they can easily fall into loss if sales falter. They tend to have significant tangible and intangible assets and the resultant depreciation and goodwill amortisation charges are prior and non-negotiable items. Other candidates include manufacturing, pubs, chemicals, mining and transport. For example, a car manufacturer's direct cost of components and labour is high and gross margins are small. There is not much fat left over to drop to the bottom line. Ford and General Motors have flirted with bankruptcy because the economics of their businesses are not good. High fixed cost can be due to office, computer and employee overheads in a service company, such as an investment bank. Where a company has an inherently high level of fixed cost, the strategy should be to increase revenue rapidly and move way above the high break-even point. A no-frills airline like Ryanair has done this with a rapid increase in its planes, which boosts marginal revenue but the fixed costs of administration, seat booking, head office, etc. are already covered and do not rise proportionately.

3m. One-off action provides revenue for years: competitive advantage rated 2

'Some genius invented the Oreo. We're just living off the inheritance.'
Ross Johnson, president of RJR Nabisco, commenting on 'America's favourite cookie'.

One of the highest-rated business models is when a one-off action leads to revenue streams for years. The market often either does not appreciate the significance of the event or, instead, gives it far too much credence. This provides an opportunity for the investor or shorter, respectively. The action can be due to a change in strategy in the existing business, or through an acquisition. Patents allow companies to enjoy the fruits of their labour for a maximum of 20 years, an example being Alexander Graham Bell and the patent for telephones. Mars chocolate bars were first sold in the UK in 1932 and still sell by the million today. Others have also been very inventive but competition soon knocked them off their perch, like Henry Ford with his mass-produced Model T car.

Another example is Albemarle & Bond, which spent several years ploughing profits back into opening its pawnbroking shops. This depressed the profit and the market was unimpressed by this 'jam tomorrow' story. However, once the rollout was largely complete at 50 outlets, the reinvestment stopped and the profits and share price rose dramatically. All this information was in the public domain. Richmond Foods made a £10 million investment by buying the rights to sell ice cream under the very powerful and valuable Nestlé brand. The products are derivatives of the chocolate brands sold and heavily marketed by the big brother. It provides a new and stable revenue stream for years.

However, a one-off action to produce revenue streams for years is not risk-free, as numerous cases of failure in the faddish consumer sector with restaurants, bars, clubs and health spas have demonstrated. This same strategy but using acquisitions is also littered with disappointment. The acquisition route is likely to be most successful in an area where the company already has competitive advantage, rather than a new area where they have to go up the learning curve but competitors do not. The TMT mania raised a mountain of cash through new issues, which promised an investment in a new economy that would provide riches for years, and shareholders are still waiting for the revenue streams to materialise.

3n. Public perception: competitive advantage rated 4

Like it or not, public perception of a company can be very important. If this were not so, then there would be no role for the myriad of financial public relations firms and it is very unusual for a company not to employ one. By definition, perception may have little to do with the truth. Companies that are badly perceived will not tend to attract investors and, since a share price is simply the point where demand and supply meet like any other product, the share price can suffer. Banks receive a mauling by the press during a recession because of dire tales of businesses and individuals unable to repay their loans. This can lead to political repercussions, such as windfall taxes and legislation, which are unhelpful to an investor.

Oil companies are as unpopular as OPEC, although the blame for the high price and occasional erratic supply of oil can be sometimes due to government (tax) or campaigners (Prudhoe Bay, Alaska). Shell was boycotted, for example, to protest about disposing of installations in the North Sea. In comparing companies within a sector, Virgin's charismatic and popular chairman, Sir Richard Branson, was always going to win its spats with British Airways, with its dirty tricks campaign, and its tussle with lottery organiser Camelot over bribery allegations. EasyJet is viewed in the same positive light, as it also has a high profile and likeable founder. Warren Buffett has by far the lowest remuneration of any CEO of a major company, at $100,000 a year. He is perceived as being the investors' champion and acting in their best interests. Fourteen thousand enthusiastic shareholders flock to his Berkshire Hathaway AGMs in Omaha. Compare that to the AGMs of some other companies where the board of directors probably needs counselling after a roasting from shareholders. This is increasingly the case and is usually because of poor corporate governance, as detailed below.

Ethical investors' black list includes tobacco, alcoholic beverages and firearms. Environmentalists and animal rights campaigners attack various activities, such as pollutants and fur farms. Railway operators have become a standard joke and receive much media criticism. Financial services companies are often in the spotlight with hard luck stories. Their bad publicity is compounded by scoring own goals caused by scandals, such as miss-sold pensions and the collapse of Equitable Life. Companies also receive bad press when something goes wrong, like accidents or tainted products, like Perrier water. The correct response is to be frank, honest, admit the wrong and promptly rectify the matter. The temptation is to 'do a Nixon' and cover up, which merely provides an ongoing and wonderful story to the media. However, remember 'what goes around comes around' and a company that has received poor publicity but has a sound business model may be an excellent value play in due course when the brouhaha has died down.

3o. **Recreate the company:** competitive advantage rated 2

'It is very easy to endure the difficulties of one's enemies. It is the successes of one's friends that are hard to bear.'
Oscar Wilde

Companies that recreate themselves in order to lower cost and/or differentiate themselves can have dramatically improved economics. This is easier to spot in hindsight rather than in advance because the change is only an avowed intention at the beginning. However, when some progress is obviously being made then investors may be tempted to buy. A good example is US's General Electric, which re-engineered itself three times under Jack Welch. He decided that they should be the number one or two in a business or withdraw. Next, the strategy was to take work out of activities and, lastly, to sell solutions rather than physical goods. Disney re-created itself by capturing more value from films, increasing the value added at theme parks, diversifying its activities, such as cruise ships, and moving increasingly into merchandising and retailing, which was more lucrative. Another illustration is the revitalisation that Stuart Rose achieved when he became CEO of retailer Arcadia in 2000. Hornby's strategy of dealing with the problem of high cost in the UK was to transfer toy production to China and it also improved quality. Radstone Technology re-created itself by changing its commodity computer products so that they became rugged and suitable for military use.

Equally, there are all too frequent cases where the transmogrification has been disastrous. Many UK companies have found that the US is a graveyard of ambitions in trying to reinvigorate companies by increasing scale or global reach. Examples are Stagecoach and Midland Bank. Marconi is, yet again, the classic example, where management was encouraged by investment banks to ditch its traditional business and buy into electrical wizardry when TMT was raging. As a result, Marconi fell apart, a sad end for what was once one of the biggest UK companies. Quality of management and their real motivations are a good clue as to whether a company's re-creation will succeed. This is not at all easy to evaluate but companies where 'employee' directors are fixated with empire building are best avoided.

3p. Strong cash flow: competitive advantage rated 3

Cash flow is the life-blood of any business because it is needed for operations, reinvestment, acquisitions and dividends. Excess cash can be returned to shareholders through share buy-backs that should enhance earnings per share, which can be an important driver of the share price by increasing demand for the shares. Some companies are better at generating cash flow than others. Those with strong cash flow typically do not have to spend heavily on fixed assets but rely more on the brainpower of employees. Engineering, manufacturing and construction companies tend to use a great deal of capital and net cash flow is usually poor, an example being Barratt Developments. Conversely, Telecom plus is a reseller of multiple utilities with a modest head office and a commission-only sales force. It generates strong cash flow that is not needed in the business and so the dividend payout is high.

Cash flow is not a panacea, however, since it can be very misleading. The snag is that it is often impossible to tell if good or bad cash flow is symptomatic of a business' fortunes. Please see chapter 8 for more details. However, it is always sensible to look at cash flow over a number of years, since this will be more telling than reading too much into just one year.

4. Management

'Surround yourself with the best people you can find, delegate authority, and don't interfere.'
Ronald Reagan

Management, or enterprise, is arguably the most crucial of the four factors of production because it is the most creative and value-adding ingredient. The other three factors of production are land, labour and capital. Assessing management is not easy because the tools to do so are imperfect, such as the annual report. Meeting them is helpful but just how good someone is at their job can be very different from how they appear. Some investment gurus choose not to meet management, as they consider it pointless, given the spin that will result, and prefer other analytical methods, such as talking to competitors. There are clues to management capabilities, however, that can shape an investor's opinion, as detailed below. The company should be avoided if an investor has an uncomfortable hunch that all is not well with management, even if he cannot quite pinpoint the reason.

4a. Auditors, opinions and accounting policies:
competitive advantage rated 3

It is vital to consider the audit carried out on a company and the accounting policies that have been adopted by the board of directors. The auditor's opinion should be that the accounts show a 'true and fair' view. These two words do not mean the same thing. A true view would be to say that the profit is at a record level. A fair view would add that this was mainly due to a one-off asset sale that will not be repeated. Note that the auditors do not guarantee or certify the accounts but merely express an opinion. Neither do they say the accounts are 100% accurate. Instead, the auditors' aim is that the accounts should be materially correct, probably with an error tolerance in the range of 5% to 10% depending on whether it is a profit and loss, or balance sheet, item.

The auditor's opinion will almost invariably be unqualified. This does not mean that the accounting policies are not without criticism. For example, they may contravene an accounting standard. This contravention will be disclosed in the notes to the accounts but the auditor's report will not usually guide you to the problem, merely saying that the accounts show a true and fair view *given the accounting policies that have been adopted by the board of directors*. For example, Lloyds TSB does not amortise goodwill on its Scottish Widows acquisition and this is a departure from the requirement of the Companies Act 1985 that all goodwill should be amortised. Goodwill is covered in chapter 8. Therefore, notice if any policies do not comply with accounting standards or the Companies Act. A qualified opinion is a red flag and needs to be investigated. It is often the case that bankrupt companies receive an unqualified opinion in their last set of accounts, so auditors are no guarantee of sound financial health.

There is usually too little detail to fathom the effect of accounting policies and any changes need to be watched. Some changes may be perfectly reasonable, such as depreciating assets over a shorter time. Be cautious if the accounting policies change frequently and particularly if any increase income or assets, or reduce expenses and liabilities. Avoid the company if you cannot understand the effect of the change in policy.

The auditors' opinion only covers the financial statements and notes in the annual report. The rest, being principally the directors' report, is outside their scope, although they will study it. They should object if there are any claims that are in conflict with the accounts and this provides some reassurance. The directors' verbiage at the front should always be taken with a big pinch of salt because it tends to err on the side of truth rather than fairness. They are almost invariably 'spun' with the help of financial public relations companies to put the results in the best possible light. For example, see if you can spot a graph or table of statistics showing anything, such as sales or customer satisfaction, which has a down year. If there is a down year, then the table will invariably be excluded. There are very few exceptions to this spin, the best example perhaps being the letters to Berkshire Hathaway shareholders by Warren Buffett.

4b. Changes in professional advisors: competitive advantage rated 4

Companies have various professional advisors, such as stockbrokers, financial public relations companies, auditors and bankers, and some turnover is inevitable as fees and service change over time. This is not necessarily a worry but keep a sharp eye out if this happens frequently, as it may be that unsavoury practises are afoot. The change could be due to the advisor not wanting to do business with the company any more. Alternatively, the company may want frequent change so that advisors do not have enough time to understand what is happening.

By far the most critical appointment is that of the auditors and any change should be treated suspiciously. This is especially true if it is from one of the big four firms, namely Deloitte & Touche, Ernst & Young, KPMG and Pricewaterhouse Coopers, to a small practice and the audit fee is very material to them. The danger is that they will be obliging because they do not want to lose this important client. The fraudulent Versailles, for example, used a small, regional firm. Also, the level of expertise of auditors will vary markedly, with the cream in the big four. Sometimes, however, a smaller firm is chosen deliberately because it is a sector specialist and can add value to the company. Auditors have significant leeway in agreeing the presentation and content of accounts, so there can be considerable horse-trading.

Any of the big four can be expected to provide a good audit but mistakes and fraud do occur, such as in BCCI, which was riddled with corruption. The US authorities accused Enron of robbing the bank and their auditors, Arthur Andersen, of driving the getaway car; they paid the price of being so helpful and have since ceased to exist. That remarkable episode should have provided a wake-up call to the surviving auditors that their independence is crucial and their report is to the shareholders who, in theory, employ them.

4c. Conflicts of interest: competitive advantage rated 2

'Prefer a loss to a dishonest gain: the one brings pain at the moment, the other for all time.'
Chilon, Greece, 6th century BC.

Companies should be avoided that have conflicts of interest. These are almost invariably the result of directors' actions and take a variety of forms. Related party transactions can be harmless, for example, when a non-executive director provides arm's length professional services, like legal or property advice. Be wary if the amounts are material. Directors' holdings in a subsidiary or associated company should be viewed with suspicion because money may be siphoned off in ruses, such as management fees or inflated transfer pricing. The worry is compounded if the subsidiary or associated company is overseas and especially if it is in a tax haven with strict secrecy laws.

Another warning is if a company depends on the benevolence or licence arrangement of another company that is partly or wholly owned by the directors. Be distrustful if the company has bought, or intends to buy, any such company. Royalty payments should be carefully examined because this takes revenue off the top and should be on commercial terms to a genuine, unrelated third party. Also, be alert to a company that seems to be operating in a profitable sector yet makes little or no profit. One such company was paying inflated prices for various goods and services and the directors were being paid off on the side. This only became known after a takeover, when the new directors discovered the fraud but it was not made public.

Conflicts of interest usually arise when there is a dominant shareholding by the board, typically over 50%. The temptation is to treat the company as a personal operation at the expense of the minority shareholders. Such dominant shareholder companies should be avoided anyway. Fortunately, most of the above unsavoury arrangements will have to be disclosed in the annual report so it is always essential to read it. Such companies do exist today but are a rarity. Examples of companies with past conflicts of interest are Polly Peck and Versailles, both of which went bust. Do not rely on an investment recommendation in the media to point out the conflicts, as they are usually negligent in this regard.

4d. Corporate governance: competitive advantage rated 2

Corporate governance has been a hot topic for years and the tempo has increased. The excessive payments made to so called 'fat cats' have been whipped up in the media and led to shareholder revolts at AGMs, such as GlaxoSmithKline and British Gas, which featured a pig that was greedily feeding and named after the CEO, Cedric Brown. Government has been concerned about the issue for over a decade but precious little action has resulted because it feels that this is generally a matter for shareholders. This attitude may change. Shareholders faced a three-year bear market until 2003 and many felt outraged at the fall in their fortunes and the rise in those that are the entrusted stewards of their money. The stock market fell by 25% in 2002 but the remuneration of the FTSE 100 boards of directors rose by 25%. Arguably, the reaction is largely a moral one to be left to each individual investor. However, corporate governance should be scrutinised carefully as it has important implications as to the attractiveness of a share, as discussed below.

Checks and balances

It is a prime tenet of good, democratic government of a country that there are strong checks and balances. This is most evident in the US, which has a written constitution and powerful states that can oppose the Presidential executive and judiciary. This is not the same in the UK, where power is largely centralised in the prime minister. Nevertheless, the splitting of the governing party, judiciary and police forces, with recourse to various European bodies, does provide checks and balances. Without them, chaos can rule, as is so evident in the developing world and in recent communist countries.

This principle also applies to companies. It is vital that there are checks and balances because the shareholders own but do not run the company. That task is delegated to professional managers. The snag is that the latter control the levers of power and shareholders have to trust that they will use them wisely. In an age of spin, the tendency has been for these stewards to put the best possible interpretation on their performance. They also help themselves from the pot, in many cases excessively so. Therefore, if an investor sees an instance of poor corporate governance, then that is a red flag about what else might be happening that is sleazy but hidden from view. The following are examples of what to spot and can be used as a checklist the next time an investor reads an annual report.

Audit and remuneration committees

There should be audit and remuneration committees, comprised of non-executive directors. This is standard practice today for larger companies. The audit committee should preferably be chaired by a qualified accountant. The auditors should have the right to hold meetings with the audit committee and without executive directors being present. This encourages frank exchange of views and can highlight problem areas that executive directors may wish to gloss over.

Board composition

'Here lies Robert Maxwell. He lied everywhere else.'
Private Eye, satirical magazine.

The splitting of the chairman and CEO jobs is a check and balance of paramount importance. It is crucial to be able to fire under-performing CEOs. A compliant board may dodge the issue and the company's fortunes can then suffer from mismanagement. The task of firing the CEO is a matter for the board as a whole but the chairman should take a lead role. If there is a blocking vote by the CEO and it seems unlikely that he could be fired, then the company should be avoided. True, the board could dispense with a strong non-executive chairman but, in practice, it would likely be keen to avoid damaging publicity. An example of problems resulting from the chairman also being the CEO is the collapse of Robert Maxwell's empire and WorldCom, which was the largest ever fraud. Avoid any company where the chairman is also the CEO. The finance director is a critical counterbalance and any company that does not have one, although very rare, can be dismissed out of hand.

Non-executives can be an important source of protection for shareholders, in addition to that provided by institutions, and they should form a majority of the board. Since the latter appoints the non-executives, the worry can be that they are cronies and will lack independence. It is reassuring if there is a heavyweight and talented non-executive with a reputation to protect. It is an encouraging sign that he would want to be associated with the company in the first place and the expectation is that he will object to inadvisable actions. However, the FTSE 100 boards are crammed with the great and the good but that has not prevented innumerable instances of bad corporate governance. However, it may have been worse if some strong non-executives were not there.

There should be a nominated senior non-executive director who should be available to answer shareholder grievances. Be wary if some directors have the same surname because family members can act as a concert party and lack objectivity. Smaller companies argue that their size does not warrant complying with the recommended corporate governance and they do have a point. However, this is one factor to weigh up in deciding whether to invest in companies of such a size.

An extreme example was one company that was once entirely composed of non-executive directors. Managers were invited in to make their reports and then left the meeting. Carpetright has a strong line up of non-executives and Plasmon has the former CEO of IBM UK on its board. Do not necessarily be swayed by titled people being on the board. Talent counts, rather than titles.

Directors' contracts

'Don't forget the golden rule. He who has the gold makes the rules.'
Anon

There are various bodies, like The Association of British Insurers, that have issued corporate governance guidelines and they recommend that directors do not have a service contract longer than 12 months. Generally, this has had the desired effect and the vast majority of companies have now toed this line. However, there have been high profile cases where this has been breached, an example being Tesco. The non-executive directors at Domino's Pizza had three-year contracts. Investors should consider avoiding companies that breach the guidelines.

Directors' remuneration

There are two ways to evaluate remuneration. The first is the absolute sum paid. This is typically in the millions for the board of a blue chip company. It may represent only a tiny percentage of profits and so is immaterial to the shareholders' interests. Nevertheless, it is a red flag if the sums are excessive. The directors will argue the going rate has to be paid for the job and they have a point. Therefore, compare the remuneration for like-sized companies and avoid those where it is materially higher. Also, consider the rate of increase over the last few years. It may indicate that directors are being greedy if the increase is rocketing. An underpaid director is a rarity indeed. There are clearly many instances of abuse and these certainly break the corporate governance guidelines. This extends beyond pay to bonuses, pensions, contract terms and, above all, share options. What the directors take off the table is not available for shareholders and a keen eye should be placed on the remuneration report in the annual accounts. The problem in the UK is not as acute as in the US, where astronomical remuneration of $30 to $60 million is common for CEOs, and share options can run into the hundreds of millions. Share options are discussed in chapter 8.

Investors may take a particularly dim view of paying special bonuses to directors for merely doing their job. The £10 million payment to Chris Gent of Vodafone for the £100 billion takeover of the German Mannesmann comes to mind. Spending shareholders' money is the easy bit. Making the acquisition work is another matter. If that payment had to be made it should preferably have been when, and if, the acquisition proved to add shareholder value and that would take some years. Such acquisitions resulted in £119 billion of goodwill on Vodafone's balance sheet but competitors, like mmO2, have written off billions of pounds in assets, in no small part due to struggling with their ruinously expensive 3G licences.

The other way of looking at remuneration is as a percentage of pre-tax profits. This is more applicable to smaller companies where the remuneration can be a very material amount. A typical percentage can be around 15%. The shares may well be avoided if the percentage is nearer 25%. Avoid companies where there has been a breakdown in corporate governance, such as occasionally comes to light, like a CEO putting home help on the payroll or luxury accommodation made available for private use by executives, even if the abuses have since been rectified.

Directors' share dealings

'I have always thought the actions of men are the best interpreters of their thoughts.'

John Locke, philosopher.

Words are one thing and parting with one's cash is another. It is always revealing to examine directors' share dealings because they are concrete evidence of how they judge the likely prospects of their company and can be a key driver of share prices. Dealings by the chairman, CEO and finance director are particularly worth noting. The selling of a small amount of shares by one director is not a problem. A significant reduction is a warning sign. Do not be reassured by any statement as to why the sale was made. These vary but include divorce, buying a house and institutional demand. You have no way of knowing whether this is the real reason or not so be cautious. They never say it is because the shares are overvalued or about to hit hard times! Cluster selling by directors is a powerful warning, especially if it materially reduces their stake.

Selling share options is trickier. Options are usually cashed in at the first available opportunity, which does not provide a ringing endorsement of prospects. After all, who would sell a goose that was laying golden eggs? It may be that the directors want to spread their wealth and not have too much tied up in the same place as they earn a living, which is understandable. Maybe if only part is sold then that is reasonable, given that the overall stake is growing. If there is cluster retention of options by directors then that is a very positive sign.

Lastly, there may be many reasons to sell a share but there should be only one reason for buying and that is to make a profit. True, a purchase could be made to demonstrate to the market that the directors are backing the company. These transactions may be modest and, if so, can be largely discounted. A large purchase by one director is a powerful signal, especially if it is a maiden purchase. Cluster buying by directors of material amounts is very telling and may be an indication that they know something the market does not, like a general expectation of a takeover. Significant directors' stake building, especially if there is cluster buying, can be indicative of good news flow that has not yet been made public or may signal that the shares are undervalued.

Directors' share options

Share options merit a separate section (please see chapter 8). However, suffice to say that The Association of British Insurers' guidelines state options should not exceed 10% of share capital over a ten-year period and no more than 3% in any one-year period. This is widely flouted and is a prime method of accounting for growth. A distinction can be made between options for the Board alone and for the rest of the employees. There is more objectivity in the latter because the recipients do not have the awarding power. Nevertheless, it is all paid for by the shareholders as compensation and should be considered in its entirety.

Just what is acceptable is a matter for each investor, some being more concerned than others, but one view is that options exceeding 10% of share capital should be unacceptable and the culprit avoided. Watermark and Interlink Foods, for example, have had share options amounting to 15% of the capital. On the other hand, Telecom plus, Hardys & Hansons and Hitachi Credit are rare, as they do not have directors' share options.

4e. Excellent, honest and well-motivated management:
competitive advantage rated 2

'We look for first class businesses accompanied by first class management.'
Warren Buffett

Management should be excellent, honest and well-motivated. One example is BP, which is widely considered to have had an excellent CEO in Lord Browne. Honesty has had its currency depreciated in the last few decades. Management should be well-motivated and this can stem from personal drive as well as their financial stake, which is preferably their own money invested rather than freeloading with share options. Not being greedy with remuneration is an important yardstick.

Good management is hard to assess by an outsider but it does tend to show in the results over a number of years and vice versa, when a company has been struggling. First-rate management is a necessary but not a sufficient condition for a successful company, however. Good management will struggle to make any headway in the sunset industries of engineering and textiles, for example. Some businesses are simple and have such attractive economics that they can hardly fail to succeed no matter who runs them, such as mortgage banks.

It is particularly attractive when management is heavyweight, given the size of the business, and this indicates an ambition to grow it. This is reinforced if the managers have made their reputation elsewhere and have chosen a company that they want to revitalise. Admiration increases if they then take a considerable stake in the company with their own money, rather than rely on share options. An example of all these facets is found in aerospace company Umeco.

4f. Follow the man when a talented director moves on: competitive advantage rated 4

When a talented director moves on it is a good idea to follow him. He is likely to be able to work his magic elsewhere and an example is Lord Harris. His life has been in carpets and he built up a three-store family firm into Harris Queensway, a major retail chain which was sold for £450 million in 1988. He then started Carpetright, which now dominates the market. Charles Wigoder developed Peoples Phone and sold it to Vodafone for £77 million. He moved on with his winning team to run Telecom plus, so there was an impressive track record that was likely to be repeated, which has been the case. Another illustration is Aero Inventory, a small support services aerospace company, which attracted Frank Turner as chairman, who was a Rolls-Royce director. His skills can clinch deals through experience and extensive sector contacts. The principle is also evident in fund management where a star can make all the difference to performance. Following talent is not always a panacea for success if the sector economics suddenly deteriorate, as happened to Umeco after the US terrorist attacks.

4g. Modest head office: competitive advantage rated 4

'The bigger the headquarters, the more decadent the company.'
Sir James Goldsmith, billionaire businessman.

Modest head offices help competitive advantage with low-cost activities. Thus, the classic example of a company to avoid is one that has a palatial head office. This symbolises whether the directors are maximising long-term profit for shareholders or running it for themselves. If the head office is sumptuous then expenditure that a shareholder cannot see might be on the same scale, like lavish expense accounts and first-class flying; this was the case with Boo.com, which blew a fortune in record time, aided by such extravagance. Fine head offices are particularly the norm with financial service companies, as they want to give the impression of solidity and they will be around to honour their promise to return customers' money years hence. Conversely, engineering companies' head offices can be dire.

The British Airways' head office is an opulent glass tower at Heathrow. It seems to be living up to its business model of being a full-cost carrier and is struggling. Ryanair closely watches the pennies with its low-cost business model and has grown very quickly. Warren Buffett has a tiny office and a handful of staff in low-cost Nebraska. Telecom plus has a spartan office in north London. Although opulent head offices are extremely attractive places for the directors to strut around, they can give potential customers a feeling of wanting to do business with them. Therefore, there may be some justification for the expenditure.

4h. Past success: competitive advantage rated 3

Past company success is a reasonable indication that the company has competitive advantage. This is easiest to measure by looking at the financial performance, such as growth in profits and dividends, combined with conservative financing and no hiccups or disastrous diversifications. Long-term, unbroken pre-tax profit growth speaks for itself at Morrisons Supermarkets, with 35 years, and Belhaven, with 12 years. Such a pedigree will be largely due to a successful business model, a promising sector and management that is reliable and competent.

Past failure can be straightforward to spot. Are the accounts free of exceptional items or does this occur regularly, as with technology companies like NSB Retail Systems? Does management wheel out unlikely and repetitive excuses, like a strong currency, lack of tourists or the early arrival of Easter, and acknowledge no blame on their part? Do they want to return funds to shareholders via share buy-backs, like Diageo, or husband it for empire-building acquisitions? Are directors being fired on a regular basis, implying there is strong discord in the boardroom? Matalan, for example, has had two CEOs in two years.

4i. Shareholder values: competitive advantage rated 2

Management should have the interests of the shareholders uppermost. This was clearly the case with Lord Weinstock when he ran GEC but was not evident in his successors, who saw it re-named Marconi and collapse in short order. Another example was Racal, which did so much to increase shareholder value by de-merging Vodafone in 1991, selling the rump for a decent price and returning the cash to shareholders. This was a recognition that Vodafone could grow faster outside the group, achieve a higher rating and become a gorilla. BT decided not to de-merge its mobile subsidiary mmO2 until 2001, by which time it was too little, too late. There was something new at Racal that seemed to promise an increase in shareholder value but not at BT.

A shareholder-orientated company maximises the return to shareholders rather than to the directors. It will have excellent communications, a clear, clean annual report that is easy to understand and directors who are reasonably accessible. Sadly, there are not many like this today. There are any number of companies that only pay lip service, if that, to shareholder values. Destroying value may not be due to conflicts of interest but to incompetence or 'hard luck' excuses. It all adds up to the same thing. A real clue is whether the company is maximising long-term profits for shareholders, or running the company for short-term share price maximisation to bolster directors' remuneration and share options. There are warning signs if the company is badly run, such as freely spending shareholders' money, and should be avoided. Instead, look in the accounts for reassurances like good attitude, conservative accounting policies and modest remuneration. In this regard, illustrations include Morrisons Supermarkets, Hardys & Hansons and Warren Buffett's Berkshire Hathaway.

4j. Something new: competitive advantage rated 2

Something new, like a product or change in management, can be a significant share price driver. A change in management is most striking if there is widespread change at the top, with a new team sweeping out failures and reinvigorating the business. The catalyst could be just one appointment and changes in chairman, CEO and finance director are usually the most significant. It is not easy to gauge their impact but keep an eye out for subsequent announcements that indicate a change of strategy. Those close to the market, such as analysts and institutions, are better placed to assess the change because they have personal dealings with the board. If the share price starts to move up, then that may indicate a vote of confidence.

Something new can result from: strategies; contracts; processes; outsourcing; buying from low-cost countries; suppliers; customers; alliances; acquisitions; takeover talk; and consolidation elsewhere in the sector. Healthcare company Celsis restructured by selling its loss-making hygiene operation to focus on the high potential of rapid diagnosis of contamination in consumer products, such as medicine and shampoo. This also boosted recurring revenue on long-term contracts and tied in customers. This strategy was very successful and the profits and share price rapidly increased.

Something new can be bad as well as good news. Stagecoach's acquisition of US coach for $1.2 billion in 1999, for example, was new but proved a millstone round its neck, as is common with many acquisitions. News is very often a catalyst for share price movements both up and down. Profit warnings are the worst form of bad news and, unlike some news, they can sometimes be anticipated. For example, when the overcapacity in high street pubs and price discounting became evident, a profit warning from other sector players was likely. Early indications of a slow-down in the technology sector after the bubble burst in 2000 could reasonably be expected to affect the other players who had yet to issue a profits warning but duly did so. The September 11th terrorist attacks in the US led to profit warnings and some subsequent collapses in aerospace companies. It is good practice to sell on a first profit warning because they tend to come in threes.

5. Products

Products are the most obvious way of achieving competitive advantage by lowering their cost, for example by removing unwanted features, or differentiating in a way that adds more value to the customer than the cost of differentiation.

5a. Brand loyalty rather than a well-known name:
competitive advantage rated 2

'Few competitive advantages are as difficult to fight as a brand name. An economic advantage can be overtaken eventually, a patent may be lifted, but a great brand can be sustained for years.'
Mike Kwatinetz, investment advisor.

A brand is a name, term, sign, symbol or design, or a combination of these, which identifies the goods or services of one group of sellers and differentiates them from those of competitors. The top ten world brands, according to Business Week, are Coca-Cola, Microsoft, IBM, GE, Intel, Nokia, Disney, McDonald's, Marlborough and Mercedes, with a total brand value of $385 billion. The likes of Toyota, Gillette and Sony were in the next ten places. Brands are very valuable as they encourage consumers to buy one particular product rather than a competitor's. Their motivation is based upon trust and familiarity. This does not mean that the branded product is better value, indeed often it is not, but it is differentiated, giving a competitive advantage. For example, supermarket own-brands are cheaper and usually higher quality than branded products but the latter are still bought.

If a brand can command loyalty then consumers will choose it in preference to a similar brand that has poor loyalty. Virgin is likely to have better brand loyalty than British Airways, which has done much to undermine its reputation. Brand loyalty is not the same as a well-known name that, in spite of its recognition, does not have great competitive advantage, such as Lastminute.com. Belhaven has the best selling beer in Scotland and its quality is a non-negotiable item as far as the board is concerned. This has lead to powerful brand loyalty. The competition's beer tends to be insipid and has to be shifted with advertising. Guinness is another good example of brand loyalty.

Building brands can be a hugely expensive and risky business. Sir Richard Branson and Ryanair, for example, either self publicise or have cheap advertisements, respectively, which generate their own free media coverage by being newsworthy or controversial. Fund manager Nicola Horlick is a walking brand like Sir Richard Branson. She achieved her widespread recognition with her 'superwoman' tag by having a large family and a high-powered job but also by flying to Frankfurt to try to be re-instated under the glare of the media. Once the brand has been damaged, it is extremely difficult for it to be rehabilitated, as British Leyland discovered. Skoda, by contrast, seems to be managing the trick with clever advertising and by producing award-winning cars under Volkswagen's parentage.

5b. Dumbing down of products creates niche market: competitive advantage rated 4

The 'bottoms on seats' approach is widespread on the basis that mass markets mean mass profits, which does not necessarily follow at all. A mass market means catering to the lowest common denominator and thus dumbing down the product to appeal to an undiscerning customer, or to have a low selling price. The result is a product that often disappoints. This tendency is most evident in the lowering of content standards in films, television, newspapers and advertisements, employing the motto 'give the customers what they want'. The company ends up with an undifferentiated, commodity product that competes on price. This may be the reason for the struggling market share and revenue of populist, terrestrial ITV television stations, compared to the BBC and British Sky Broadcasting, which have a more differentiated product. Other dumbing down examples include food, beer and holidays. Dumbing down creates a dissatisfied, up-market audience niche, whose tastes are not being met by such products, and provides an opportunity. This is a good space to occupy, as customers will tend to be less price-conscious and margins should be higher.

Intelligence is not equally distributed in the population and, for example, only 10% of people have the ability to become a manager. The up-market audience will tend to be drawn from such a socio-economic group. Supermarkets like Tesco have developed a 'finest' range of high quality foods and sell up-market drinks, such as exotic beer. Cinemas can cater for rarely-shown films and demand can be met by niche radio and cable channels. Unusual holidays are a fast growing section of the holiday market, offering adventure, walking and culture, for example, to those who eschew two weeks on a Spanish beach. Specialist financial publications cater for those tired of populist press articles for the masses that lack content.

5c. Focus on competitive advantage: competitive advantage rated 1

'Loss of focus is what most worries me. Would you believe that not a few decades back they were growing shrimp at Coke and exploring for oil at Gillette?'
Warren Buffett

The world has moved on from the fad for conglomerates a few decades ago. These were intended to have a mix of businesses in different sectors that would reduce the overall risk of the group. Success in one area could offset disappointment in another, especially during the course of the economic cycle, because businesses are affected differently. This is examined further in chapters 3 and 4. Examples included the industrial conglomerate Hanson and British American Tobacco, which owned the life insurance company Eagle Star. Conglomerates usually end up operating in various non-core activities and thus trying to compete with experts in those fields. The latter will have the competitive advantage, not the conglomerate which can be a jack of all trades and, possibly, master of none.

Today, the mantra is focus and most companies have rationalised their operations to concentrate on where they have the greatest competitive advantage. Good management is as scarce as it is expensive and non-core businesses can tie up much of the creative juices of a company, particularly if they face serious problems. In general terms, it is usually poor policy to try to fix the problem and then sell off the division. Instead, it is better to bite the bullet, sell it quickly and let management concentrate on the core business. Thus, the share price often responds when a company announces the disposal of a problem operation because profits should rise in due course. There are many instances of company disposals, such as Scottish & Newcastle exiting their disappointing and expensive foray into Center Parc, and Marks & Spencer withdrawing from overseas. Illustrations of non-core businesses in two companies that might be sold are distribution at Dicom and marine at Chemring, after it already sold other ancillary divisions. Such action would enable the groups to focus on activities where they possess competitive advantage, namely in software and countermeasures, respectively.

5d. Growth in profits for a decade or more: competitive advantage rated 3

Typically, investors will want to ride the growth in a company's share price and, when that stalls, sell and move on to the next opportunity. The up trend in the share price typically lasts a couple of years but eventually all the good news is in the price. This method of short-to-medium term investing incurs transaction costs and takes time, effort and skill, as well as possibly triggering capital gains tax. Buying and holding a fund is one way to invest long-term but another is to invest in a company that keeps on steadily growing profits for years and whose share price keeps up with the pace.

Such companies are not common and are hard to spot. However, an investor will chance on them with a long-term holding in a company. The best example is perhaps Warren Buffett's Berkshire Hathaway, which has increased $19 of book value to $56,000, or by an average 22% compound, for 40 years. The shares started at $15 and have hit $90,000. There are 1,900 companies in the UK stock market but only 15 have enjoyed a decade-long growth in earnings per share:

- Alliance UniChem
- Associated British Ports
- Barratt Developments
- Berkeley Group
- Henry Boot
- Bunzl
- Cattles
- Enterprise Inns
- Forth Ports
- Greggs
- Johnson Matthey
- Johnston Press
- MITIE
- Provident Financial
- Sage

The list is short because so many growth companies have had a profits interruption, given the testing economic conditions since 2000. There is no guarantee that their record will continue, especially for those prone to a recession, such as Barrett Developments and Berkeley Group, but this list is a useful hunting ground. What is interesting is that the candidates cover so many different sectors and reflect their competitive advantage derived from individual business models rather than because of a common tailwind. Indeed, this list may suggest candidates appropriate for a well-diversified portfolio for an investor wanting to use steady, long-term growth as an investment method.

5e. Launching new products: competitive advantage rated 2

'I think they'll live up to their name.'
Warren Buffett's opinion of junk bonds.

Companies that can launch successful new products have attractive business models. They expand the market and maintain its dynamism and growth. Examples from the past include credit cards and Boeing's 747 jumbo jet, which carries more passengers over greater distances and reduces the need for refuelling stops. Technology and pharmaceutical companies are at the forefront with revolutionary products like the internet or blockbusters, an example being the £14 billion spent on cholesterol drugs. The Japanese constantly unveil new, refined, cheaper consumer electronics, including digital video cameras, DVD players and plasma televisions. Alcopops from the likes of Diageo have been very successful in combining a sweet soft drink with alcohol to encourage the young to turn from the former to the latter and familiarise them with a strange new taste.

Many companies expand existing operations by bolting on new products, like Virgin adding mobile phones and financial services to its airline and entertainment empire. Banks did the same by offering life insurance and other financial services. Supermarkets are constantly bringing out new ranges, such as ready-to-cook meals to satisfy busy customers, and internet shopping with home delivery. Disney's aim is to reinvent cruising by making the ship itself the destination, cramming it full of branded characters and entertainment.

Some businesses are basic and new products are difficult to launch, for example the heavy industries of mining, coal and metals. The profit zone is in selling services, like financing and insurance, on the back of mature, physical products, such as cars and 'white' and 'brown' goods like refrigerators and furniture. In recent years, one of the most expensive attempts to launch a new product was for 3G phones, which allow mobile internet access, but whether it is at a price that consumers want to pay is another matter. The jury is still out and companies like Vodafone have a great deal at stake.

5f. Lean manufacturing: competitive advantage rated 3

Lean, or just-in-time, manufacturing was developed by Toyota in the 1980s and the objective is to make the necessary type, quantity and quality of goods at the required time. It reduces or eliminates: waste; overproduction; warehousing; excess stock; obsolescence; defective goods; transport; and waiting time. This cuts down the capital tied up in stocks. Lean manufacturing depends upon having efficient systems and no disruptions in the supply chain. Therefore, strikes or stock-outs could be a problem. An even more targeted method of production is to produce only when there is a specific order and this can apply to computers, planes, ships and some cars, like BMW. Mass-market manufacturers, like Ford, produce in the hope that the goods find a buyer.

Lean manufacturing helped Japan to achieve global competitive advantage. It has been emulated elsewhere, an example being Hewlett Packard in the US. In the UK, industrial gas supplier BOC improved its service to customers by establishing gas production infrastructure at their locations, rather than transporting gas to them. Both companies gain, as BOC reduces the cost of its logistics and the customer has reliable, just-in-time supply.

Buying stock in anticipation of demand may be necessary due to the pattern of demand and logistics but it can increase risk. McDonald's cooks more or less to order, whereas supermarkets have to stock up in anticipation of demand. Clothing retailers, like Next or Marks & Spencer, need a lead-time of months to design and ship a range from low-cost countries like Mauritius. This time lag can run foul of changes in taste and weather, leading to unwanted stock that has to be cleared in a sale. Combining longish lead times with fickle demand is a tricky business and can lead to profit warnings. This is one reason why retailing is a higher risk sector.

5g. Like-for-like sales growth: competitive advantage rated 3

Like-for-like sales growth features mainly in the consumer sectors, such as retail and leisure, and is a useful gauge of a company's business model. Such internal, or 'organic', growth is from existing units rather than rolling out new units. Beware of like-for-like numbers that are touted by management, as various measures can be used and you should expect the company to report those that are most favourable to them. For example, one supermarket chain featured BOGOF, which is 'buy one, get one free', and included both items in the like-for-like growth, even though the cash in the till was half this. The market takes a dim view of falling like-for-like sales and it is a strong sell signal. The shares can drop precipitously, as was the case with Pizza Express which was subsequently taken over. Existing shareholders then face the gall of a cheeky takeover at a low price, rather than the chance of eventual recovery.

Be very suspicious if a company that normally reports like-for-like numbers suddenly omits them. This is unlikely to be an oversight and the conclusion is that they are poor or negative and is a sell signal. Also, have a suspicious mind when it comes to management's explanation why like-for-like sales have not matched the previous year. They are likely to be excuses, such as the weather, rather than reasons, such as poor competitive advantage and customers going elsewhere. Also, look at real growth, so that if the economy has grown 3% in the year and a company has reported 8%, then it outperformed by 5%. Thus, like-for-like growth of only 1% in this case would mean the company is slipping.

It is useful to compare and contrast similar companies in a sector to see which is consistently reporting respectable like-for-like sales. Tesco tends to lead the pack in supermarkets and is beating the like-for-like sales of stragglers, such as Sainsbury's. Telecom plus has reported very strong like-for-like sales from its distributing agents and has been a key profit driver.

5h. Low depreciation and amortisation: competitive advantage rated 3

'It makes me laugh when I hear investors say, 'Well, it's a non-cash item. A write down, I don't care about'. This is management telling you it has made a $50-$60 billion mistake in buying a company.'
James Montier, global strategist on goodwill write-offs.

Attractive businesses achieve a high return on capital employed. Heavy industry, like manufacturing, engineering and steel, are generally unattractive because they need huge amounts of capital locked up in land, plant and machinery to produce the goods. This results in high depreciation that hits the bottom line, regardless of the revenues earned. Such fixed cost can be lethal in a recession. It is a non-cash item in the current period but an expense nevertheless. Cash was paid to buy the asset originally and will be paid again when it is replaced. Indeed, the rate of replacement in a mature business will be roughly equal to the annual depreciation charge. As a rule of thumb, there is more margin of safety if the depreciation charge is a fifth or less of pre-tax profit, as in the case of brewer Hardys & Hansons. This should provide some cushion if profits dip. By contrast, the engineer Tomkins has depreciation of almost half of pre-tax profit. Amortisation of goodwill is very similar to depreciation and is discussed separately in chapter 8, given its importance.

Service businesses tend to use less capital and are often more attractive investments. Telecom plus does not need significant fixed assets and depreciation is only around 5% of pre-tax profit. Services are not a panacea, however, as the key employees can leave a brain-powered company. Also, some service companies can be regarded as modern 'factories' because they have significant fixed assets in offices, computers and cars. Nightclubs and bars have expensively fitted out complexes that depreciate quite fast but only really have decent trade for a few hours a week. The assets are idle for the rest of the time. Compare that to factories, which work flat out, 24 hours a day and maximise the use of the fixed assets. The overriding issue is that the profit zone for Western manufacturing has moved overseas where costs are lower. Services have been largely protected from such competition, as they are difficult to import, and retain their pricing power. Incidentally, that is why inflation will continue to be an endemic problem to a greater or lesser extent, given that services are four-fifths of the economy, and so deflation is highly unlikely in the UK.

5i. Maximising profit from different revenue streams: competitive advantage rated 2

A business model is attractive if it maximises profit by optimising different revenue streams. Companies typically have greater profit from some revenue streams than others and the trick is to combine them to maximum effect. For example, a corner shop does not make much from selling cigarettes but needs to stock them to lure in customers that also buy higher margin goods, like sweets and alcohol. It is very useful to compare and contrast two companies in the same business and choose the one that has the more attractive revenue streams. For instance, mobile phone companies have subsidised handset sales to encourage growth in the very high margin calls. Thus, a mobile phone company that has significant hardware sales should be less appealing than one that concentrates on call revenue.

The hardware sales in information technology company Dicom are not very profitable. However, they do lead to follow-on sales of profitable software and there should be emphasis and growth in the latter with the former ticking over.

Similarly, Radstone Technology manufactures computer boards for others under contract and the profits are low. However, this helps to pay for the infrastructure that produces the high-margin, rugged computer boards. Some supermarkets are increasing the sales of more profitable lines, like clothes and music, and adding new revenue streams, such as financial services and telecommunications, rather than just increasing low-margin, mature, food sales. A case in point is Tesco, which has a favourable sales combination compared to Somerfield. Tobacco company Gallaher has a good balance of premium brands, like Benson & Hedges, as well as protecting market share with discount brands, such as Mayfair. It is important for a restaurant chain to succeed in drink sales, which are four times as profitable as food and are much less labour-intensive. Chains like Deep Pan Pizza and TGI Friday's seek to delay the customer going to the table and have them linger in the 'cocktail' bar to maximise the revenue from drinks. Whether this merely serves to irritate customers is a moot point.

A finance company may be over-exposed to profitable but risky loans that will result in bad debts. Broadcastle, for example, aims to have a blend of high-, medium- and low-risk loans that should maximise the profit after bad debts. The same applies to banks like Northern Rock and Lloyds TSB. Similarly, oil exploration and productions companies, like Dana Petroleum and Premier Oil, have plentiful proven reserves to offset the risk of drilling for new wells, compared to companies whose fortunes stem mainly from drilling, such as Faroe Petroleum.

5j. Moving up the value chain: competitive advantage
rated 2

'Put six bottles of port by my bedside and call me the day after tomorrow.'
A note to his butler from William Fiennes, 15th Baron Saye and Sele, and ancestor of Sir Ranulph Fiennes, the world's greatest living explorer.

Moving up the value chain can be an attractive business model, as the aim is to capture more profit for the company that is at present enjoyed by others. This is the basis for the classic, vertically integrated company that seeks to control the product from inception to the ultimate consumer. Thus, Shell and BP are two oil majors that produce crude oil and process it into finished products which they sell themselves.

Belhaven and Hardys & Hansons are vertically integrated brewers that make the beer and sell it in their own pubs. Generally, this model in the brewery sector has been eschewed in favour of outsourcing non-core activities. Therefore, one-time brewers, like Whitbread, have become retailers and buy in the product from the likes of Interbrew. They have deemed that the profit zone is not in the production of a commodity item like beer but in retailing skills, which provide higher profit margins and direct contact with millions of end consumers. Dicom is moving up the value chain away from distributing and selling hardware and into earning licence fees from software. Coca-Cola moved up the value chain by emphasising selling direct to the consumer on higher margins and away from the low-margin bottling business, part of which was floated some years ago. The fact that it was floated is an indication that it lacked value to Coca-Cola.

Japanese car companies started with motorcycles, then cheap and cheerful cars, but have moved up the value chain into luxury cars, such as Toyota with its Lexus brand and sport utility vehicles (SUV), a fast growing segment of the market. General Electric and Ford have moved into lucrative financing services for their products, which was possible because they had access to the end consumer. This reduced their reliance on physical products, which are exposed to intense competition. Corus has covered steel with finishes, such as plastic, to capture this added value rather than just produce basic metal. Therefore, consider if the company is moving up the value chain or being pushed back down it by others with greater competitive advantage.

5k. Owning the standard: competitive advantage rated 1

Owning the standard means that a product is built by various companies within agreed parameters and is a wonderful business model. This puts the owner of the standard in pole position to dictate sector structure, pricing, terms, development and relationships with suppliers, customers, other sectors and government. Standards can be open or closed, so that in the former case the company will license others to produce but not in the latter case. Companies with first mover advantage often own the standard and they may be able to set the rules to suit themselves.

Microsoft owns the standard in operating systems and some applications software. IBM also owns various computer standards. In the battle over videos in the early days, the VHS format developed by JVC became the standard, trouncing Sony's incompatible Betamax. The acceptance of Dolby noise-reduction circuitry as an industry standard was due to Mr. Dolby awarding cheap licences. Earning royalties from the standard is a low risk and very profitable business model. It also piggybacks on the efforts and growth of others. For example, Microsoft has benefited enormously through the rapid growth in sales of personal computers, egged on by equally rapid obsolescence which results in a short replacement cycle. The snag is to carry on owning the standard, given the threat that a competitor may develop a 'better mousetrap'. Technology can result in obsolescence of the standard, examples being cassette tapes giving way to compact discs and video cassettes succumbing to DVDs and digital video recording.

5l. Product differentiation: competitive advantage rated 1

'Your premium brand better be delivering something special or it's not going to get the business.'
Warren Buffett

This chapter covers differentiation in all its facets and product differentiation is emphasised here specifically, given its importance. Differentiation is covered at the beginning of this chapter and, to re-cap, it can be anywhere in the value chain and not just in the product itself. It could be in bulk buying, flexibility, marketing, staff morale, location, etc. The difference adds value to the customer and is the reason why he buys, rather than going to a competitor that does not add such value. These values can conflict. For example, a national chain of estate agents, such as Halifax, may appeal to customers who want a choice of houses for sale in different parts of the country, compared to a competitor that only has a few offices. However, the sales tactics of a chain may be poor or lack personal service. Therefore, the small competitor may add more value overall.

Tesco is a good example of offering a differentiated product with its internet shopping. It will deliver to up-market customers in unmarked four-by-four vehicles, as some prefer not to have a Tesco van outside their house but do not mind a high status vehicle, presumably because of snobbery. This is a prime example of a company taking great care to listen to what the customer wants. It is also in Tesco's interest because these affluent customers will tend to buy the finest goods and not be price conscious. A 'corner-shop' electrical repairer may be happy fixing a household appliance that a big store, like Comet, will not fix. Some cars have a three-year warranty, compared to others that have only one year. A regional airport may have limited destinations but saves the hassle and distance of going to a major hub. Differentiation is all about standing out from the crowd with a product that is unmatched, with features that customers want and for which they are motivated to pay a premium price. Otherwise, the product has the characteristics of a commodity that may or may not sell and price is the main or sole means of competing. Therein lies a deeply unattractive, profitless zone.

5m. Rolling out a consumer chain: competitive advantage rated 3

'I watch where the cosmetics industry is going and walk in the opposite direction.'

Anita Roddick, founder of The Body Shop.

Rolling out a consumer chain is an attractive and fairly common business model. The company starts with one or two outlets to test that the formula is a winner and then the profits bankroll additional outlets. When they are established, the like-for-like sales will tend to be pedestrian so the growth does not stem from this but from adding new outlets. Eventually, competition and saturation of the market mark the end of the growth phase and it is time to sell. Just when to buy can be tricky, as there are many failed examples, so the best approach is to see concrete evidence of success and ride the story until you think it is going to change for the worse.

Examples of successful rollouts include: Merchant Retail's simple formula with The Perfume Shop, selling discounted fragrances; Domino's Pizza; Ask Central, with its pizza restaurants; JD Wetherspoon pubs; Matalan and Peacock discount clothes stores; The Body Shop cosmetics; and supermarkets like Tesco. Failed examples include: any number of health clubs (Holmes Place); nightclubs (Po Na Na); and discount clothes (TJ Hughes). The reasons for failure vary and can be due to: rapid expansion; gearing; misjudging the market; pricing points set too high; inadequate management; overcapacity; intense competition; accounting irregularities; and adverse changes in the economic cycle. Dealing with transactional, or one-off, consumers in the retail market is always tricky. However, this model does lend itself to scuttlebutting because you can try the product for yourself, talk to staff and judge the footfall. Please see chapter 7.

5n. Secondary profit zones: competitive advantage rated 3

A company's profit zone may not be obvious because it can be secondary to the front line product, which is a 'taster' or loss leader to lure the customer. Secondary profit zones are widespread and include: retailing for airport, plane and ferry operators; travel insurance and currency exchange for tour operators; casino wins for hotels; financing and servicing at car dealerships; warranties on electrical goods; appliance servicing from utility companies; corporate investment work at stockbrokers; tax and financial advice from auditors; on board revenue for cruise ships; and soft drink and popcorn at cinemas.

A prime example is the internet, where services are often free and the profit comes from advertising or selling follow-on services, such as professional versions of firewalls or superior features like increased storage capacity. Similarly, the profit zone in media may not be the front-line product, for instance a television programme or film, but stems from lucrative branded products that the show promotes. A classic example was Avesco's stake in the 'Who Wants To Be A Millionaire?' television show, which was a smash hit. It was rolled out all over the world and the profit zone was twofold. The first was the premium rate phone calls from thousands of members of the public wanting to be contestants and the second was from merchandise sales. However, its popularity has suffered due to being shown too frequently.

Children's television characters, such as Noddy which is owned by Chorion, are another example of secondary profit zones, which create demand for products that carry these brands. The profit margin for such merchandise is attractive and it can be sourced cheaply in low-cost countries like China. There is no shortage of competitors' toys trying to grab the child's attention and one way to spread the risk is to brand other goods, such as yoghurt. Children's characters can be a chancy business as failures are high and the product needs refreshing. Children are erratic and the most difficult customers in the world. However, the audience is constantly refreshed as new children replace those that have grown up and are outside the target age group. Parents can feel comfortable letting their children watch such harmless programmes. It can be risky to stock up on merchandise in anticipation of a promising film, as Character Group found with a flop like Dick Tracy, in spite of Madonna's starring role, or tired re-makes such as Star Wars. More promising is a classic brand turned into a film, examples being Spiderman and The Incredible Hulk.

5o. Superior product or service: competitive advantage
rated 2

'I'm very proud of my gold pocket watch. My grandfather, on his deathbed, sold me this watch.'
Woody Allen, comedian.

Having a superior product or service is a great source of competitive advantage. In a world of intense international competition, it is difficult to have superior products. Pharmaceutical companies can achieve this with new blockbusting drugs, like GlaxoSmithKline's anti-ulcer drug Zantac, in a way that a commodity product, such as petrol, cannot, in spite of advertising claims to the contrary. Coca-Cola was a superior product for decades until consumer tests showed that Pepsi was preferred. Coca-Cola then decided to change the formula to launch a new Coke, which was a disaster. Not that the taste was so much to blame but management misunderstood that Americans thought of Coke as a symbol of life that they 'owned' and they disliked someone trying to change that. It was forced to revert to its old and superior product. Some thought that this was just a clever ruse to achieve free publicity. However, the CEO candidly said 'We are not that smart and we are not that dumb'.

An example of a superior service is British Sky Broadcasting's premier league football. It trounced the second division matches that doomed ITV's digital aspirations, which paid too much for something that could not command a premium price. Superior products displace obsolete products, such as compact discs' conquest over tapes and vinyl records. A superior product is not enough because, in addition, the marketing war has to be won too. A good example was Sony's failure with its superior Betamax video recorder compared to JVC's VHS version. JVC achieved critical mass by licensing VHS to other manufacturers whereas Sony kept Betamax to itself. Microsoft is a story of marketing rather than invention. They have been masters at the former and not renowned for the latter. Competitors had superior products that Microsoft acquired or shut out (see the case study in appendix 2). Sellotape provided Scotch with strong competition in the UK, and some overseas markets, because it used hand-tearable cellulose film, whereas Scotch used PVC that needed a dispenser to enable it to be torn.

A superior product can launch a company into hyper-growth. Virgin and high street electrical stores like Currys could not stock their shelves fast enough when mobile phones and video recorders, respectively, hit their hyper-growth stages. It can be very rewarding to invest in a company at the start of such growth and sell when it tails off. In addition, these sorts of products are easy to scuttlebutt, which means assessing products by testing them yourself, as explained in chapter 7. Maintaining the lead can be an uphill struggle, as is the case with Intel that has to forge ahead on all fronts to stop the likes of AMD snapping at its heels.

5p. Supported by a famous personality: competitive advantage rated 5

Popular 'stars' of often-dubious merit are promoted in a world of intrusive, mass media that far exceeds anyone's capacity to absorb more than a tiny portion. It is becoming more difficult to have 15 minutes of fame. The masses crave someone to follow and admire. The support for a product by a famous personality enhances its stature by implying that it is trustworthy. In addition, maybe some of that star's aura can rub off on to the consumer by association. That, after all, was the point behind Bruce Willis, Arnold Schwarzenegger and Sylvester Stallone setting up Planet Hollywood, which was valued at £2 billion at its peak. Yet, this was only a hamburger chain with modest profits and soon crashed to earth. A look-alike product, Fashion Café, was established by famous models with similar results. The business model relied not on expensive advertising but on the publicity from free media that is anxious to cover something new about stars. The drawback was that fashion is fickle. Consequently, the story was soon old and no longer newsworthy. Name association has promoted a wide variety of goods, examples being Paul Newman and Linda McCartney branded food. Formula One racing drivers are often required to drive the streetcars of their sponsors and say with a straight face how wonderful they are. Nor is this a new phenomenon, an example being Christmas trees, which were popularised by Prince Albert in 1846 and then the masses wanted one too.

Financial gurus like Jim Rogers and Sir John Templeton (see chapter 9) can be very influential in raising money for new funds. Nicola Horlick's celebrity status, mentioned above, enabled Société Générale Asset Management to differentiate its investment product and it raised £5 billion of new funds. Stelios Haji-Ioannou is the charismatic founder of easyJet and often appeared in a television series about events at his airline that raised its profile for free. Sir Richard Branson has been very successful in generating eye-catching publicity, such as with his balloon flights. This draws the crowds to his Virgin airline, mobile phones and financial services because his products are differentiated, trusted and perceived as offering value for money.

When the crown of fame slips, however, it can damage the product. Michael Jackson hit bad publicity some years ago and the squeaky-clean Pepsi promptly dropped him in its advertising. Negative publicity surrounding Mohamed al Fayed has probably done little to enhance the status of Harrods, which he owns.

5q. Unique selling point: competitive advantage rated 2

'It is the greatest mathematical discovery of all time.'
Albert Einstein referring to compound interest.

A unique selling point, or USP, can clinch the sale by making the choice a 'no-brainer'. There is some aspect of the product that satisfies the demand more completely than the competition. USPs can be hard to achieve and can be copied, so the triumph may be short-lived. An investor should ask what is the USP of this company. If there is no answer, then you should avoid it. USPs can apply to the product regardless of who makes it, or it can be specific to how an individual company makes it. Here are some examples of the former. A USP of cassette tapes was that customers could play pre-recorded music but also record their own and this fuelled growth for whoever made the machines and cassettes. A USP of railways is that there is no other effective way of travelling quickly to a large city because of congestion, parking and slow buses. A USP of a regional airport is its lack of hassle compared to that of a major airport. A USP of e-mail is immediate, worldwide, free communication compared to 'snail mail' letters. Internet shopping's USP is cheaper prices and home delivery. Commercial television's USP is that it offers advertisers the opportunity to target mass audiences, unmatched by other media like newspapers or radio.

Here are some examples of USPs that are specific to individual companies. A USP of some broadband or information technology companies, like Nildram, is that they offer round-the-clock support, whereas some competitors have more limited service, like Gateway. A USP of a retail outlet may be free, on site parking, such as a supermarket, compared to a high street store, like Marks & Spencer. Further, it might, like Tesco, offer internet shopping or be open 24 hours a day. One company might have deeply discounted special offers, whereas another might rely on reward cards to ensure repeat custom, as in Tesco's case. A USP of a type of car may be the lack of a waiting list or wide availability of one option that is essential to some buyers, like automatic transmission in Mercedes Benz's small cars. A car manufacturer like Ford has a USP by offering to buy the car back from the customer at a set price after two years and also giving discounts. A USP could be free insurance or breakdown assistance. Freeview offers free digital channels compared to paying for British Sky Broadcasting. Premier Direct specialises in selling books and fancy goods conveniently in offices and thus saves time and travelling.

Also, question whether the USP is in fact a USP or an illusion. For example, in the TMT mania, many claims of USP were in fact proven to be false when consumers showed that they could manage with the products they had, for example Windows 98 rather than XP operating systems. If there is a USP then wonder how important it is and if it can readily be copied. If so, then the USP might be transitory. Whole sectors can have USPs providing competitive advantage. Genuine USPs of long duration are the most attractive, such as patented products in pharmaceuticals.

6. Suppliers

Companies enhance their business models by having power over suppliers rather than the other way round. Low cost is of paramount importance and suppliers hold the key to this source of competitive advantage. Generally, in a world full of competition and overcapacity, suppliers do not have the whip hand.

6a. Bargaining power over suppliers: competitive advantage rated 1

A company's bargaining power over suppliers is crucial because it can improve the price, quantity, quality, reliability and timely delivery of inputs. Company power increases the more the inputs are commodity items and are subject to price competition. In addition, the company, rather than the supplier, should add the value. Thus, a restaurant buys commodity items like vegetables, meat and drink, all of which are widely available and subject to intense competition. It has power over suppliers and adds the value by processing them into expensive meals. Similarly, Radstone Technology takes commodity computer boards and adds value by making them highly durable to withstand battlefield conditions. Richmond Foods buys commodity raw ingredients and manufactures ice cream, adding value with the Nestlé brand.

Gorillas tend to have bargaining power over suppliers due to their size and can secure discounts for bulk orders, for instance better television advertising rates. Such critical mass can be achieved through acquisitions which enable greater volumes to be bought. An example is Luminar, which greatly increased its food and drink requirements when it acquired Northern Leisure for £330 million. Becoming a bigger fish can also enhance the stature of a group so that it receives preferred customer status. Thus, it might obtain better terms from a bank due to an improved credit rating.

Power can be due to having a big brother that enables a company to punch above its weight by piggybacking on their much larger orders. Retailer Premier Direct sourced low-cost goods from the Far East with one of the world's largest direct sales companies, leading to cost savings of up to 70%. Bargaining power can accrue to those with sound business models who take action when competitors are struggling. For example, full service airlines fought for their very survival after the US September 11th attacks and low-cost competitors, like easyJet and Ryanair, bought planes cheaply as demand for them evaporated. Suppliers have power when they can restrict an essential product, such as OPEC and oil.

6b. Buying opportunistically: competitive advantage rated 4

'Fire the whole purchasing department. They'd hire Einstein and then turn down his request for a blackboard.'
Robert Townsend, author of *Up The Organisation*.

Some companies can take advantage of supplier weakness and buy opportunistically when demand is poor. This is more significant when the cost of inputs is high and if buying can be timed. Supply may be seasonal, an example being heating oil. Its low summer demand means weak prices and this is a good time to buy. Similarly, a utility reseller should achieve lower rates when the supplier has surplus capacity, such as telecommunications at the weekend. Supply also varies according to the economic cycle and bargain prices can be had in a recession for assets, like property, as well as for companies that can be taken over. It is a favourable time to hire talented people, a key supply in white-collar companies, and acquire choice locations for a consumer roll-out like Merchant Retail's Perfume Shops. Cash is king in such situations.

Supply may be time-sensitive because the product or service cannot be stored. Examples include perishable goods, like food and drink, and fashion goods past their sell by date. It affects services like transport, media, entertainment and leisure, with scheduled services, such as flights or holidays. It is the premise behind Lastminute.com's business model, which offers cut prices to stimulate demand for travel and entertainment that has to be quickly shifted or it will never be sold. Some marginal revenue is often better than none to the supplier, although cut pricing can undermine the normal pricing structure. Conversely, a supplier of goods which are not very sensitive to time, like information technology, does not face this problem and is not under the same threat.

6c. Not dependent on a few suppliers: competitive advantage rated 2

A company's business model is strengthened if it is not dependent on a few suppliers but has a good spread, with back-up contingency plans and substitutes. The danger is that an important supplier stops selling and the company can be in dire straits. Long-term supply contracts can be a useful hedge to ensure continuity. Companies should be awash with eager suppliers because competition is generally fierce. This may not be so when supply is disrupted, an example being a mining company facing political or security problems in hostile territory. There again, the supplier may have an effective monopoly or cartel, an example being De Beers and diamonds.

Supply problems can be due to seasonal or unexpected events, such as lack of water in a drought. Strikes at suppliers can be very damaging and one at BOC, for instance, years ago seriously threatened the manufacturing sector, which depended on industrial gases. The car strikes in the 1970s are legendary and, more recently, a petrol blockade meant that supply to garages was cut off. Even something as obscure as a lift maintenance strike has been a problem in using office blocks. A postal strike is bad news for companies that heavily rely on mail to do business. E-mail and telecommunications are excellent substitutes. Air travel is an essential supply for companies in a global economy. This is frequently curtailed by strikes, politics, war, instability and fear of flying due to terrorism. Video conferencing is a formidable substitute that is likely to grow in importance. It is also free in its basic form, examples being Microsoft and Yahoo Messenger, which use a personal computer and a camera.

Licences awarded by others, such as the government, can be a wild card resulting in a company losing its supply. A car distributor has little power, as it operates with the consent of the manufacturer, and supply may be withdrawn at any time. Countries can impose restrictions on imported goods, like electronics and cars, or they can arise due to trade quotas, embargoes, blockades or the common agricultural policy. Scarcity can also result from uniqueness and inability to increase supply, like car parks or seats on rush hour transport. Planning restrictions and lack of available land limit the power of property companies, like Land Securities. Airlines and BAA have very limited power to increase the supply of runways, as evidenced by the inquiry into Terminal 5 at Heathrow, which lasted a decade.

Conclusion

We have now examined how business models can be configured in a company to provide competitive advantage via low cost and differentiation throughout the value chain. However, companies do not operate in a vacuum and their sectors can provide an important tailwind for success. Therefore, we now analyse sectors to find those that have strong competitive advantage.

CHAPTER 2

Business models: investing in sectors with strong competitive advantage

Business model of a sector

*'Competitive advantage comes from being different. Increasingly, difference
comes from the way people think rather than what organisations make.'*
Dr. Kjell Nordstrom, author of *Funky Business.*

A business model describes a sector's competitive advantage and depends on
factors or capabilities that drive consistent outperformance. This depends on
having good economics, management and products plus power over customers,
competitors and suppliers, which result in strong competitive advantage. These
same headings were used to analyse the company business models in chapter 1.

The profitability of a company is largely determined by being in a sector with a
sound business model. An attractive sector has the ability to mould the world for
its benefit, rather than weakly reacting to pushes and shoves over which it has no
control. It will contain many companies that are profitable, due to low costs
and/or doing something different, examples being banks, oil, tobacco and
pharmaceuticals. If a sector has a weak business model then most companies are
unprofitable, examples being engineering, automobiles and household goods.
The product itself is but one important ingredient and straightforward products
can be attractive investments, e.g. beverages, whereas those that seem exciting
can be unattractive, e.g. technology. This chapter looks at these power points in
alphabetical order and one of the business models may be applicable to *numerous*
sectors, for example beverages, tobacco and mining. This is followed by some
examples of sectors that should be avoided. The merits of *individual* sectors, such
as telecommunications, are analysed in chapter 4.

65 sector business models

The table below lists each of the power points for ease of reference and provides
a checklist for investors to score sectors easily. There are 65 business models to
assess the competitive advantage of sectors and this list is not exhaustive. These
are analysed in detail after the table below. Please note that, in order to provide a
comprehensive picture, some aspects in this sector-wide analysis inevitably
overlap with those of their underlying companies (chapter 1) and the individual
sector analysis (chapter 4), although this has been minimised as much as
possible.

All business models are not equal

As explained in chapter 1, all business models are not equal, as some are more powerful than others. Consequently, the table scores them on a rating of 1 to 5, with 1 being the highest and 5 the lowest. These ratings are subjective and could arguably be higher or lower, to an extent, but a top-rated business model would unlikely to be relegated to the bottom or vice versa.

The points are awarded depending on the power of the sector to achieve low cost and/or differentiate itself so that it adds value. Above all, it is crucial to be able to control its revenue streams. Consequently, those that score the maximum 1 are: rivalry; substitutes; value added; recession resistant; addictive or highly compulsive; long-term and opaque pricing; make once and sell many times; and moving up and down the value chain. Medium scorers include consolidation and demographics. At the bottom of the pile are those with poor competitive advantage because they are commodity-type businesses that have serious flaws or do not add value, such as dying sectors.

Sector business models table

Sector business models	Competitive advantage (1 highest, 5 lowest)	Illustrations
1. Competitors		
1a. Collaboration	2	Information technology, oil
1b. Consolidation	3	Stockbroking, banking
1c. Entry and exit barriers	2	Oil and gas, aerospace
1d. Rivalry	1	Telecommunications, food retailing
2. Customers		
2a. Elasticity of demand	2	Beverages, leisure
2b. Elasticity of supply	2	Telecommunications, construction
2c. Materiality	3	Automobiles, aerospace
2d. Motivation	3	Retailing, financial services
2e. Predictability of demand	2	Tobacco, retailing
2f. Size and number	3	Mortgage banks, aerospace
2g. Substitutes	1	Tobacco, internet
2h. Sticky customers	2	Utilities, banks
2i. Value added	1	Beverages, chemicals

3. Economics		
3a. Deflation and inflation	3	Tobacco, pharmaceuticals
3b. Demographics	3	Healthcare, leisure
3c. Global potential of a sector	2	Mobile phones, supermarkets
3d. Government spending	3	Health, transport
3e. Hubs and spokes	3	Media, oil
3f. Legislation and regulation	4	Financial services, utilities
3g. Low-cost overseas production	3	Automobiles, electronics
3h. Market size	3	Banks, diversified industrials
3i. Megatrends	2	Energy, leisure
3j. Outsourcing to third parties	3	Airlines, television
3k. Recession resistant	1	Tobacco, life insurance
3l. Self-reinforcing	4	Financial services, engineering
3m. Spending other people's money	4	Entertainment, government
3n. Technology	2	Electronics, food
4. Management		
4a. Ability to attract top talent	3	Dot coms, financial services
4b. Intellectual capital	3	Advertising, information technology
5. Products		
5a. Addictive or highly compulsive	1	Tobacco, gambling
5b. Commodities	5	Sugar, distributors
5c. Crazes	5	Emerging markets, property
5d. Crossing the chasm	3	Mobile phones, automobiles
5e. High growth markets	2	Mining, pharmaceuticals
5f. High value product	2	Software, stockbroking
5g. Intellectual property rights and proprietary products	2	Pharmaceuticals, consumer goods
5h. Internet threat	3	Music, retailers
5i. Obsolescence	3	Tobacco, technology
5j. Long-term and opaque pricing	1	Life insurance, support services
5k. Make life easy	3	Supermarkets, leisure
5l. Make once, sell many times	1	Information technology, financial services
5m. Monopoly, oligopoly and cartels	2	Oil, utilities
5n. Must-have products	2	Information technology, music
5o. New products	2	Electronics, transport
5p. Positional goods	4	Automobiles, clothing
5q. Research and development to maintain lead	3	Aerospace, pharmaceuticals

5r. Recovery plays	4	Banks, TMT
5s. Product pipeline	3	Automobiles, tobacco
5t. Toll bridge – intangible	2	Software, support services
5u. Toll bridge – tangible	2	Transportation, leisure
6. Suppliers		
6a. Cost of inputs compared to selling price	2	Pharmaceuticals, food retailing
6b. Excess capacity weakens supplier	3	Telecommunications, financial services
6c. Moving up and down the value chain	1	Beverages, oil
6d. Weak and numerous suppliers	2	Food retailing, leisure
7. Sectors to avoid		
7a. Attracts capacity in the good times	5	General insurance, telecommunications
7b. Based on a quirk that politicians can remove	5	Retailing, banking
7c. Being the bacon in the sandwich	5	Distributors, food producers
7d. Dying sectors	5	Engineering, textiles
7e. Endless restructuring	5	Heavy industry, airlines
7f. High depreciation and amortisation of goodwill	5	Steel, telecommunications
7g. Long tail liability insurance	5	General insurance, reinsurance
7h. Prone to the economic cycle	5	Builders, cyclicals
7i. Prone to litigation	5	Tobacco, health
7j. Regulated	5	Transport, utilities
7k. Unethical	5	Beverages, tobacco

We now look at each of the sectors in detail. A sector should enjoy multiple business models and be scoring well on these to be highly-rated, as this strengthens its overall competitive advantage. For example, pharmaceuticals' competitive advantage is rated 1, as it has a top score in such business models as entry and exit barriers, value added and recession resistant.

1. Competitors

'A horse never runs so fast as when he has other horses to catch up and outpace.'
Ovid, Roman poet.

Sectors are attractive where the profitability is captured by the participants and not frittered away by strong competition, which results in low prices. If the latter does happen then the customers capture the profitability instead. Unfortunately, the days of making easy money have gone and now global competition is generally as fierce as it is widespread. This has been due to, inter alia, lowering of trade barriers, free currency movement, competition regulations, technology and rapid industrialisation of some developing economies. This has empowered customers, who are increasingly more demanding, at the expense of companies. The implications are far-reaching and have not yet run their course. It has hollowed out the profitability in those sectors that have poor competitive advantage, examples being textiles, distributors and manufacturing. Others are squeezed by ever more powerful gorillas, such as food producers by supermarkets. Some customers are not wanted because they can no longer be profitably served. Various business models have been abandoned, for instance relying on products rather than services. Clearly, no longer is it relevant to have a mission statement just to 'increase sales' or 'create a bigger empire', as these are no panaceas for profitability.

Therefore, sectors vary and some have greater intensity of competition than others. A reasonable assumption is that those sectors with the highest profit margins have less intense competition. These are, in order, tobacco, pharmaceuticals and health, and utilities. This concept is more fully explored in chapter 4.

1a. Collaboration: competitive advantage rated 2

Sector profitability can be enhanced by the collaborative behaviour of the participants, such as choosing not to compete in certain areas and thus avoiding a backlash. Microsoft collaborates by code-sharing with preferred partners who are not competitors, examples being printers and cameras, and are thus outside its sphere of activities. The dominant players may act paternally, like Coca-Cola, and desire a stable and profitable environment for all in the sector and act accordingly, for example, with pricing, expansion policies and setting technical standards. There may be a cartel operating that enables all the participants to earn super profit, e.g. OPEC, or a more informal cosy relationship, e.g. petrol retailing. Companies can collaborate in joint ventures and thus share the risk. Such partnerships can enhance trust and reasonable behaviour, with 'milestone' payments made when progress is made. Joint ventures are not generally very attractive, however, as a company loses some control over its destiny and partners can be unreliable. Joint ventures are evident in oil, aerospace and biotechnology. Generally, fierce competition has weakened collaboration between companies within a sector, an example being clothes retailing, and is the exception rather than the rule.

1b. Consolidation: competitive advantage rated 3

'Why anybody thinks they will produce a gazelle by mating two dinosaurs is beyond me.'
Tom Peters, author of *In Search of Excellence.*

Consolidation is an ongoing trend in some sectors, driven by their economics. They may have no choice if they need to reduce capacity and competition or reap economies of scale, such as achieving critical mass. This could be a spur to increased profitability and a re-rating. Consolidation may be due to empire building by CEOs in some cases. Some sectors have not consolidated and have a large number of participants with no one being dominant.

Consolidation is prevalent in sectors at different times and recent activity has been in stockbroking, oil, banking, food retailing, media and pharmaceuticals. Some undergo consolidation where emergent gorillas grow by bolting-on acquisitions. This may increase competition or not, depending on how the participants behave. For example, the cigarette sector in the US has been threatened by price-cutting by struggling competitors. Increased size is a driving force in banking and life insurance to cope with international competition, or the need for global reach. The regulatory burden is a large overhead that cannot be easily afforded by small players. In such an environment, takeovers are inevitable. Supermarket chains are consolidating to achieve economies of scale in order to compete. Utility companies need the critical mass of millions of customers and consolidation quickly helps to achieve this. Commercial terrestrial television is consolidating into a single ITV company, given the merger between Granada and Carlton, so that it can compete with the BBC and British Sky Broadcasting.

Investing in a takeover target is usually a more attractive investment than the gorilla in a consolidating sector because of the takeover premium. It is particularly attractive if the number of targets is small. A bidding war may ensue over who will acquire the limited number of players still left in the market and this drives up the take out price. Thus, a minor company in the life insurance sector like Friends Provident would be more attractive than a gorilla like Prudential, all things being equal. Similarly, in mortgage banking, smaller players like Alliance & Leicester and Bradford & Bingley are targets, as is Gallaher in tobacco. It may be worth thinking of buying a struggling company in the hope of a takeover but be aware that a white knight may take years to come to the rescue, if at all, and a takeover price could be lower than the current price if the target's fortunes decline further. Therefore, it is sensible to invest in a company because it is attractive on its own merits, with the possibility of a takeover thrown in as a bonus.

1c. Entry and exit barriers: competitive advantage rated 2

Sectors benefit from high barriers to entry because they keep out competitors that may otherwise undermine profitability by increasing capacity and lowering prices. The barriers may be because the existing companies in a sector have locked in the customers, suppliers or distributors, for instance in oil and gas. Switching costs may be high and incur risk or inconvenience, a feature of information technology. A newcomer may fear retaliation if the companies then overlap sectors, such as media and entertainment. Government can impede newcomers to protect home markets, as the French did by limiting Japanese cars. Brands may be very important and the cost, time and risk are too great for newcomers to build their own, e.g. newspapers and cars. The sector may be dominated by a few gorillas, with propriety products, that put a moat around the business. A newcomer may find it impossible to gain comparable proprietary expertise, let alone exceed it. Some sectors need global reach, huge economies of scale or capital to operate, examples being international advertising agencies and pharmaceuticals, and this makes it very difficult for a small company to gain a foothold and grow.

Sectors also benefit by having low barriers to exit so that firms who want to leave can easily do so. This reduces capacity and enhances profitability. Exiting is easier when the costs of doing so are low, for instance in support services or software, where it might mean closing a rented office and firing mainly temporary staff. At the other extreme are sectors where the fixed cost is very high and it might be cheaper to carry on than close down, examples being power generation, car plants, mines, aerospace and defence. Exiting will be easier if the player has other sectors on which to focus, rather than having to face annihilation.

In conclusion, it should be hard to enter the sector but easy to leave it. Information technology is a case in point, where know-how and proprietary products can make entry hard but it is straightforward to close down.

1d. Rivalry: competitive advantage rated 1

'I would rather see a battalion enter the field than him.'
Duke of Wellington's estimation of Napoleon.

Great rivalry tends to undermine profitability and such sectors should generally be avoided. This could stem from low growth or fighting over declining demand. There could be overcapacity, e.g. telecommunications, or a dominant gorilla that is determined to crush opposition, e.g. British Sky Broadcasting. Some players may see the sector as a loss leader to make profits elsewhere, e.g. holiday companies cut prices but make money in travel insurance. The balance of power may be uneven, so a struggling player with poor competitive advantage may resort to desperate action and thus increase the rivalry. Price wars can develop where competition is intense, with adverse effects on share prices. This occurs frequently in food retailing and has featured in newspapers, tobacco and pubs.

Rivalry can feature when there are large fixed costs and low marginal costs. This structure means that prices can be cut significantly to produce some contribution to the fixed costs. An example is air travel where the cost of filling the seat is minimal but the overheads are enormous. This price-cutting can become an expectation by the consumer, who increasingly becomes resistant to paying the full fare, e.g. last minute holidays. This undermines the long-term health of the sector. Rivalry is very likely in profitless sectors where little value is added. The participants are cornered and panic, with disorder resulting in ruinous competition. This tends to be particularly evident in a recession and sectors include construction, household goods and textiles.

2. Customers

Sectors are preferred where the companies capture the value added rather than customers. This depends on the balance of power and the ability of the sector to add value to customers that induces them to pay a premium price. If the companies have little power and the customer is king, then the sector will be a profitless zone.

2a. Elasticity of demand: competitive advantage rated 2

'Every time I reduce the charge for our car by one dollar, I get a thousand new customers.'
Henry Ford

It is important to have some understanding of elasticity of demand and supply. We start with elasticity of demand, which shows how demand for products varies according to the price charged. Typically, the demand for a product increases as the price falls and vice versa. Elastic demand means that demand changes more than the change in the price. Unity elasticity means that demand increases by the same percentage as the price change. Inelastic demand means that, as the price changes, there is little change in demand and power generally rests with the companies, not customers.

Sectors with high elasticity of demand are unattractive because customers can be unreliable, such as leisure (health clubs) and retailers (jewellers). Demand falls by a greater percentage than the price increases so turnover drops overall. Generally, luxury items have high elasticity of demand so sales can fall dramatically in a recession, as survival rather than prestige become uppermost in customers' minds. Yachts are a good example. However, the demand for some luxury goods, like diamonds and gold, can actually rise as the price rises, since they can become a status symbol.

Sectors with inelastic demand are attractive because customers will be reliable. Demand falls by a lesser percentage than the price increases so turnover rises overall. Tobacco, petrol and alcohol are examples and are subject to swingeing tax that only dents demand, rather than curtailing it seriously. Staples of life, like food and utilities, also have inelastic demand. Customers may lack price sensitivity and thus have inelastic demand. For example, the product may be a low-ticket item, such as sugar, or the customer may be prosperous and not fight to save costs. Another reason for inelastic demand may be that the product may add great value, for instance a car, or have a powerful brand, like Coca-Cola, that provides a compelling motivation to buy.

The demand for shares and other stores of wealth, like housing, usually increases as the price rises, the opposite of normal economic theory. This peculiarity is covered in chapter 6 on technical analysis.

2b. Elasticity of supply: competitive advantage rated 2

Elasticity of supply measures how much the supply of products varies according to the price. Elastic supply means that supply changes by a greater percentage than the price change. Normally, companies increase the supply when the price is raised as they can increase profits. Unity elasticity means that supply increases by the same percentage as the price rises and vice versa. Inelastic supply means that as the price changes there is little change in supply.

Sectors with elastic supply are attractive because output can easily be increased or decreased to meet the demand from customers. One example is software sold on a compact disc or downloaded from the internet. This extra cost is minimal but the revenues can be high, as the software may add great value. Such sectors are eminently 'scalable' to meet changing demand. Other scalable sectors include pharmaceuticals, tobacco, telecommunications, retailing, media and financial services.

Sectors with inelastic supply are generally unattractive because companies lack the power to change output to meet demand. This is because it is not easy to increase the supply in the short run. The result is that an increase in demand is not met by an increase in supply but by an increase in the price, as customers chase what is available. A good example is construction and house building, as planning permission and actual construction can take years and, even then, only marginally increases the total stock. This means the sector's operating risk is high, creating booms and busts, and is best bought just after a recession when prices are at rock bottom.

The ideal sector has inelastic demand, so the customer is not deterred by higher prices, and elastic supply, so that output can be raised easily if demand does increase. Tobacco is one such sector.

2c. Materiality: competitive advantage rated 3

Sector power tends to increase when the ticket item is low. Customers are less inclined to seek alternatives if the price and any savings are modest. Thus, petrol is a low-ticket item compared to a car and the customer will therefore be much choosier with the latter, as they also have to live with the consequences for years, compared to the former. Very large ticket items put the sector in a weak position since the customer is likely to be powerful and will negotiate hard. Examples include aerospace, defence and shipping, plus some aspects of automobiles and transport. Also, the operating risk is high because of the disproportionate effect if a very large sale is lost. If the item is a small component of the overall product then the customer's power tends to lessen, even if the cost is significant, e.g. seats with televisions on an airplane compared to the enormous cost of the engines.

2d. Motivation: competitive advantage rated 3

Customers have power if they are motivated to seek the best deal and such fussiness increases price competition to the detriment of the sector's profitability. In retailing, for instance, shoppers can spend hours traipsing around comparing prices and what is available. Others go straight in and buy at first glance, such as a low-ticket, repeat purchase item like a newspaper. Motivation usually is greater when the amounts involved are material, so customers will generally spend more time choosing a big-ticket item like a holiday. Upset customers will be motivated to go elsewhere, and maybe even on worse terms, out of spite and this is a feature of, for example, financial services, automobiles and leisure. They will often spread the word to anyone who will listen and thus deter others from buying. Upsetting customers is to be avoided at all costs. Prosperous customers are to be preferred, as they tend to haggle less than those who are struggling, and thus they enhance the sector's profitability. The internet has increased customers' motivation to drive a hard bargain, since they can easily compare prices and read reviews of products, and this has increased competition.

2e. Predictability of demand: competitive advantage rated 2

'You go to bed feeling very comfortable just thinking about two and a half billion males with hair growing while you sleep. No one at Gillette has trouble sleeping.'
Warren Buffett.

Some sectors have predictable demand for standard products, such as food and tobacco, which are largely commodity products, non-seasonal and recurring revenue is high. This lends stability to the sector and companies have more control. The products need little innovation and sell themselves. Utilities are another example but demand has peaks and troughs, so, for example, demand for power is low in the summer and expensive infrastructure is idle. Ice cream sales peak in the summer but capacity is evened out somewhat by storing winter production. Customers can stock up at keener prices when there is excess capacity, e.g. oil and off-peak electricity rates. Water, by contrast, has much steadier demand. Telecommunications and transport have to meet peak demand, which is very costly. Seasonal demand also affects the airline and holiday sectors. One strategy to deal with seasonal demand is to have offsetting products, for example skiing and sun holidays, or allow competitors to satisfy peak demand.

Some sectors are subject to transactional or one-off customers, whose demand alters with bewildering and unanticipated speed, leading to the sector's grip on power slipping. An example is retailing, where fashion and the search for something new leads to fickle customers and demand can suddenly drop off a cliff. Media is also a prime candidate, especially if it targets the capriciousness of youth, searching for identity, confidence and role models.

The predictability of demand is heavily influenced by the economic cycle. In a recession, customers may want to buy but cannot if they are financially stretched. The recession resistance of sectors must be carefully considered at each stage of the economic cycle and this is explained in chapter 4. Defensive sectors, like tobacco, are very attractive if the economy is about to enter a recession and vulnerable sectors, such as construction, should be avoided.

2f. Size and number: competitive advantage rated 3

The size and number of companies in a sector compared to that of customers affects the balance of power. The ideal is a few powerful gorillas in a sector, like mortgage banks, and a myriad of small, weak customers. Information technology can also benefit similarly, with companies like Microsoft not facing powerful suppliers or customers. It needs little in the way of the former and the latter number in the hundreds of millions.

If the customers and their orders are large, then they will tend to be in a strong position, for example the government buying pharmaceuticals and defence hardware, such as ships. The aerospace sector has few aircraft manufacturers and the number of customers is limited. This can be awkward if a customer is lost and particularly affects military suppliers. Sectors are risky which are over-reliant on too few customers. This applies to food producers and processors that sell to the dominant supermarkets who can divide and rule. Therefore, supermarkets have the best of both worlds as they have power over their suppliers and millions of small customers.

2g. **Substitutes:** competitive advantage rated 1

Sectors that have no, or limited, substitutes are the highest-rated business model and include tobacco, oil and gas. The customer's bargaining power increases if he can substitute the product. Choice increases competition and he can easily shop elsewhere. Substitutes provide choice but the cost of switching can be a deterrent. For example, a company car fleet is cheaper and easier to run if one manufacturer supplies it and this is an impediment to switching. The propensity to do so will be less if the substitute's attractions are marginal or perhaps not long-lasting. For example, switching from oil to electricity may be attractive today but uncertain in the future due to changing prices. The customer may lack motivation to switch because he is uninformed, happy at present or there is a risk involved, for example, in changing to a new computer system. There are also time costs of substituting, due to researching the options available and implementing the change. The new economy opens up powerful, new substitution opportunities for customers and threats for companies, such as buying on the internet.

2h. **Sticky customers:** competitive advantage rated 2

A 'sticky' customer is one that carries on buying because impediments inhibit him from going elsewhere. They are attractive, therefore, as they will be reliable and weak, putting the power in the hands of the sector. The result should be a high level of recurring revenue that can be relied upon if there is a recession, if the price increases or if the product deteriorates. This stickiness can arise if the cost and value of the product are not easy to evaluate, for instance life insurance, or if there is uncertainty or lack of knowledge. Banks have sticky customers because of the inertia of changing, plus the time to re-establish credit cards, direct debits, overdraft limits, etc. This is why the banks are so keen to grab students, as they will tend to stay for decades.

Utility and telephone customers have sticky customers due to the hassle of switching and the trust that is felt towards the incumbent. The information technology sector also tries to lock in customers by building in incompatibilities. Plane manufacturers have sticky customers if they are their sole supplier because airlines do not relish the cost and trouble of running separate fleets. At the opposite end of the scale are tourists who are here today and gone tomorrow and are transactional, or one-off, customers. Such fleeting customers also feature in the retailing, leisure and hotel, media and entertainment sectors, making them less attractive investments.

2i. **Value added:** competitive advantage rated 1

'The key to survival is to learn to add more value today and every day.'
Andrew Grove, Intel.

Sectors which have power add significant value by offering differentiated products to customers who are prepared to pay a premium price. This has the highest competitive advantage rating. Sectors should strive continually and relentlessly to increase the value they add and long-term winners include: beverages; food retailing; pharmaceuticals; tobacco; oil; gas; banks; and financial services. The value added must not only be valuable to the customer but must have the ability to beat overseas competition or their terms of trade will deteriorate. The value added could be a premium brand, such as Gordon's Gin, Guinness or Pepsi, the taste and image of which many prefer over cheaper supermarket brands. Another example is information technology that increases productivity or re-engineers the production process. On the other hand, commodity products, like mining and chemicals, add little value and price is at the forefront of negotiations. Therefore, such sectors typically have little power.

3. Economics

Sectors that tend to out-perform will have good economics that result in strong competitive advantage. This means that they manage to combine the four factors of production, namely land, labour, capital and enterprise, in a manner that adds value to the customer, resulting in profit for the shareholders. This is discussed more fully in chapter 4.

3a. **Deflation and inflation:** competitive advantage rated 3

Deflation in the economy as a whole is an unlikely prospect in the UK, as explained in chapter 3. However, it can and does affect some sectors. Falling prices are a two-edged sword. On the one hand, the cost of inputs to a sector may fall but so too might its selling prices. This constantly squeezes margins if the latter falls more than the former. Margins can be held if the input costs are falling in step with the selling prices. A good example of a deflationary environment is information technology and electronic goods where prices have dropped steadily for years, yet the specification of the products has increased. Telecommunications is another sector where prices have fallen dramatically due to excess capacity and alternative providers, like the internet. This is wonderful for the consumer, of course. Supermarkets have also suffered some food price deflation and have countered by expansion into higher margin products like clothes. Favourable sectors have solid pricing power, such as patented drugs, and can resist deflation.

Inflation also provides winners and losers. Winners would be those sectors that have low input costs and have pricing power, like tobacco. Estate agents receive a percentage of the house sold and the fee increases in line with the house but for no extra work. Indeed, the work will be less in a boom with houses selling fast. Banks are beneficiaries as they finance larger loans needed to buy the inflated asset. The losers are sectors that suffer increased costs but lack the competitive advantage to pass them on by raising prices. Manufacturing and engineering are instances, as these 'screwdriver' industries struggle to compete with low-cost areas, like Eastern Europe, Latin America and the Far East. Generally, losers are those that have a large labour force and high replacement costs of fixed assets, such as chemicals and transport.

3b. Demographics: competitive advantage rated 3

There are ongoing and numerous changes in demographics, which create multi-year tailwinds. One is the increase in the number of old people, which fuels demand for products like retirement homes and healthcare. The number of workers as a proportion of pensioners has been declining over the years and the ratio is expected to fall from 5:1 to 2:1 in due course. More single person households have benefited house builders and increased demand for microwaveable food. There has been a rapid increase in university education, which has lead to more accommodation, campuses, lecturers and recreational facilities. The population's real disposable income increases by a third in real terms every decade and has lead to increased car usage, more roads, congestion charging, traffic management systems, more petrol stations and car dealers. There has been an increase in time available, at least for the non-working population, which has supported media and leisure activities like recreation centres and television. Overall, the sectors that benefit from favourable demographics include: food producers and retailers; pharmaceuticals; healthcare; construction; automobiles; general retailers; leisure; media; entertainment; and financial services.

3c. Global potential of a sector: competitive advantage rated 2

A compelling innovation can create the conditions for global potential for new sectors, examples of which include oil, banking, pharmaceuticals and insurance in the distant past. More recently, technology and a changing economy have spawned brand new sectors or sub sectors, such as mobile phones and information technology, with rapidly emergent gorillas like Vodafone and Cisco. It can be extremely rewarding to buy at an early stage into these potential giants before their promising product turns into a blockbuster. Hold the shares for this hyper-growth stage and sell just before everyone else realises that the market has become mature. The most likely hunting ground for hyper-growth is in technology, given the potential economics of the business, which include innovation, scalability and very high added value. However, technology is tremendously difficult to predict and change happens at an increasingly fast rate. Supermarkets have been slow to demonstrate their global potential. However, they may now be starting to do so, given Tesco's expansion into Europe and Asia, which generates £6 billion of sales, representing a fifth of turnover, and is growing fast.

3d. Government spending: competitive advantage rated 3

Sectors can be attractive that are highly favoured by government, which employs one in five of the workforce and spends 40% of GNP. Its immense power provides a good tailwind and vast amounts can be poured into 'untouchable' government priorities, almost regardless of whether money is being wisely spent or if the service should live within the means of the country. Such immunity from criticism is a great protection against cuts, although a recession will present some hard choices. The prime examples are health and education, which are likely to remain very buoyant for decades to come. Pharmaceutical, support services, construction, real estate and information technology are some of the beneficiaries of the government's largesse. There can also be a tailwind from a change in political emphasis, such as the shift to public transport, which favours train and bus operators, and away from cars.

Government contracts are not a panacea, though, as Government often drives a hard bargain since enriching companies is at the very bottom of its priorities. In addition, policies do change that can adversely affect the economics of a sector, as seen in railways (Railtrack), nuclear power (British Energy) and defence (BAE Systems). There is also the political risk if a company is seen to be profiting from public services and union opposition to activities like outsourcing and private finance initiatives are downsides. However, there is no risk that the debtor will default.

3e. Hubs and spokes: competitive advantage rated 3

'Capitalism without bankruptcy is like Christianity without hell.'
Frank Borman, astronaut and CEO of Eastern Airlines.

Knowledge is power and it is better to occupy the space at the hub or centre of a wheel, rather than at the end of a spoke, out on the rim. This is a 'switchboard' business model, bringing together many buyers and sellers who need an intermediary to connect them for a fee. A good example is a stockbroker or financial advisor channelling money from investors into companies. A central position gives a clearer overview of what is happening and provides more power to control events. An information provider that gathers material from a wide variety of sources, like Reuters or Williams Inference, will have a better overview than that of the individual providers.

Those at the centre of the action, such as the integrated oil majors like Shell, have the power to control the fortunes of support services that feed off its success, for instance drilling. Such peripheral service companies that are beholden to a big brother are not in a powerful position, as the crumbs from the table can be removed. Supermarkets have the same powerful central position compared to food producers. The US government largely developed, and still pays for, the huge internet engine that powers the backbone of the system. This is a generous act but it also puts its agencies in pole position to monitor all traffic for its own reasons, which it does to gather intelligence and prevents other countries from doing the same.

3f. Legislation and regulation: competitive advantage rated 4

Legislation and regulation drive demand in some sectors in order to comply with requirements of the government, EU and trade organisations. Health and safety legislation has benefited various sectors by increasing demand and includes airport security, extra personnel, fire escapes, seat belts and smoke alarms. For example, marine safety dictates that certain boats must have radio, distress flares and life jackets on board, which fuels non-discretionary demand for such products.

Sector-wide stipulations increase the cost of doing business, such as in the highly regulated insurance and financial services sectors. This creates a level playing field in that all participants have to comply but the cost is onerous, although it can create a useful barrier to entry. Starting a new life insurance company, for example, is very difficult due to tight regulations as well as the high critical mass needed. Rules inevitably increase over time as the power and reach of government increase remorselessly, given extra momentum with European legislation. In the travel sector, for example, IATA, the regulatory body, requires companies to have a high cash backing that is put into a bond and is an effective barrier, inhibiting new entrants and the growth of small companies.

Powerful sectors can influence regulations in a way that suits them. Generally, it is best to avoid sectors that 'work for the government' and instead choose those where the government creates the demand instead, as in marine safety above. Heavily-regulated sectors include utilities and real estate, given planning requirements, and lightly-regulated ones include beverages and leisure.

3g. Low-cost overseas production: competitive advantage rated 3

Sectors that can source production from low-cost areas, like Eastern Europe and the Pacific Rim, can gain competitive advantage. These include clothing, textiles, toys, cars and electronics and their prices often fall relentlessly. Companies that can but do not do this will wither. Service companies produce locally and their costs are largely incurred locally, an example being leisure parks, and this restricts their ability to benefit from cheap countries. However, some can employ low-cost overseas labour, such as telecommunications, software development, and insurance and banking call centres. An engineering consultancy can sell its wares locally but can have designs drawn up in China. Local service industries are generally insulated from low-cost overseas areas and this lack of competition is a powerful source of their ongoing pricing power.

Countries should concentrate on producing goods and services where they have international comparative advantage and trade where they do not. This produces a 'two plus two equals five' result and all countries benefit. Unfortunately, governments do not like the political repercussions of lame duck sectors that have lost their competitive advantage and instinctively try to support them. This is a foolish and painful lesson, learnt in the UK in the 1970s and 1980s. The arrival of Margaret Thatcher, the reduction of trade barriers and a freely convertible currency largely sorted out the problem. It persists, though, in various forms around the world and examples include the common agricultural policy in the EU and the restriction on Japanese cars in countries like Italy. Western Europe is becoming increasingly less attractive for inward investment, as companies respond by avoiding their high production costs in favour of low-cost areas.

The high growth of the Pacific Rim resulted in a rise in demand for some goods for the first time from that region. This is lead by a burgeoning middle class that now wants goods and services like oil, western prestige brands, air travel and holidays in the US and Europe. Sectors will prosper which cater to this trend, which is set to continue, and include oil, beverages, leisure, tobacco, insurance and financial services.

3h. Market size: competitive advantage rated 3

'Since the industrial revolution began, going downstream and investing in businesses that will benefit from new technology, rather than investing in the technology companies themselves, has often been the smarter strategy.'
Ralph Wanger, CEO of The Acorn Funds.

Size matters and large national or global markets provide huge opportunities, stability and headroom for growth for sectors like banks, pharmaceuticals, oil and gas. If the market is mature then there are opportunities for smaller growth companies to prosper within it, yet all participants can be profitable. On the other hand, small markets may hardly be worth the bother and have limited growth prospects, such as diversified industrials, forestry and paper, although they can offer profitable niches.

All markets once started small and creating a new one from scratch is risky. The profit zone in a sector being transformed is often outside the core business. Therefore, the safety play is to provide mundane items like 'picks and shovels' to the pioneers on the front line and let them bear the start-up risk, e.g. railroads and canals in the industrial revolution. A more recent example is mobile phones, with their picks and shovels provided by various players like Metnor, which integrates and commissions sites for mobile phone networks, or CRC, which repairs mobile phone handsets. The ideal market is one that is established and taken seriously but is still a long way from maturity, thus providing growth opportunities for all players but with diminished risk. Information technology was a prime candidate until the sector burst in 2000 but, at some point, it should have its day in the sun again.

3i. Megatrends: competitive advantage rated 2

'Huge numbers of baby boomers have sophisticated tastes. They want less of the cheap fattening foods at places like McDonald's. As soon as their kids are old enough, they go elsewhere.' .
Cheryl Russell, demographer.

Sectors with attractive economics feed on powerful and ongoing megatrends, of which three have been covered above, namely demographics, government spending and low-cost overseas production. Such a rising tide lifts all boats. Sectors which are powerful cater to where populations are spending their time and money. This means a good tailwind for the likes of telecommunications, energy and leisure. There are short-, medium- and long-term trends. One of the latter is rising energy prices, with an ever expanding and wealthy world population, and new sources of supply very limited. Indeed, some argue that was the reason for the 2003 Iraq war, since that country has the second largest oil reserves in the world. Indeed, as an American comedian quipped 'how did our oil get under their sand?' The Middle East will continue to help itself to the first cut of the world's wealth. The upshot is that it is preferable to invest in producers rather than users of energy, since the former receives the high price paid by the latter, so one should prefer oil companies to automobiles. On the other hand, information technology hardware prices fall inexorably, which makes investing in the sector more risky than in the software users. Pharmaceutical companies enjoy buoyant conditions as the demand for new and increased quantities of drugs inexorably increases. The prices are protected by patents for a maximum of 20 years. They also have the advantage of being typically bought with someone else's money, in this case by the government for the public. The UK is the only developed country where there is no cost to the customer. Sweden, for example, makes a nominal charge for visiting a doctor. With zero or subsidised cost to the customer, demand for healthcare is infinite.

One international megatrend is the realisation that currencies and terms of trade of the developing world will continue to deteriorate against those of the developed world. For this purpose, many of the low-cost countries of the Pacific Rim, like China, are excluded as they can compete. Therefore, it is unattractive to use strong currencies to invest in operations in long-term weak currencies, for instance the South African Rand. This can be turned to an advantage if the production is locally financed but traded in dollars, such as gold, diamonds or oil. Another trend is that countries which are open to free trade will prosper in contrast to those that do not. The UK has a very open economy, for example, and is amongst the leaders in attracting inward investment into Europe. A US trend is the increasing problem of obesity and the young now face the prospect of having a shorter life expectancy than that of their parents, which is also a trend in Russia due to unhealthy lifestyles. This US trend has led to threats of lawsuits against hamburger chains like McDonald's and the need to avoid high-fructose corn syrup in favour of a healthier lifestyle. This is a positive tailwind for various businesses including health foods, gyms and lawyers.

A favourable tailwind is a great boon to a sector and the leading example over the last two decades has been technology. It has created new products, like personal computers, camcorders and smart weapons, and computer chips have permeated into a wide variety of existing goods, such as cars and home appliances. The internet has been a disaster area for investors but that is more a fault of foolish people than its underlying, unique advantages. It is increasingly a must-have product, egged on by faster speeds and ease of use. The enthusiasm for technology boiled over in the TMT mania that ended in 2000 and it is now a dirty word, given the scale of losses and the over-investment. This will take some time to unwind and for investors' painful memories to fade. The trick will be to make money out of it but the tailwind is there, although it has passed its hyper-growth phase and is becoming a mature sector without new killer applications.

Sectors that lack a good tailwind include chemicals, manufacturing, engineering, mining and steel, which are discussed below in the section on sectors to avoid. These are mature, lack differentiation, suffer poor pricing power and face intense international competition. They are under threat from imports and are prone to the vagaries of the economic cycle, which adds extra risk.

3j. Outsourcing to third parties: competitive advantage rated 3

Sectors are favoured which outsource non-core activities to specialist third parties to reduce cost and this is a phenomenon that has gained ground in recent years. Conglomerates with a myriad of activities were once fashionable because it was argued that diversity would ensure smoother results, since a downturn in one area could be offset by growth elsewhere in the group. That notion has been discarded in favour of sectors that focus on core activities, allowing them to excel and compete effectively, and outsource non-core activities.

There are numerous examples. Some airlines buy their in-flight goods from specialised providers, rather than making these themselves, allowing them to concentrate on flying planes. They also delegate the task of co-ordinating the supply of thousands of components to specialists in that area. Television companies commission some programmes rather than producing them all in-house, as they are, in effect, publishers of content rather than content providers. Professional firms, like accountants and lawyers, delegate training to companies which enable staff to pass difficult exams. Companies outsource back office routines, such as office maintenance, cleaning, clerical work and catering. Others have outsourced their tax affairs and information technology. Vertically integrated brewers effectively outsourced production of beer to concentrate on retailing it to the end consumer. This is further covered in chapters 1 and 4.

3k. Recession resistant: competitive advantage rated 1

A recession severely reduces demand and sectors suffer accordingly. It is a crucial attribute of a good sector that it has strong control over its revenue streams. This is achieved by having power as outlined in this chapter. The recession resistance of each sector is scored in chapter 4 and is briefly summarised here. Long-term contracts and a high level of repeat business are two ways of controlling revenues. When economic conditions deteriorate, the customers are still buying. Sectors that are product-driven are less dependent on the economic cycle. An example is tobacco, where the customer is addicted to the product so demand remains strong. Another is food retailers, as people have to eat. Utilities are also necessities. Life insurance has long-term contracts with sticky customers. Mortgage banks have long-term contracts too and avoid the horrendous bad debts on commercial loans suffered by the clearing banks in a recession. Mortgage banks will be hit by repossessions but this is offset to some extent by mortgage indemnity insurance, which is taken out by the borrower with an insurance company. Mortgage banks have a very attractive and shrewd business model that allows their risk to be transferred to another company at the customers' expense.

Sectors that are most prone to a recession tend to be those that sell big-ticket or luxury items that consumers can defer purchasing. These include construction, real estate, automobiles, holidays and information technology. Engineering and house building, for example, are not highly-rated at the top of the economic cycle when profits are booming because the market is aware that the quality of these profits is poor and will be hammered in a recession.

3l. **Self-reinforcing:** competitive advantage rated 4

'There are three ways of losing money. Racing is the quickest, women the most pleasant, and farming the most certain.'
Lord Amherst

An attractive sector is one that is self-reinforcing, where thriving demand produces healthy profits. These pay dividends so the shareholders are pleased, as well as funding investment in products and infrastructure, which further stimulates demand in a virtuous circle. Raising new capital for expansion and new ventures is not a problem, as an air of confidence reigns. Examples include financial services, oil and tobacco. A moribund sector, like engineering or coal mining, does not have these attractions and each year suffers a death by a thousand cuts with redundancies sapping talent and depressing morale. There is little prospect of raising new capital, as shareholders have been disappointed, and would be throwing good money after bad. Thus, the two types of sectors tend to diverge increasingly over time as the gap between them widens. There is a third type that is stuck in the middle, such as building materials and general retailers, where life is as unexciting as are the returns to shareholders.

3m. **Spending other people's money:** competitive advantage rated 4

Demand tends not to be sensitive to price if the customer is spending someone else's money. People are typically very careful how they spend their hard-earned cash but they look less carefully at the cost, if at all, when the expenditure is borne by someone else. Indeed, the higher the expenditure the better sometimes, as it can impress one's peers. Sectors that supply business entertainment, travel and conferences can be very attractive, although such extravagance tends to stop in a recession. Appealing to a non-working spouse spending the working spouse's money can also be effective for luxury brands like watches and pens.

The biggest hitter of them all is the government that has no shortage of wish lists on which to spend the taxpayers' money, not all of it wisely. The Millennium Dome is a good £0.8 billion example of where this can lead. Another white elephant was the £1.3 billion cost of Concorde, which was some way over its £160 million budget. Sometimes the lesson is learned, an example being when the UK government would only sanction the Channel Tunnel if it was privately financed, thus saving taxpayers the £9 billion bill. Government spending increases remorselessly in line with economic expansion and especially under left-wing governments that increase the overall percentage of GDP confiscated in taxation. Sectors which stand to benefit accordingly are beneficiaries of public spending and include health and transport. A change of government may, and a recession would, curtail these good times.

3n. Technology: competitive advantage rated 2

'There has obviously been a great disservice done by the gross misallocation of capital in the TMT sector around the world. We went from a world where the focus was on EBIDTA (earnings before interest, taxes, depreciation and amortisation) in valuing these companies to PS (price to sales) to one focused on EPS (earnings per share). I define EPS in this way, 'the estimated probability of survival'.
Marc Gabelli, fund manager in 2001.

All companies to a great or lesser extent use technology but information technology is a sector in its own right, as analysed in chapter 4. It has proved to be no panacea for success, as the TMT debacle illustrated only too vividly in various products including optical fibres, 3G mobile phones, internet sites, routers and cable and satellite television. Its profitability has been hollowed out by a variety of factors, including overcapacity, lack of paying customers, too much capital employed in worthless goodwill, government greed and inappropriate products. Nevertheless, cutting edge technology can be crucial for TMT companies to try to stay ahead of the intense competition in areas like computers and semiconductor chips.

Technology can be a major source of competitive advantage for non-TMT companies as it can be used to re-configure the value chain to lower cost and differentiate. Technology is beneficial if it improves companies' economics, such as increasing the value of the product to the customer, or if it allows first mover advantage. For example, one major confectionary conglomerate would allow any technology expenditure by managers to improve efficiency but would not allow the hiring of a single extra person. Technology was seen as a one-off expense but an extra person would be paid year after year, which was both a high and an inflation-linked cost. There has been a megatrend generally to swop technology for people and to run lean businesses. The result has been that the remaining employees have to work long hours to compensate for lack of bodies. In the UK for example, the average working week is 44 hours, the highest in Europe.

Technology has changed the ability of companies to offer new products, an instance being selling complicated financial services, such as insurance and credit cards, over the phone. This lowers cost, cuts out middlemen and makes life easy for the customer. Satellite navigation and anti-lock brakes are car innovations that entice the customer to pay a premium price. The quality of the product can improve, for instance the delivery time of information via the internet. There is a substitution effect so that e-mail, for example, has relegated personal 'snail mail' letters to only 5% of the total post, the rest consisting of junk and business mail. Mobile phones have displaced call boxes. Some companies, like banks, can use technology more than others, like mining, but to have a sound business model it is necessary to employ it more effectively than the competition. Technology is prevalent in sectors that either add value through brainpower or are services and they include pharmaceuticals, telecommunications, aerospace, electronics, automobiles, media and entertainment, support services and financial services. The remaining sectors are more product-based and technology has less impact, examples being food, tobacco and utilities.

4. Management

'Take our 20 best people away, and I will tell you that Microsoft would become an unimportant company.'
Bill Gates, co-founder of Microsoft.

The quality of management in a sector is perhaps the most important ingredient of business success. It is difficult to assess by an investor but it does tend to be reflected in profits growing consistently above the market norm. Please also see management in chapter 1, section 4.

4a. Ability to attract top talent: competitive advantage rated 3

Attractive sectors are those that can attract top talent. Bright people want to go where the future is promising and offers the opportunity for personal enrichment and promotion. For instance, it has been estimated that a quarter of MBA graduates in the TMT mania went to work for dot coms, which were seen as an outstanding opportunity at that time. Indeed, that was a signal to short the sector. Some of the best talent is drawn to the City with its allure of high salaries and a glamorous career. Rocket scientists have been lured into investment banks to help write trading software. Few such individuals are drawn to a life in a struggling, northern, manufacturing company. Also, do not forget the influence of a spouse in deciding what job an individual does and where they want to live. Leafy Surrey is a more attractive proposition than an inner city. There are regular lists of the top 100 large and small UK companies to work for and is a strong endorsement that is likely to attract top talent. The winners include Bacardi-Martini, Asda, Volkswagen, Honda UK, St. James's Place, Morgan Stanley and Landaround.

However, good management is not a panacea, as Warren Buffett pointed out: 'When management with a reputation for brilliance tackles a business with a reputation for poor fundamental economics, it is the reputation of the business that remains intact'. Therefore, good management needs to be combined with a good business. Failing sectors will suffer a brain drain, compounding their economic problems.

4b. Intellectual capital: competitive advantage rated 3

'The information revolution has changed people's perception of wealth. Intellectual capital is far more important than money.'
Walter Wriston, CEO of Citicorp.

Brainpower is all-important in an economy where four fifths of the national income is provided by services. Some sectors have more intellectual capital than others and it can be a very valuable source of competitive advantage in today's tough world. Intellectual capital is more important in sectors where the business is complex, such as oil, and less so in straightforward ones, like retailing. Other examples of high levels of intellectual capital include advertising, information technology, financial and professional services, including bankers, accountants, lawyers and insurers. Intellectual capital is very hard to measure, although there have been some attempts at accounting for human assets, dating back to the 1960s with Rensis Likert's work. Nevertheless, it is useful to be aware of this intangible asset and question whether the sector has clever people or dullards.

Information technology companies tend to score well. Intellectual capital can be hard to retain because the assets go down in the lift every night. Nevertheless, the number of applicants for top jobs vastly exceeds the vacant posts and companies will continue to have the power. For example, a newspaper advertisement for a senior position resulting in 700 applications is not unusual, so leavers can be replaced since no one is indispensable.

5. Products

A sector with strong competitive advantage simply has products and services that customers want to buy which add value to their lives. Powerful products make for a powerful sector. Sectors widely differ in their ability to achieve this and how much profit they can capture from their activities.

5a. Addictive or highly compulsive: competitive advantage rated 1

An addictive or highly compulsive product has dedicated customers that are glued to it, queue up to buy it and are not easily deterred by price, which are very attractive attributes. Consequently, it has the highest-rated competitive advantage. The prime example is tobacco where the consumer is addicted and punitive rates of taxation do not deter such inelastic demand. Alcohol is another legal drug that has various levels of compulsive consumers who are little deterred by heavy taxation. Gambling can be highly compulsive for some but it is not in the same league as tobacco.

The internet is increasingly compulsive and a survey found that half of respondents said they could not do without web access for more than two weeks. Some sections of the population, such as youngsters, find certain products like video games and mobile phones to be compulsive. Petrol has inelastic demand because of the compulsion that people have to drive to work or for everyday life and recreation. National characteristics can determine demand so, for example, the Chinese and Americans tend to have a greater propensity to gamble than the British.

5b. Commodities: competitive advantage rated 5

Commodities like metal, sugar, coal and bulk chemicals are unattractive. They lack competitive advantage because they are undifferentiated. They are subject to volatile, internationally-set prices, often in dollars, which leads to a currency risk. The focus of producers therefore tends to be on trying to lower costs in order to sustain profits and the major controllers of supply can have an advantage. The ability to achieve this is limited, as costs tend to be similar throughout the industry. Commodity sectors tend to have low barriers to entry and the weaker players threaten the profitability for all participants by competing with the only weapon they have left, which is to discount prices.

Some business can be described as having commodity characteristics, even though the product is not strictly a commodity. Their activity is like a commodity, in as much as there is little to distinguish it from competitors and the underlying items are handled like commodities, such as distributors of computers. This 'box shifting' activity does not add much value and, consequently, customers are not prepared to pay handsomely. They have little power and should be avoided.

5c. Crazes: competitive advantage rated 5

'There seems to be an unwritten rule on Wall Street: If you don't understand it, put your life savings into it. Shun the enterprise round the corner, which can at least be observed and seek out one that manufactures an incomprehensible product.'
Peter Lynch

Crazes are a peculiar phenomenon that spring up unannounced and are unpredictable, only to disappear just as fast. Sectors that are subject to them can have good and lean years. Examples of craze products include Atari and its Space Invaders, Pokémon, video games, Cabbage Patch dolls, stamps, paintings, classic cars, pop groups and celebrities. Such activities are high-risk but some companies have a 'picks and shovels' approach feeding off the growth. Examples are public relations companies, insurers and auctioneers.

There are also crazes not just for a product, such as Dutch tulips in the seventeenth century, but also for a company or sector, which lead to manias. Examples over the last few hundred years include: the South Sea bubble; Robert Law's Mississippi scheme; railways; canals; Poseidon gold mine; emerging markets; technology; and property. Speculators can make money out of the foolishness of others in a mania but must fully recognise the great risks involved. This is not an activity for widows and orphans and does not have any of the margin of safety hammered home in this book. Nevertheless, speculators should buy, if so inclined, when the mania becomes apparent and ride the curve upwards. Set a tight stop loss and get out when it is triggered. Do not be tempted back in as the whole idea is to leave the last 10% for the greater fool. The brilliant Sir Isaac Newton forgot this rule after he sold his South Sea shares, doubling his fortune to £14,000. Unfortunately, greed lured him back and he lost a staggering £20,000, at a time when wages could be just £1 a year. He could never bear to hear the South Sea Company referred to for the rest of his life: 'I can calculate the motions of the heavenly bodies, but not the madness of people'.

5d. Crossing the chasm: competitive advantage rated 3

'Technology companies should be valued at a discount to the shares of companies like Disney and Coca-Cola, which have long-term earnings.'
Bill Gates

Sectors which are powerful cross the chasm from just having ideas, or a product with limited scope, into mass markets. A good example is Microsoft, which turned a formidably frustrating, expensive and difficult to use personal computer with limited scope or widespread appeal into a 'must-have' product for office workers and home users alike. Previously, a user had to know what to do next and type in a complicated instruction onto a blank screen. Windows lets the computer know what to do next and presents a menu of options for a user simply to click on. The electronic sector has produced an impressive variety of products that have become every day items, such as compact discs and digital televisions. Each successive product cycle maintained the momentum of growth. Mobile phones made the leap from being huge, impracticable, expensive and limited boxes to a miniaturised, 'must-have', mass-market product that adds tremendous value.

Ford crossed the chasm by manufacturing mass-produced, cheap cars a century ago. Previously, they were hand-crafted, expensive and for the privileged few. Low cost was reinforced by promoting just one colour, black, although any colour could be ordered, contrary to popular belief. Ford preferred black because it was cheap and quick-drying, rather than because of its aesthetic appeal. The wooden packing cases containing the US kits for UK manufacture at Old Trafford were re-used as the floorboards and side panels and are another example of low-cost production. Spotting a sector that is just about to enter such hyper-growth provides a wonderful opportunity. This was one of the underlying premises behind the TMT mania and, with that gone, it is not apparent where the next hyper-growth will appear. Nevertheless, the TMT sector seems the most likely candidate at some stage, given its dynamism and scalability.

5e. High growth markets: competitive advantage rated 2

This chapter's sections on low-cost overseas production (3g) and crossing the chasm (5d) are subsets of a wider desirable attribute of a sector, namely to have a high growth market. This means a favourable tailwind of profitability available for the companies therein and is infinitely preferable to a stagnant or dying sector that faces a war of attrition. Those sectors that have enjoyed high growth in profits over the last five years are detailed in chapter 4. The list is likely to be quite different over the next five years as the economic cycle unfolds and there are different winners and losers. The list is as follows, in decreasing order of growth in profits: mining; construction and building materials; pharmaceuticals; health and personal care; banks and speciality finance; software and computer services; support services; oil and gas; telecommunications; tobacco; food producers and processors; beverages; electricity and other utilities; foods and drug retailers; automobiles and household goods; leisure and hotels; general retailers; chemicals; aerospace and defence; transport; information technology hardware; electronic; electrical and engineering; media and entertainment; life assurance and insurance. The growth rates start at 14% with mining and goes down to minus 20% for insurance.

The sectors with the highest growth in profits are not necessarily those with the highest profit margins. For example, tobacco has the highest margin at 27% but had a pedestrian five-year growth rate of 8% compound. Pharmaceuticals combine the best of both worlds with a margin of 25% and a five-year growth rate of 12% compound. Growth can be high in profitability or turnover. The former is far more important than the latter because only profits can increase shareholders' wealth. Also, high growth in turnover carries a wealth warning, since the infrastructure tends to increase rapidly to keep pace with actual or anticipated growth. The trouble is that the growth may fade away as competition starts to undermine revenues. The business model may be flawed or management may not have had time to bed the business down and learn which markets can profitably be served. The fixed cost is then left to hit the bottom line and profit warnings are the order of the day.

5f. High value product: competitive advantage rated 2

Powerful sectors add high value to the customer and this is especially effective if the cost is small and/or one-off. An example is software that is bought once at modest cost but used countless times. Personal computers are now cheap and add great value because they are so versatile. They are increasingly being used beyond the old remit of document processors, internet information and e-mail and now used as a telephone, radio, and television and for person-to-person (P2P) music and video file swopping. The purchase decision becomes a 'no-brainer' if the usefulness of the product far exceeds the price. High prices can be charged when such a product first hits the market to capture value from top end consumers. Later, when this demand is satisfied, competition increases and prices drop to stimulate mass demand, an example being colour televisions.

Switzerland is landlocked with high production and transportation costs. The population is highly educated and skilled. Their competitive advantage needed a product that contained significant added value during production that could be captured by them, rather than suppliers or customers, yet was inexpensive to transport so ideally would be small. These constraints led to the success of their watch industry, with the likes of Rolex, until the Japanese became interested. A variation of this is the high number of transactions business model. This means selling high value products where the cost and effort involved is similar to selling low value products. The company can add a modest percentage for its efforts that does not materially increase the high price to the customer but does represent a material fee for the company. Estate agents and stockbroker commissions are good examples. The value of houses, or a large share transaction, dwarf the fee charged by these middlemen, so customer resistance is minimised.

5g. Intellectual property rights and proprietary products:
competitive advantage rated 2

'Somebody said to me, 'But the Beatles were anti-materialistic'. That's a huge myth. John and I literally used to sit down and say, 'Now let's write a swimming pool.'
Sir Paul McCartney

Intellectual property rights (IPR), such as patents, copyrights and trademarks, are intangible assets like goodwill and may be recorded in the balance sheet if purchased from another company. They will not be shown as an asset on the balance sheet if 'home-grown', although they may be very valuable nevertheless. IPR can be a potent method of putting a defensive moat around a sector. It prevents competition because new entrants have to build their own IPR and this can be very difficult and risky.

Patents are prevalent in many sectors and include telecommunications, oil, gas, aerospace, defence, electronics, pharmaceuticals and technology. They may be a stalwart of the business or may only apply to minor applications. The advantage of the patent may not be apparent in the product that is sold. Therefore, whereas it may help to lower cost and inhibit competitors, it may not add any perceived value to customers. They are crucial to pharmaceutical products because new drugs take years to develop and to obtain regulatory approval. The average cost is a staggering £0.5 billion each and this increases by 10% a year. The super profits earned when the patent is in force for up to 20 years can then fund more research and development. When the patent expires, generic drugs can then compete on price. Patents are not foolproof, however. Some countries, like India, do not recognise drug patents and generic forms of Western drugs are produced within the patent period and then sold worldwide at knock down prices. BT is another example, as it filed a 1978 patent on the hyperlink on a computer page that directs a user to a hidden page. The hyperlink is widely used and is a cornerstone of the internet. It is usually underlined or in a different font and the cursor turns into a hand icon. The US courts have refused to recognise this patent or the colossal royalties that might otherwise accrue to BT.

Copyrights apply to products like software and music. Trademarks are a word, name, symbol, or device used by a company to distinguish their goods from those of competitors. Examples include consumer goods like Coca-Cola, Shell petrol, Hilton hotels and Cadburys' chocolate. Proprietary products are produced with a firm's expertise and, although they may be unpatented, they can be very difficult to emulate. This can lead to head-hunting of top management to find out how a competitor operates. Formula One racing cars are one example. Sometimes a product, or production method, will not be patented, as they would then be in a public document. Competitors could shamelessly copy them, especially in lax foreign countries, such as in the Far East, or slightly alter them so that the patent is not technically infringed but essentially a copy is made all the same. In addition, patents do expire. The formula for Coca-Cola has not been patented. Microsoft is perhaps the best example of a company that does not patent but instead hides the computer codes to safeguard its proprietary products.

5h. Internet threat: competitive advantage rated 3

'I look for businesses in which I think I can predict what they're going to look like in ten to fifteen years' time. I don't think the internet is going to change how people chew gum.'
Warren Buffett

Internet shares rocketed in the TMT mania and have since crashed back to earth but the invention is more popular than ever. There is great reluctance by consumers to pay for software or using internet sites, other than online buying, as they have become accustomed to free services. This technology and attitude is a threat to any product that can be sold or downloaded online. For example, sales in the music sector are falling because records are being distributed for free on the internet using websites like Limewire, which allows millions of people to share billions of files. The gorillas have retaliated by shutting down sites like Napster and are attempting to sue individuals. The profit zone has moved from the shareholders to the public.

This trend will only strengthen with download speeds and number of users both increasing. Some music companies have increased prices to make up the revenue shortfall, which is a strange business model as it further motivates free downloading of a more expensive product. Others are allowing downloads for a small charge.

The growing power of the internet means that buyers and sellers can interact directly and do not need a middleman providing information or services, such as a travel agent. The ability to compare prices of products increases competition and puts the traditional 'bricks and mortar' retailers under great pressure. Their response has included 'if you can't beat them, join them' and many now also sell online at keen prices but this undercuts, and cannibalises, their own high street shops. Buying online is quick, convenient and goods are delivered to your door. Six per cent of all sales are now via the internet and this is growing fast. Many sectors are affected and include: beverages; food and general retailers; telecommunications; utilities; automobiles; leisure; media; entertainment; support services; information technology; and financial services. Some sectors and companies are affected more than others and investors should be wary of those that are losing ground. Ironically, this threat does not extend to old economy sectors like chemicals, construction, oil and gas.

5i. Obsolescence: competitive advantage rated 3

'The only big companies that succeed will be those that obsolete themselves before someone else does.'
Bill Gates

The sector operating risk is greatly reduced if the product does not become obsolete. New launches are expensive and a successful outcome is uncertain. Products that do not become obsolete include food and tobacco and can be relied upon to deliver solid revenue streams that underpin the reliability of profit forecasts, thus minimising surprises. These are usually staples of life and have remained essentially unaltered. The downside is that the markets are mature with limited growth.

Other sectors are not so fortunate and obsolescence is ever-present, so they operate in a constant state of flux. Participants have to relentlessly innovate and market their products skilfully to stay ahead of the competition. Technology and telecommunications are cases in point with the rapid increase in the power of computers and fibre optics, yet prices drop inexorably. This phenomenon was observed by the co-founder of Intel and is now remembered as the famous Moore's Law: the number of transistors per square inch on integrated circuits doubles every year. Intel took this to heart and competes by trying to keep one step ahead of the competition by constantly innovating with faster and cheaper chips. Such product obsolescence increases the risk/reward ratio of affected sectors. The growth potential is very high, as demonstrated by the rapid dominance of gorillas like Cisco and Vodafone. Automobiles and aerospace are examples of sectors where the threat of obsolescence means that they have to work hard just to stand still. Fashion goods, such as clothes, depend on obsolescence to wheel out new ranges with a life expectancy measured in months.

5j. Long-term and opaque pricing: competitive advantage rated 1

Products with long-term contracts or commitments lock in the customer and is one of the strongest business models. Life insurance has this characteristic where savings, pension and life products earn premiums from the same customer over decades. Further, the pricing is opaque because customers lack information about how much the product really costs, as commissions are deducted from premiums so no bill is presented to the customer. Payouts are uncertain and far in the future. This makes it very difficult for a customer to make a rational buying decision and much is left to crossing fingers, relying on a brand and hoping for the best. This applies to all companies in that sector, so trying to shop elsewhere does not ease the customers' plight. No wonder then that life products are 'sold' to the customer rather than 'bought'. Compare this to transactional, or one-off, products like a restaurant meal, where the cost and benefits are immediately apparent. The customer is thus empowered as to whether he has received value for money and can then decide to return, go to a competitor or cease buying. Sectors that feature long-term contracts, which can extend up to as long as 25 years in some cases, include construction, aerospace, defence and support services. Opaque pricing is prevalent in financial services, such as banks and reinsurance.

5k. Make life easy: competitive advantage rated 3

'The question is, then, do we try to make things easy on ourselves or do we try to make things easy on our customers, whoever they may be?'
Erwin Frand

Sectors that make life easy are attractive in a world full of hard work, long hours, commuting and constant demands on time. People who are 'time poor and cash rich' will pay for products that save time, examples being broadband internet and the now defunct supersonic air travel. Making life easy also appeals to those who are 'time rich and cash poor', notably retirees. A prime example is the wide choice offered by supermarkets that enables customers to purchase most of their needs in one shopping trip, with convenient locations and free parking. Compare that to the old days of fighting traffic in congested towns, trying to find a parking place, trudging round endless stores on a cold, wet high street and lugging the weight of shopping back to the car. Leisure complexes combine multi-screen cinemas, restaurants, sports bars, bowling alleys and nightclubs all under one roof in a safe environment, again with easy car access and parking. This is a long way away from the local 'flea pit' showing one film a week.

Cars in the early days did improve life but a dozen punctures on a 20-mile trip was common, so it did not make life that easy. Compare that to today where cars are reliable, usually only need servicing every 10,000 miles and many motorists have never had a puncture. There are countless other products that make life easy including: air-conditioning, which, for example, made living in Florida possible; automatic gearboxes in cars; answerphones; and e-mail, which allows free global communication. Companies also buy to make life easy, such as delegating non-core activities to support services providers or backing up the entire computer records off site in case of disaster. Sectors that benefit from making life easy include: beverages; food; telecommunications; electronic and electrical; automobiles; household goods; general retailers; leisure; media; entertainment; transport; and financial services.

5l. Make once, sell many times: competitive advantage rated 1

Sectors which have the highest-rated competitive advantage make a product once and then sell it many times. Information technology is a case in point, as once software has been written it can be produced at very little extra cost and sold by the million, especially if installed in computers as standard. Financial services products have the same characteristic and are essentially quite straightforward. Once the product line of bank accounts and financial products is open for business, they can be sold for years and, like software, are eminently scalable to deal with increased demand. Tourist attractions are another instance and indeed, for historical sites, like a castle or mansion, the whole point is not to change the product, as its uniqueness is the selling point. Once a telecommunications network is in place, the traffic can be sold many times.

Transport journeys and holidays are the opposite and can only be sold once and, awkwardly, at a specific time. Similarly, music, film, fashion and media sectors continually have to create new products for a faddish consumer. This makes the operating risk high and there are a large number of flops.

5m. Monopoly, oligopoly and cartels: competitive advantage rated 2

Monopoly, oligopoly and cartels allow sectors to earn super profits and can be very powerful. The sector has a stranglehold on the product and the number of participants is one for a monopoly, several for an oligopoly and a group for a cartel. The super profit is achieved by restricting production and thus keeping the price higher than the equilibrium point, where demand and supply would otherwise be equal at a lower price. They are attacked by governments that are keen to stop abuse and accomplish this through increased competition and regulation. They have existed since the earliest times and are much less of an issue today. Oil has been rife with such a structure, for example Standard Oil until its break up in 1911. OPEC is a cartel that was spectacularly successful in the 1970s and 1980s. It literally had the world over a barrel until the higher prices and self-inflicted recession reduced demand. In addition, squabbling over quotas and increased output by non-OPEC members led to supply and demand being brought back into balance at lower prices. UK petrol retailing is an area thought to be operating as a cartel and has been investigated by the authorities.

Utilities, such as telephone, gas and electricity, are natural monopolies, as it made no economic sense to have more than one line or pipe laid. These sectors have been privatised and thrown open to competition in the last two decades and prices have fallen. Microsoft was ordered to split its activities, since it was judged to have monopolistic tendencies with its operating systems and software, but this has not been put into effect. An example of a minor monopoly is one where customers have no choice, as with leisure parks, such as Disney, which forbid customers bringing their own drink and food, forcing them to buy on site. Motorway service stations can have the same, though limited, power.

5n. Must-have products: competitive advantage rated 2

Sectors are attractive where the customer must have the product, almost regardless of the macroeconomic backdrop. Technology had been a prime example, although many products have been shown to be nice-to-have rather than must-have after the TMT fallout in 2000. The dream two decades ago was a personal computer on every desk, which seemed fanciful. It readily became apparent that this product was essential, cost effective and had to be bought regardless. It sounded the death knell of secretaries, once a major occupation, as computers empowered individuals to do this work instead. It also had the key attribute that it made no sense to have computers on half the desks so everyone had to have one, once the decision was taken to introduce the technology. Laser printers allow fast and quiet copies to be made from the desktop and increase efficiency compared to their clattering mechanical predecessors.

The growth of compact discs over cassette tapes is an example of a must-have product substituting the original product that initially propelled sales. Eventually, demand is satisfied and the must-have product becomes mature. The must-have product can be new or an updated version. For instance, some companies want to strike a balance between the significant cost of computer and software upgrades against their benefits and many decide to miss one upgrade and wait for the next one. Wonder drugs, like penicillin and anaesthetics, open up fresh markets and fuel demand because of their revolutionary properties. They are thus product-driven and not dependent on the economic cycle.

Specialised, unique applications or providing cost effective solutions to a major problem are typical features of must-have products. However, not all of them have pricing power. Food producers and utilities are essential to life but there are many suppliers of these commodity products and so competition has often resulted in low pricing power.

5o. New products: competitive advantage rated 2

'Necessity is the theme and the inventress, the eternal curb and law of nature.'
Leonardo da Vinci

Some sectors are more dynamic than others and are constantly bringing out new products that stimulate demand, whether from scratch or when old products reach the end of their cycle. There are many examples of new products including jumbo jets, microwave ovens, mobile phones, drugs and the national lottery. Technology is at the forefront of introducing new products and services. Examples are software applications, high performance computers and business solutions, like supply chain management. The most attractive new products or services have killer applications and become essential products, rather than refinements of old products. Thus, Windows 95 was a revolutionary product that enabled the personal computer to be used with ease. Windows XP has improved on this original product but it is only an improvement, rather than a killer application.

Consumer electronics have reaped the advances in technology with a bewildering range of products that became mass markets, such as DVD players. Car manufacturers desperately increase the specification of their products but, although much more refined, it still does what it did a century ago, which is to travel from A to B. Other sectors have old economy products that struggle to innovate or cannot do so at all.

5p. Positional goods: competitive advantage rated 4

Positional goods are luxury items that are wanted because of the status conferred on the consumer, rather than the particular merits of the product or representing value for money. Consequently, they are attractive businesses as high margins can be earned from catering to the tastes of snobbish consumers. Beware of an economic downturn, though, when such spurious demand can fall off a cliff. There are many examples of positional goods. Oysters were cheap in the UK when they grew plentifully several hundred years ago. They were then devastated by disease so became expensive and thus today they are a symbol of affluence. The same concept applies to lobsters, which were once so plentiful on coral reefs that this disdained food was given to the dog. Similarly, medieval lords were constrained by law as to the number of times a week that they could feed salmon to their serfs, given it was then so abundant. Rolex watches, diamond rings, Rolls-Royce cars, exclusive addresses, personal number plates and art are other illustrations, with some being bought as gifts, safe in the knowledge that they will be well received. Holidays, such as skiing and sailing, and exotic destinations are a means of differentiating yourself from your peers.

Positional goods are most evident in the minefield of fashion where brands are intended to enhance status. The Japanese have a love affair with western brands, like Saville Row tailoring, and the Chinese often leave brand tags on sunglasses. Care must be taken not to stretch the brand too far, as Gucci found out when its brand was spread over 3,000 products and lost its mystique. The same may happen in due course when up-market car manufacturers, such as Mercedes and BMW, entered the bottom end of the market. Toyota's approach to this problem of brand dilution was to use its brand on ordinary cars and create a new one for its prestigious Lexus luxury cars.

5q. Research and development to maintain lead:
competitive advantage rated 3

Some sectors need to plough back a large percentage of profit into research and development to generate new products and maintain their lead. These include aerospace, automobiles, pharmaceuticals and technology. GlaxoSmithKline, Microsoft and Toyota each spend £3 billion a year on research and development. Intel is a good example in computer chips, where high expenditure is essential to keep ahead of competitors. Research and development expenditure is not a panacea, as there is no certainty that it will lead to the production of goods and services that customers want at a premium price. However, it is an indication of a dynamic sector that may enter hyper-growth, such as mobile phones. Sectors may be more attractive which avoid heavy research and development cost and which have lower operating risk, an example being food retailing. Be wary of companies that capitalise the cost on the balance sheet as an asset rather than write it off as an expense to the profit and loss account. Rolls-Royce capitalised the cost of developing its RB211 engine in the 1970s, rather than expensing it, and subsequently went bankrupt.

5r. Recovery plays: competitive advantage rated 4

Sectors that are out of favour can be very attractive recovery plays, providing that they still have long-term attractions. Buy when the sector has shown tangible evidence of rehabilitation in investors' eyes by using basic technical analysis and do not try to pick the bottom of the market. Also, try to buy value and this is especially true with recovery plays because that will guard against opportunistic takeovers or any further woes. Therefore, solid asset backing, high and well-covered dividends, cash in the bank and some growth in profits are safeguards. This subject is covered in chapters 5 and 6.

Sectors have their moment in the sun and then wane. Sometimes this can be because of loss of international competitive advantage and the decline is terminal, as is the case with shipping, textiles, coal and steel. In others, it can be because of temporary set backs that lead to profit warnings and plunging share prices. Such setbacks can be self-inflicted, such as price wars in supermarket or tobacco sectors. It could be due to overcapacity, as in general insurance or high street pubs. Another reason could be simply a stock market bubble in a sector. Most sectors are prone to the economic cycle. It is important to know where you are in that cycle and which asset classes to hold. Thus, the likes of banks, house builders, manufacturers, leisure and recruitment companies should be sold at the top of the cycle and bought after the next recession ends, as discussed in chapters 3 and 4.

5s. Product pipeline: competitive advantage rated 3

'A good negotiator lets the other person think they are getting the best deal.'
Anon

Consider the length of the pipeline needed to bring new products or services to the market. It takes a long time to develop and launch a new car and is an expensive, risky business. Nevertheless, the Japanese achieved a four-year product cycle, unlike most of the competition that had an eight-year cycle. Pharmaceutical companies also have a long-term pipeline. The snag is that a competitor may launch a new product first and steal the market. Also, by the time the product is ready, demand may have moved on or been swamped with overcapacity, for example semiconductor chip manufacturers, mobile phones and general insurance. Technology, telecommunications, aerospace and mining sectors tend to have long pipelines.

At the other end of the spectrum, supermarkets and retailers have a timescale measured in months to bring out new products. Pipelines tend to be less of a problem when the product is stable, as demand can be more accurately forecast and innovations will be few, such as a commodity product like tobacco. Although it is an oversimplification, long pipelines increase the chance of wasted expenditure and dubious demand. The shorter the timescale, the more attuned and tailored the product is likely to be to the available demand.

5t. Toll bridge – intangible: competitive advantage rated 2

Toll bridges can be intangible or tangible and they levy a charge for using a facility. They are very desirable business models, as they tend to be low risk by feeding on the labours of others. An intangible toll bridge applies to services, ideas and permissions, rather than physical assets like a road. License fees, such as for software, are a good example where customers pay to use patented or proprietary products. The licensee, rather than the licenser, has the risk of combining the factors of production to make a profit and the licenser sits back and watches the money roll in. Brands can be licenced to create demand for an otherwise undifferentiated product. For example, children's characters are used to sell a host of products from toys to clothing. Support service companies pay to use utilities' trusted brand names to sell associated products, as do distributors of financial services products, such as life insurance. Search engines, like Google, charge a toll bridge fee for advertisers' web links displayed on the results page and the fee increases according to the number of hits by interested customers.

5u. Toll bridge – tangible: competitive advantage rated 2

Tangible toll bridges charge a fee for using a physical asset. A characteristic of tangible tolls is that the provider often has an effective monopoly and can earn super profits. Therefore, they do tend to be regulated. A main attraction is that once the facility is built it feeds off natural growth in the economy and demographic factors, like an increase in population, so revenues increase with little increase in costs. Road and bridge tolls have been around for centuries. Airports have runaways that planes have to pay a landing fee to use. This is an attractive and low risk way of riding on the back of the remorseless growth in air travel, compared to the high risk of airline companies. Cruise ships pay a toll per passenger when they dock at ports. A car park feeds off the demand for shopping or train travel. Eurotunnel is a painful reminder that not all tolls are a money-spinner. The economics of the internet are unusual in that no charge is made to the user for using its backbone, although there is a cost of access through internet service providers.

6. Suppliers

Sectors aim to capture the profit from their activities, rather than surrender it to suppliers. Attractive sectors therefore have control over their suppliers so it is important to understand where the power lies.

6a. Cost of inputs compared to selling price: competitive advantage rated 2

Supplier power is less important if the cost of a sector's inputs is low compared to the selling price. The suppliers are weak because their involvement is marginal. For example, pharmaceuticals add most of the value during production rather than from suppliers, as do services that generate their own output with little recourse to suppliers, such as professional firms and information technology. Sectors can have many suppliers for the myriad of inputs they need and their strength varies. A sector can cope with powerful suppliers where their impact on the value chain is minimal. The sector should have weak suppliers where their impact is significant. For example, suppliers to supermarkets have a major impact but they are weak because the supermarkets have the whip hand.

6b. Excess capacity weakens suppliers: competitive advantage rated 3

The supplier might be in a poor negotiating position if it needs to shift high volumes, especially if they are time sensitive, and this puts pressure on prices. For example, 95% of telecommunications capacity is not being used and this excess capacity weakens suppliers. This is very different to oil companies that depend on volatile and uncontrollable supply and price of crude oil from the likes of OPEC, which has at times seized the profit for itself by cutting capacity. There is generally no shortage in the supply of goods today, although this is less true of services. This abundant supply is the cornerstone of the intense competition that companies face. For example, a stroll round a shopping complex will reveal the overcapacity in outlets for women's clothes and shoes. Other sectors that have overcapacity include automobiles, technology and financial services.

6c. Moving up and down the value chain: competitive advantage rated 1

Suppliers may be wary of being too greedy if they fear that the sector they serve may move down the value chain into their territory in order to capture the value added. For example, a pub company may start its own brewery rather than buying from a supplier. Similarly, the sector may fear that the suppliers may move up the value chain into their territory, for example a brewer moving into pubs. Likewise, a Kuwaiti oil company moved into petrol retailing with its Q8 chain and this would help to secure demand from the end user. Some sectors' participants, like Dell and Amstrad, eliminated the middleman by selling direct and the internet is a rapidly emerging force in this area. Such companies have more control over their destiny and access to the end user, who can be sold follow-on services, such as warranties and financing. Sectors that have moved up and down the value chain include: utilities; leisure and hotels; media and entertainment; information technology; and financial services. Such moves should be with the aim of moving into profit zones and thus maximising long-term profit for shareholders, rather than due to conflicts of interest, like empire building. It can be psychologically very hard to abandon markets but there should be no hesitation if the prospects are poor.

6d. Weak and numerous suppliers: competitive advantage rated 2

The ideal position is for the sector to have a small number of powerful gorillas that buy from weak, numerous and competitive suppliers, on the 'divide and rule' principle, examples being supermarkets and beverages. The amounts ordered should be varied to stop suppliers from becoming complacent and the gorillas should ask for many quotes. Sector power increases if there are low costs of switching between suppliers, for example buying utilities, or if the suppliers are locked into unattractive terms. Switching is easier if the sector can substitute inputs, for example outsourcing production to China. Sectors with weak and numerous suppliers include pharmaceuticals, aerospace, retailers and support services and are thus attractive on this score. Conversely, the supplier's hand is strengthened if it can sell to others, such as software that cuts across all sectors and is thus not dependent on just one sector. Cinemas in the UK, for example, have few and powerful suppliers, since just six distributors control 90% of all films, and the cinemas have no control over the type of films made, meekly having to show what comes down the pipeline and hoping the audience will like it.

7. Sectors to avoid

Just as there are attractive sectors with strong competitive advantage, there are those that should be avoided. Some of this has been touched on in this chapter and is included here for completeness. Here are a few examples.

7a. Attracts capacity in the good times

Sectors that attract capacity in the good times are risky. In the bad times, the resultant overcapacity leads to price-cutting and threatens the profitability of all the players. General insurance is a good example. This sector has its own cycle, which is independent of the overall economic cycle. Assume that the sector is in equilibrium, demand and supply are in balance and the sector is earning normal profits. Then an event happens like the terrorism of September 11th and the $50 billion of underwriting increases premiums. Injecting more capital to take advantage of this opportunity increases underwriting capacity. This eventually leads to falling premiums and underwriting losses. There is no swing producer to regulate this huge market, as there is with Saudi Arabia and oil. In the technology wonderland of excess in the 1990's, fortunes were spent on fibre optic telecommunications leading to immense overcapacity. Also at that time, demand for semiconductor chips seemed sky-high and the response was to build very expensive factories, many of which faced a future of idleness.

Real disposable income increases by one third each decade and this affluence has fuelled demand for cruising, the fastest growing part of the holiday market at 8% per year, and propelled the US-based Carnival into the FTSE 100 index. There has been a massive increase in the sector's capacity over the last decade. New ships are being launched at the rate of one a month and 40% are mega-sized at over 100,000 tons, such as the 150,000-ton Queen Mary 2 which cost £0.4 billion. The break-even point of this business is high, as fixed costs are substantial. The cabin prices will have to be heavily discounted in the next recession and losses will mount. However, unlike general insurance, it will not be easy to reduce capacity, as cruise ships have no alternative use, although this will be less of an issue for some of the older ships, which can be mothballed. Such cyclical businesses are best bought as recovery plays just after the economic cycle has started to pick up again after a recession. They should be sold just before the cycle peaks.

7b. Based on a quirk that politicians can remove

Sectors are vulnerable which are based on the largesse, or lack of it, of politicians. Frequently, such largesse can be removed and increases the operating risk. For example, BAA was a prime sufferer when duty free allowances were removed on travel within Europe a few years ago at the behest of the EU. It lost revenues at its airport shops and issued a profit warning. Offshore banking was opened up after Margaret Thatcher abolished exchange controls when she came to power and proved a boon to tax havens. OECD governments are clearly unhappy about them and have brought strong pressure to bear.

New financial services have grown on tax quirks such as BES, VCT, PEP and ISA that have been encouraged and discouraged, as the mood has suited governments. Other areas affected include the private finance initiative, which was started by the Conservatives and has survived under Labour. However, it has not been a smooth ride and opposition has come from many quarters. Import quotas have been applied when a trade row flares up, such as between the EU and the US. The Common Agricultural Policy is an eccentricity that was devised to protect marginal farmers and has had profound effects on agriculture. Fishing is heavily regulated with quotas. Politicians wax and wane on all sorts of issues. Examples include: the fifth terminal at Heathrow; more homes to be built in the south; congestion charging; environmental taxes; and redistribution of council tax. Be aware of the risk and generally avoid sectors that are prone to government fiat.

7c. Being the bacon in the sandwich

Avoid being the 'bacon in the sandwich' and being eaten by jaws either side of it. Distributors in general face this problem, a good example being car dealers. They add little value and are stuck between powerful suppliers and price sensitive, informed customers, leading to wafer-thin margins. They are supplied by a small number of powerful gorillas that manufacture the cars and, because they award the franchise, have power over the distributors so can dictate terms. The car buyer is well informed and has access to alternative suppliers via the newspaper, internet or cheap imports. Cars are also big-ticket items and buying tends to be postponed in a recession, so the sector has high operating risk. Resellers of utilities, such as phone calls, can be in a similar position. Another illustration is food producers and processors. Although they do add value, they are at risk from being squeezed between suppliers on the one side and mighty supermarket customers on the other. Some food producers do have competitive advantage, like Inter Link Foods, which works more as a partner with the supermarkets, adding value through innovation and quality and is not overly reliant on one or two gorillas.

7d. Dying sectors

Dying or sunset sectors have poor international competitive advantage and should be avoided. Coal, steel, engineering and textiles are in long-term decline, as is manufacturing in general, which is now only a fifth of the economy and dwindling. The cost of production is too high compared to low-cost producers of the Pacific Rim and elsewhere. Chemicals is another unattractive sector which is dying in the UK, with commodity products and import substitution. These heavy industries have large work forces, whose cost is continually and materially rising. Instead, concentrate on higher-growth, sunshine sectors that have international competitive advantage. These include: beverages; pharmaceuticals; tobacco; food retailing; telecommunications; oil; aerospace; leisure; media; support services; information technology; banking; and financial services.

7e. Endless restructuring

'Constant reorganisation can create the illusion of progress while producing inefficiency and demoralisation.'
Petronius, Roman author.

Avoid sectors that have endless restructuring which results in heavy 'exceptional' costs. There are three types of restructuring. Firstly, the sector may be stuck in the middle with poor competitive advantage, or worse, be in long-term decline, as is the case with heavy industry, from which there will be no recovery. Secondly, restructuring may be sector specific due to a major event, such as the terrorist attacks of September 11th, which resulted in some airline bankruptcies, or a country's default affecting banks. Lastly, restructuring may be due to the sector's inability to withstand the economic cycle, so that those with poor recession resistance suffer in a downturn. These last two types may offer recovery plays for a contrarian investor.

Restructuring costs can have a habit of appearing every year and are, in effect, normal operating costs. They also tend to be excluded by management in its yardstick of performance but they destroy shareholder value all the same. Take the view that all the costs in the income statement count and concentrate on the actual bottom line, rather than a more optimistic number the directors prefer to highlight without the 'nasty bits'. Endless restructuring is proof that competitive advantage is under threat and a transition to the promised land may or may not happen. Let another shareholder go down that road rather than you. Gorillas can be more prone to this than smaller companies. Restructuring them can take a Herculean effort and the risk of failure is high.

7f. High depreciation and amortisation of goodwill

Sectors that suffer high depreciation and amortisation of goodwill are prime candidates for reporting losses in bad times. Since these are fixed charges, there is precious little that management can then do to improve the situation. The poor results may prevail for a long time, as the write-offs can extend for up to 20 years.

Depreciation is prevalent in sectors that are heavy users of capital and need substantial fixed assets. Thus, candidates include: telecommunications; utilities; steel; mining; oil; gas; aerospace; engineering; leisure; and transport. Goodwill is prevalent in sectors that have embarked on an acquisition spree, particularly at the top of the market when valuations were high, or in a consolidating sector. The best example is TMT, where astronomical sums were paid for companies with poor business models and precious little in net assets. Other sectors include beverages, pharmaceuticals, tobacco, utilities, oil, gas and financial services. Goodwill is discussed in chapter 8.

7g. Long tail liability insurance

Long tail liability insurance, or so called 'property casualty' insurance, should be avoided at all costs. It is hard to think of a more unappealing business. The premiums are received today for unknown and potentially unlimited liabilities years ahead, so an underwriter has no idea what the costs are going to be and budgeting is pure guesswork. A player entering this area may just be providing capital and relying on the lead underwriter's judgement, not that it will have much idea as to the outcome of events. Therefore, control has been delegated to a supposed expert. The premiums are often reinsured round the market and each broker takes a commission cut. The premium can be a shadow of its former self by the time the residue is received by the player and they take time to be paid, as the reinsurers earn interest by sitting on the money. The liabilities, by contrast, come down the line fast and are the full 100%, unlike the whittled down premiums.

Some of this merry-go-round was exposed in the Lloyds of London scandal in the 1990s, when unsuspecting names were sucked in to meet several catastrophic liabilities, notably the Piper Alpha oil rig blowing up in the North Sea. The US market is the most litigious in the world and the courts go after deep pockets on the most flimsy and ludicrous of excuses. Liabilities can emerge years later that were unknown at the time, such as asbestosis which has bankrupted companies. Avoid companies in the Lloyds insurance market or being a 'name', as well as companies that have reinsurance activities. The space to occupy when the premiums are hard is that of a broker placing the reinsurance for a fee. It does not need much capital and it rides on the back of this increasing revenue. In addition, it is not exposed to the considerable underwriting risk.

7h. Prone to the economic cycle

Avoid sectors that are prone to the economic cycle and are thus cyclical. Recession resistant sectors are very attractive as they have far better control over their revenue streams. The time to buy cyclical companies, like builders, is at the bottom of the cycle and then sell at the top. This is fully covered in chapters 3 and 4.

7i. Prone to litigation

Avoid sectors and countries that are prone to litigation, which is itself a growth industry. The cost of litigation and the awards made can be staggering, especially in the US. In addition to the financial costs and the damaging publicity, lawsuits tie up endless amounts of top management time that should be spent creating shareholder value. The sector most exposed is tobacco and avoid companies that have US operations, notably British American Tobacco. The US government is fighting to wring $280 billion out of the tobacco industry for allegedly conspiring to promote smoking for 50 years. Avoid general and reinsurance companies exposed to US risks, like Royal & Sun Alliance and its exposure to workers' compensation and asbestos claims. The UK is turning more litigious, as it tends to be affected by trends in the US over time, and this can be expected to increase. The NHI, for example, pays £1 billion damages a year for contamination of patients in hospitals. This provides an opportunity for companies that provide solutions, such as Biotrace and Celsis.

7j. Regulated

'If you have ten thousand regulations you destroy all respect for the law.'
Sir Winston Churchill

Avoid sectors that are regulated by the government or other authorities, a point emphasised by Warren Buffett. Such a powerful body can undermine the profits materially, unexpectedly and quickly. As a result, such sectors have high operating risk and are unlikely to achieve a decent rating. Railtrack was placed into administration because the government suddenly stopped the agreed subsidy that is needed to run the system. It instead preferred a 'not-for-profit' organisation, which seems likely to cost a fortune. British Energy was brought to its knees by a new wholesale market imposed by the regulator which meant that its price did not even cover the costs.

Utilities and television are regulated with pricing and conditions set for a typical five years. This is unattractive as the regulator is a wild card and may be keen to impose swinging price cuts or reallocate licences for political or other reasons. Where the regulator has largely withdrawn, for instance in telephone calls, he has left behind a sector that is subject to fierce competition. Financial companies are regulated by the FSA and the costs of compliance are onerous. The trend towards more regulation will increase inexorably, egged on by the EU, whose influence is set to increase.

7k. Unethical

Some investors wish to avoid unethical sectors, such as gambling, guns, alcohol, military activities and tobacco. This subject has been well-aired and is a moral decision in the main. The absence of such investors reduces demand for the shares, tending to lower the price and increasing the return for those investors who are not deterred. Alcohol, tobacco and petrol are the usual suspects for 'sin' taxes and governments have not lost their zeal in increasing such taxes and claiming 'it is for your own good'. These sectors have their pricing in the hands of government, which is, prima facie, unattractive. On the other hand, as explained above, all three have robust, inelastic demand that is little dampened by price increases.

CHAPTER 3

Shifting deck chairs on the Titanic

'You better start swimming or you'll sink like a stone, for the times they are a'changin.'
Bob Dylan

We have examined in the first two chapters the business models of companies and sectors that result in strong competitive advantage. The next step is to assess how they fare during the course of the economic cycle, as this determines when they should be bought and sold.

The first part of this chapter examines how the economic cycle can seriously enhance or damage your wealth. It is vital to select the appropriate asset class and sector. Investing in the wrong sector at the wrong part of the economic cycle can lead to a catastrophic loss of capital. The second part is to analyse how asset classes behave in a typical economic cycle and identify opportunities.

1. The economic cycle

'Most other fund managers refuse to believe that the cycle exists any more: they believe that consumers can go on spending indefinitely.'
Peter Webb, Eaglet investment trust.

Share selection can be compared to shifting deck chairs on the Titanic. You may have chosen a good spot to sit on the ship but that is not very helpful if it is about to hit an iceberg. Similarly, it is imperative to choose shares that will not sink when the economic cycle changes. Some understanding of this will, in all likelihood, be the most important determinant of success or failure. Sadly, all too many investors and businessmen extrapolate from the past to the future and assume that existing trends will continue. They fail to understand that the trend has a bend in it and even less understanding of when that bend may happen.

It is vital to recognise the current point of the economic cycle. Once this is understood, the appropriate asset class can then be selected. Essentially, investors should have a good tailwind behind them and this is best and most easily achieved by being in asset classes that are rising in price and avoiding those that are falling. Battling against a strong headwind is futile. Another way of riding the cycle is to be long on assets that are rising and short those that are falling. We will return to this later but first we need to examine what causes the cycle and where we are on it now.

What causes the economic cycle?

*'Change is the law of life. And those who look only to the past or the present
are certain to miss the future.'*
John F. Kennedy

The economic cycle is a normal part of life. In a typical cycle, the economy starts
with equilibrium between supply and demand in the four factors of production,
namely land, labour, capital and enterprise. Presently, companies begin to feel
confident and anticipate that profits can be improved, so they increase output.
The demand for the four factors of production rises accordingly and their prices
rise. Additionally, people foresee continued and increased demand for their
labour so they feel confident about spending on consumer goods. Borrowing
increases and this fuels the housing market. The economy starts to operate above
its long-term growth trend, which is about 3% a year. Inflation, a trade deficit and
a falling currency ensue and this threat is met by the central bank with higher
interest rates. This increases the cost of capital, one of the four factors of
production, and, with more resources earmarked for that purpose, there is less left
over for the other factors. The demand for these falls, as companies and people
tighten their belts, and recession ensues along with a severe bear market in shares
and houses. Inflation is eventually wrung out of the economy and it can once
again return to equilibrium. Then the whole process can start all over again.

Alan Greenspan's view

'Don't confuse genius with a bull market.'
Wall Street slogan.

Alan Greenspan, chairman of the Federal Reserve, assessed the economic cycle
admirably in 1997: 'There is no evidence, however, that the business cycle has
been repealed. Another recession will doubtless occur some day. History
demonstrates that participants in financial markets are susceptible to waves of
optimism, which can in turn foster a general process of asset-price inflation that
can feed through into markets for goods and services. Excessive optimism sows
the seeds of its own reversal in the form of imbalances that tend to grow over
time. When unwarranted expectations ultimately are not realised, the unwinding
of these financial excesses can act to amplify a downturn in economic activity,
much as they can amplify the upswing.'

'Clearly, when people are exposed to long periods of relative economic tranquillity, they seem inevitably prone to complacency about the future. This is understandable. We have had fifteen years of economic expansion interrupted by only one recession and that was six years ago. As the memory of such past events fades, it naturally seems ever less sensible to keep up one's guard against an adverse event in the future. Thus, it should come as no surprise that, after such a long period of balanced expansion, risk premiums for advancing funds to businesses in virtually all financial markets have declined to near-record lows.'

These words are so apt that they are well worth carefully re-reading, as it could save investors a fortune. There are mini cycles of about three to four years but the whole cycle lasts for about a decade, as evidenced by the recessions in the early 1970s, 1980s and 1990s. On this wave theory reckoning, another recession should be anticipated in the not too distant future. The reason recessions seem to occur every decade may be because it takes that long for those at the sharp end to forget the pain but, once forgotten, the assumption becomes that it will not return. Also, a new generation has not yet felt that pain and naively acts without fear until it is their turn to experience a recession. If people forget the lessons of history, they are doomed to repeat them.

A history lesson

'Truth is the daughter of time.'
Josephine Tey, author.

We should examine what has happened over the last three decades to understand where we are in the economic cycle today. The stock market boom lasted 18 years from 1982 to 2000. The 1987 stock market crash proved to be but a correction in that overall bull market. It is very unusual for a bull market to last so long and it was a response to changed macroeconomic conditions. In the 1970's there was stagflation, which is a combination of inflation and no growth. This had a number of causes, such as the quadrupling of oil prices, very strong and aggressive unions, high taxation and protected economies that restricted currency movements and propped-up lame duck industries. A new determination to tackle these problems lead to conservative parties coming to power that re-invigorated the economy both in the UK and US. They opened the borders to free trade, in the UK's case made necessary anyway after joining the EU. Currency controls were swept away and direct taxation was reduced to encourage private enterprise. The behemoths of state industries were privatised en mass. The demise of heavy industry and growth in smaller companies eroded union membership and the causes of strife evaporated, most notable amongst them being ruinous inflation. The result was that strikes became rare.

On the face of it, the economy today seems to be in fine fettle with continued growth in GNP, unstoppable increases in property prices and ultra low interest rates and unemployment. Yet, scratch below the surface and a different picture emerges. We are past the top of the economic cycle but some of the traditional measures that mark this event have yet to become evident. One that has done so is a lead indicator of trouble ahead, namely the three-year rout in the stock market up to 2003. In 1987, for example, the stock market crashed and the authorities' rapid response was to ease monetary policy by lowering interest rates. This fed inflation and then interest rates had to be increased sharply, causing the recession in 1991-92. It is not feasible for the stock market, the main yardstick of economic growth, to experience such a bear market and also have ongoing health in the real economy and property prices. Eventually, the latter will have to face up to the reality of the ominous signals that the stock market has forecast.

Greatest bubble in stock market history

'The hangover may prove to be proportional to the binge.'
Warren Buffett

Low inflation broke out in the mid-1990s. This was a puzzle at the time to many, including Alan Greenspan, chairman of the Federal Reserve, because, with the economy booming, inflation would have been expected to increase but it did not. There were a number of reasons, including a quiescent oil price, intense competition and a strong dollar making imports cheap. Also, inflation was low because most people merely extrapolate from the past. For example, if shares or houses are increasing in value then investors climb on board, as they expect this trend to continue. It seems that a key ingredient in the high inflation from the 1970s to the mid-1990s was the expectation of more inflation. People saw there had been high inflation and pushed for high wage increases to compensate, which itself then caused inflation. When that cycle was eventually broken and low inflation became the expectation, based on current low inflation, then wage claims ratcheted down.

This low inflation allowed central bankers to reduce interest rates steadily since the mid-1990s. In general terms, there is a direct and inverse relationship between interest rates and asset prices. Low interest rates result in increased asset prices and vice versa. If interest rates are low, borrowing is cheap to buy assets, such as property and shares. Also, the value of a share is the discounted net present value of all dividends that will be paid in the future. If the discount rate is lower, reflecting low interest rates, then the value of a share increases accordingly. The result was a massive increase in borrowing by companies and individuals that culminated in the stock market bubble that ended in the TMT mania in 2000. Low inflation and interest rates proved a curse, not a blessing. The booming stock market was not due to a significant increase in profits, as these had been falling since 1998, but because the PER quadrupled and reached a staggering 43 in the Standard and Poor's index. It was the greatest bubble in stock market history. The three-year bear market up to 2003 brought the PER down but was still at the same level as when the market crashed in 1929, at around 30. Then the Great Depression ensued and it took 25 years for the market to regain its 1929 heights. The ultimate arbiter of world stock market levels is the US long bond. Its yield is around 5% and should this rise significantly, to say around 8%, the markets would be in dire straits.

The curse of low inflation

History provides a powerful reminder of the curse of low inflation, as the three biggest stock market bubbles and subsequent busts, which were 1929 in the US, 1989 in Japan and worldwide in 2000, were caused by low inflation. Japan has been in a bear market since 1989 and its stock market level is but a quarter of that peak. It can take a very long time to unwind asset bubbles and it is wisest to prevent them occurring in the first place so that the economy remains in equilibrium. Unfortunately, such common sense is not that common.

Furthermore, there are serious doubts as to whether the PER is based on real numbers after scandals such as WorldCom, the failings of the defunct auditors Arthur Andersen and accounting treatment of items like share options and goodwill. If anything, in a world that has long since lost financial conservatism, a PER of 30 may well, in reality, be even higher if earnings have been overstated, thus making the stock market more overvalued. However, recessions uncover what the auditors do not and reality eventually returns. The corporate backdrop has been bleak in the real economy too. Profits in the US suffered their sharpest fall since 1929 and profits in the UK hit the lowest for 10 years after the TMT crash. The response was to cut costs wherever possible and profits have recovered, at least for now.

Followed by the housing bubble

'When you combine ignorance with leverage, you get some pretty interesting results.'
Warren Buffett

The reaction by central banks to the 2000 stock market meltdown was to carry on reducing interest rates to the lowest levels for half a century in a misguided, foolhardy and futile attempt to avoid a recession. Setting interest rates at the lowest level for half a century is, by definition, an extreme and very rare act leading to a hangover that is likely to be equally extreme and unlike anything experienced for half a century. The central banks have rewarded those that borrow at the expense of those that save and this is has produced a false and untenable economy. Spending one's way to prosperity is a peculiar notion and would not sit easily with Charles Dickens' Mr. Micawber: 'Annual income twenty pounds, annual expenditure nineteen, nineteen and six, result happiness. Annual income twenty pounds, annual expenditure twenty pounds nought and six, result misery'. Millions of consumers would laugh at such a notion, at least for now, hooked as they are on debt.

The response to this cheap money was that a mountain of it flowed into property and this led to a second bubble, which is still expanding. This was the last thing the economy needed, when the concentration should have been to unwind the stock market bubble fully. UK house prices more than doubled since 1995, with important implications for the health of the economy. The increased property prices eventually trickle down into the real economy, as wages and prices need to increase to offset the higher cost of one of the four factors of production (labour, capital and enterprise are the other three). The reaction will be to use less of any factor of production that suddenly increases in price and use more of that which is cheaper so there will be substitution, for example by producing in low-cost countries.

Reverting to the norm

'Whenever you get a wild excess on the upside, the following correction doesn't just go back to normal; it almost always falls way below normal.'
Sir John Templeton, author, philanthropist, Founder of the Templeton Growth Fund and John Templeton Foundation.

All markets tend to revert to the norm, which is the long-term trend line, and the

UK stock market was 40% above its norm in 2000. That anomaly was removed in the three-year bear market when it again hit the norm. In the previous house price boom of the late 1980s, prices were also 40% above the norm. The subsequent bust meant that prices hit the norm again by 1996 after years of falls. House prices are now even more exposed than in 1989, as they are a perilous 50% above their norm and, at some point, another bust can be expected so that prices once again hit their long-term trend line. The housing bubble could burst for a variety of reasons. Eventually, all the people and speculators who want to join in will have bought and the lack of such buyers on the margin will lead to falling prices, as confidence evaporates to be replaced by fear. Other factors could be a rise in unemployment and interest rates. The fall in prices will deter further buyers but there will be great selling pressure from speculators rushing for the exit, resulting in a collapse. Looking at how far the price of any asset is above its trend line is a good way of assessing the presence of a bubble, although Alan Greenspan has claimed asset bubbles are hard to identify until they burst, which would be a convenient defence if it were true.

Mega recession in the wings

'For those properly prepared in advance, a bear market in stocks is not a calamity but an opportunity.'
Sir John Templeton

The increase in the unrealised gain in house prices enabled consumers to strip-mine this manna from heaven and fuelled a massive increase in spending. This has kept the wheels on the economic bus, at least for now. This spending has been crucial because the consumer accounts for two-thirds of the economy. The snag is that consumers are relying on the unrealised gain being permanent but it will disappear in a housing bust, turning into negative equity. The mortgages will not vanish so miraculously and the pain of repayment if interest rates increase will be extreme, especially if there is a significant rise in unemployment. Add to that the psychological ingredient of a 'feel-bad' factor and all the usual suspects are lined up for a recession. It could be the worst in living memory, as, historically, the severest are those resulting from the deadly combination of a stock market bubble and massive over-investment and borrowing, as two bubbles have to be unwound, not just one.

The borrowing can take up to a decade to be repaid or written off and, if low inflation persists, its real value will stubbornly remain intact. By contrast, the recessions in the last half-century were not caused by low interest rates but by high interest rates which were imposed to reduce rampant inflation. Thus, we are now sailing into uncharted economic waters and a depression could result, rather than a recession. If low interest rates do persist then the unwinding of the housing bubble may be similar to the Japanese experience since 1989, which has been a long and painful economic squeeze rather than a short, sharp recession. The stock market will be in a crisis either way and this should provide a rare and fantastic buying opportunity. Recall that in 1974 the stock market dividend yield was 12% overall and that the deeply depressed shares could be bought at a further 40% discount by buying investment trusts like Foreign and Colonial.

Conflicts of interest

'Mr. Greenspan, I always enjoy your presentation because, frankly, I wonder what world you live in.'
Bernie Sanders, Republican Congressman.

The false economy has been egged on by central banks and governments, who have aided and abetted the two bubbles. Why should this be so? Central banks and governments are keen to maintain their reputations and be re-installed into power. This provides a conflict of interest, as the temptation is to try to stimulate unsustainable, short-term growth rather than manage the economy for the long-term good. Alan Greenspan admits that the power rests with the markets but that still does not prevent central banks believing they are powerful and clever enough to control the economy. Indeed, Gordon Brown, the UK Chancellor of the Exchequer, made the unbelievable claim that he had abolished the economic cycle by taking the 'tough decision' to give the Bank of England independence in setting interest rates. These words will haunt him when the recession proves him wrong. One problem is that central banks have a narrow brief to control interest rates and have but scant responsibility for borrowing levels. This lack of responsibility is truly astonishing and a solution would be to make central banks responsible for preventing asset bubbles as well as inflation. That way they could stop the bubbles in the first place rather than sorting out the mess afterwards, which is their preferred method. A more sensible attitude would be to recognise the economic realities of life, suffer a mild recession and avoid one later that will be much more severe.

Deflation

The Federal Reserve, other central banks and the media have expressed fears about deflation. It is a reality in Japan and is a possibility in Germany more than the US. It seems an unlikely scenario in the UK because inflation is a high 5% in services, which accounts for two-thirds of the economy, and their limited substitutability by consumers means that this type of inflation will probably continue. This high rate of inflation in services is offset by deflation of 2% in physical goods, which is due to intense international competition as substitutability of goods is generally easy. There are no prizes for concluding that a company has a rosier future in services than making physical goods. Should deflation in fact transpire, it would increase debt in real terms and exacerbate the unwinding of the debt bubble. The central banks are running out of room to manoeuvre to 'prevent' recession, as interest rates are low and they cannot fall below zero.

Perilous US economy

'There cannot be a crisis next week. My schedule is already full.'
Henry Kissinger, US statesman.

The US economy looks perilous as it has massive debt with very low consumer savings. The current account and trade deficits have rocketed to about 5% of GDP and this profligacy is financed by 80% of the world's savings. This largesse by the rest of the world could be withdrawn at any time and such lack of control is as dangerous as it is uncomfortable. Repatriation of foreigners' money would be unsurprising, as US interest rates are low. Further, the US stock market has recovered strongly since the three-year bear market to March 2003 but the rally has the hallmarks of being an unsustainable 'dead cat bounce' rather than the start of a major bull run. This view is based not only on macro economics but also on technical analysis, such as Elliott Wave theory, and stock market history. The dollar has tumbled and hit an all time low against the euro, with more falls likely. A weak currency means that imports cost more, so inflation should rise and lead to higher interest rates. This would burst their housing bubble and a worldwide recession would then beckon. However, it would mark the beginning of a sustainable and healthy economy, once the excesses have been eliminated.

Where are we in the cycle?

On an historical basis, we are past the top of the cycle, given the severe bear market and the economy is set for recession, which may yet be postponed by low interest rates but not cancelled. As explained above, this cycle has not been typical because of the absence of inflation. This has allowed interest rates to be kept low and so bond and property prices are high. Just how long the central banks can forestall the day of reckoning is unknown. It is unlikely that the next recession will follow the same timetable as the last three recessions because the ingredients are dissimilar and so extreme: two bubbles and ultra low interest rates.

How to find out where we are in the cycle

'Never trust an economic boom fuelled by consumer debt.'
Neal Weintraub, author of *Tricks Of The Floor Trader*.

An investor does not need to be an economist to find out where we are in the cycle. There are many signals given by business and the public. Those signals from business indicating a raging bull market and the time to sell may include:

- PER ratios and forecast increases in profit are very high
- institutional cash holdings are very low, stock market indices are beginning to falter and are far above the norm
- a mania for a sector, investment style, asset or geographical area
- bad news is dismissed and good news is a catalyst for action
- new issues are oversubscribed and trade at a premium
- the stockbroker's phone is always engaged
- inflation and interest rates are beginning to increase but are dismissed as blips
- dividend yields are at record lows

Signals from the public indicating a raging bull market and the time to sell may include:

- media and pundits are overwhelmingly optimistic
- doomsters are few, ignored or fired
- consumer and government borrowing and spending are high
- speculation in shares and housing is rampant
- advertisements abound for foreign holiday homes
- dinner party talk is boastful of success in the markets
- few can see any reason for a change
- political stability seems unending
- empty restaurant and trains seats are rare

- sudden appearance of new cars in the neighbourhood
- investors think they are geniuses, complete novices show interest in risky investments and their 'success' is highlighted in the press
- investment conferences are packed and the circulation of publications like Investors Chronicle is at a peak
- conspicuous consumption of luxury goods, such as fireworks, champagne and cigars at Christmas and New Year parties

The indicators of a bad bear market are the reverse and are excellent buy signals.

2. The cycle of opportunity

'We view our level of liquidity or gearing as probably the most fundamental decision we have to make on behalf of the shareholders of Personal Assets – much more so than which individual stocks we should buy or sell.'
Ian Rushbrook, fund manager.

We have now analysed the economic cycle and where we are in it. We turn our attention to how different asset classes behave in the cycle so that investors can profit by riding trends.

How asset classes behave in a typical economic cycle

Shares, property, cash and bonds are attractive during different stages of the economic cycle, in that chronological order, and provide opportunities. Let us assume that we are near the top of the cycle in year one, as outlined in the table at the start of chapter 4. The economy has boomed and inflation is on the prowl. Interest rates increase to combat this and now is the time to be out of shares and into cash. This is because share prices drop before the real economy falters, as the stock market is a lead indicator by anticipating the future some six to nine months ahead. Cash is king, benefiting from high interest rates and ready to take advantage of juicy prices in the ensuing recession. Property still remains robust for a couple of years but then it succumbs as well, although in this current cycle it has lasted longer as it has been propped up by ultra-low interest rates. Assuming that interest rates do rise, bonds should then be bought, locking into these high rates just as they begin to fall, which is when the recession has run half its course. Sell bonds when their prices rebound, which is approximately one year before the bottom of the recession.

Share prices have been now falling for some years in this scenario. Buy shares six months before the bottom of the recession, as they begin to rally following the lowering of interest rates to kick-start the economy. Property should be bought as the 'green shoots of recovery' become apparent. Inflation has now been wrung out of the system in this painful manner. Share prices and property rise until the economy begins to overheat. Inflation is starting to increase and higher interest rates can be foreseen. Now is the time to switch out of shares and into cash since we are approaching the top of the cycle and the process can then start all over again.

The conclusion is to be in cash at the peak of the cycle and in the subsequent recession. Then invest in bonds to benefit from falling interest rates, then shares and, lastly, property, near the trough of the cycle. Note that the best time to buy the asset is at the start of their runs and then hold them until switching to another asset class that becomes more attractive. If an investor is in the wrong asset class and, in particular, if it is bought at the end of its run rather than the beginning, then it is likely to be very costly.

Investment strategies

'If you warn 100 men of possible forthcoming bad news, eighty will dislike you right away. If you are right, the other twenty will as well.'
Anthony Gaubis, investment counsellor.

a. Hold cash and recession resistant shares

A sensible investment strategy with the economic cycle past its peak might be to hold up to, say, half a portfolio in cash with the rest in shares that will withstand a recession. Bonds and property should be sold. Shares can offer opportunities whatever the cycle, it is just that performance is much more difficult in a bear market. To be out of shares completely is another strategy. However, an investor might well then miss the re-entry point and trying to pick the bottom of markets is practically impossible. Stock markets have a nasty habit of shooting up unexpectedly. However, the shares selected must be able to withstand a recession. It is imperative, therefore, that they have sound business models in attractive sectors, as pointed out below and in chapters 1 and 2.

A long-term 'buy and hold' strategy for shares will be unsatisfactory, as it is guaranteed to be hit by bear markets caused by recessions. Unit and investment trusts that track, or quasi-track, the index will similarly disappoint. Managers rarely want to stray too far from the performance of their peers, no matter how unsatisfactory it may be. There are some funds, such as Personal Assets and RIT Capital Partners, that actively move in and out of asset classes to ride the cycle with success but they are a rarity.

b. Hedge and other funds

'Protection against adverse market conditions was provided by our liquidity, the diversity within the portfolio and the increased investment in asset classes which are less directly correlated to markets. Your company has been an investor in selected hedge funds in the pursuit of absolute and relatively consistent returns.'
The Lord Rothschild, chairman of RIT Capital Partners.

One route to consider is hedge funds, which have grown enormously in popularity and now number 6,000 worldwide with assets of $9 trillion. They have a variety of strategies to protect against bear markets. Their tools include shorting (selling shares they do not own), derivatives, futures, options and leverage. Many aim to be market neutral by being equally long and short and to make money from stock picking. They are predominantly based offshore and target high net worth individuals. FTSE 100 company Man Group is one of the leading providers with $40 billion under management. George Soros' hedge fund is Quantum and Warren Buffett ran one in his early years and said there was nothing mystical about it. Another offshore fund is Green Cay Asset Management run by Dr. Jane Siebels and is majority-backed by billionaire Sir John Templeton, the legendary global investor.

One solution for a private shareholder may be to buy an investment trust, like RIT Capital Partners, that invests in hedge funds as part of its wider remit to manage a portfolio of shares and securities. Alternatively, a private shareholder may try hedging himself by going long and short or, instead, just going short in anticipation of a bear market but this strategy is for professionals only.

CHAPTER 4

Which sectors to buy and sell during the economic cycle

'Draw a circle around those businesses you understand and then eliminate those that fail to qualify on the basis of value, good management and limited exposure to hard times'.
Warren Buffett

We now examine the competitive advantage of *individual* sectors, like beverages, rather than business models, such as moats and recurring revenue, that cut across *numerous* sectors, as discussed in chapter 2. We then discover which individual sectors to buy and sell during a typical economic cycle. The starting point is to consider UK and international competitive advantage.

UK competitive advantage

The UK initially secured international competitive advantage with the advent of its industrial revolution in the nineteenth century. This gave it first mover advantage but this waned when the rest of the world industrialised and began to catch up on the UK's first mover advantage. Other factors which strengthened its competitive advantage included language, geographical position, natural temperament of the population, reputation, history and perceptions of value.

Today, the UK's international competitive advantage is in various sectors that tend to dominate the top of the FTSE 100. They score highly in the table that follows and are beverages, pharmaceuticals and health, tobacco, food and drug retailing, oil and gas, and banks. These are followed by food producers, utilities, aerospace and defence, and life insurance. This does not mean that these sectors are attractive at all times, or that each company therein is attractive. Gems can be discovered in unattractive sectors. However, it is a useful reminder of where the competitive advantage lies and which have long-term potential. Those sectors that lack power have a low score in the table below and, unsurprisingly, include chemicals, electronics, electrical and engineering.

International competitive advantage and 'Wal-Martisation'

'While you're negotiating for a 35 hour week, remember that they have only just got 66 hours in Taiwan and you're competing with Taiwan.'
Victor Kiam, of 'I liked the shaver so much I bought the company' fame.

Asia is fast becoming the powerhouse of the world. This megatrend can be expected to last for decades and will probably intensify. From an economic point of view, the West and Asia will benefit if each specialises in those activities where it has competitive advantage and trades goods and services with other countries where it does not. China and its billion people on low wages have a powerful competitive advantage in manufacturing, not only in low cost but, increasingly, in quality too. Southern China has reached the stage of development where costs have risen and production is shifting to the north, where they are still low. Japan has competitive advantage in high-quality goods, such as consumer electronics and cars, although its manufacturing heart is being hollowed out as production shifts to low-cost countries.

Companies that can transfer production to low-cost countries have little choice but to do so or they will be beaten by the competition. If the value created can be captured by the sector, then profits will benefit accordingly. If however, they are frittered away in ruthless competition then the consumer will benefit but this may, nevertheless, increase overall demand and perhaps provide critical mass. Some sectors are unable to benefit from this megatrend and they include general retailers, transport and oil.

Intense international competition has meant that the fat in businesses is not just being cut out but is being fried out in a pan. This reflects the megatrend towards the 'Wal-Martisation' of the world. Price is increasingly the main, if not the only, matter that counts in selling goods. Wal-Mart piles them high and sells them cheap, as evidenced by sales that have reached $1 billion in a single day. Increasingly, if the correct price point is hit then customers ring the phone off the hook. Miss that price point by just a shade and the phone is silent. The internet has aided and abetted this extreme price consciousness.

Another megatrend is the dumbing down of jobs that take out the skill with easy to learn and powerful personal computers. There is great demand for cheap and cheerful bodies but much less demand for expensive middle and senior managers. This has thinned the ranks of the prosperous middle classes that spent freely and those that catered for them have seen business suffer, for instance expensive, four-star hotels in Austrian ski resorts. The cheap and cheerful chalets down the road that manage to produce a Wal-Mart type product that hits the price point remain packed. Therefore, it is increasingly important to differentiate products that add real value to the customer in order to achieve premium pricing. The alternative is to be in the Wal-Mart business with an ultra-low cost base and a very keen sense of capturing market share on a continuing basis that keeps the competition at bay. This is a difficult job to do indefinitely without hiccups. There is, however, little middle ground.

There will be a place for niche producers in the West for the likes of up-market car manufacturers, such as BMW, that have immense image and prestige. However, the long-term outlook for manufacturing is bleak. It has been shrinking faster in the UK than Germany, France and the US since 1997. It has fallen from 21% of GDP to 17%. Services, for example leisure, are difficult to import and are largely immune from overseas competition. In some sectors, like telecommunications, banking, software and engineering consultancy, the back office and call centres can be transferred to low-cost countries.

Which sectors to buy and sell during the economic cycle

The economic cycle of opportunity table, which follows, starts with the asset class to hold over the cycle, namely cash, bonds, shares and property, and this was discussed in chapter 3. Each sector is scored for its recession resistance and competitive advantage. The annual profit growth over the last five years and the profit margin is also specified.

There is a time to buy and sell various sectors, as illustrated in the table. Non-cyclical sectors are: beverages; food producers and processors; pharmaceuticals; health and personal care; tobacco; food and drug retailers; telecommunications; and utilities. They should ideally be bought in the third year of the cycle when share prices are depressed but demand for these goods is robust, as they are needed in good and bad times. Consequently, they tend to have strong recession resistance. They can then be held until near the end of the cycle and sold around year nine. Alternatively, they are candidates for holding if an investor decides to have an exposure to shares regardless of the cycle, as explained in chapter 3.

Cyclical sectors are resources, basic industries, general industrials, cyclical consumer goods, cyclical services, information technology and financials, which includes real estate. They should be bought later than non cyclicals in year five when their prices are rock bottom. Share prices then begin to increase, as the market will anticipate the end of the recession by approximately nine months. Demand will recover and will boost profits enormously. These sectors are sold earlier than non cyclical sectors, in around year eight. An investor will then be partly or fully out of the market before it begins to discount the top of the cycle when it will de-rate these recession-prone sectors harshly.

Note that the sector headings and order correspond to the FTSE Actuaries Share Indices classification for ease of reference, as this details performance, dividend yield and cover, PER and total return in summary form. This classification is also used to group all of the individual shares into sectors. Both are listed daily in the Financial Times. Thus, an investor can track sectors that are of interest and then drill down to see individual shares in that sector from a quick perusal of the paper.

There are likely to be shares that will do well in any sector and a stock picker will focus on these, rather than be swayed by sector moves. However, the job is made harder without a reasonable sector tailwind. Note that this chapter analyses each individual sector and thus complements chapter 2, as that examination of competitive advantage cuts across numerous sectors. For example, sector consolidation discussed in chapter 2 applies to banks, pharmaceuticals and oil. Each of these sectors is assessed below individually to see what competitive advantage they possess.

The economic cycle of opportunity table, overleaf, scores the recession resistance and competitive advantage of each sector over a typical ten-year economic cycle. Although these scores are subjective, they should provide a reasonable guide. The competitive advantage points are awarded in the same manner as for sector business models in chapter 2, namely the power of the sector to achieve low cost and/or differentiate itself so that it adds value. Above all, it is crucial to be able to control revenues streams.

The economic cycle of opportunity

The economic cycle			Top		Bottom		Top	
Year			1 2	3 4	5 6 7	8	9 10	
Cash			out			in		
Bonds			buy	sell				
Shares			buy				sell	
Property				buy			sell	

When to buy and sell sectors	Recession resistance	Competitive advantage *	Profit growth %	Profit margin %	Buy / Sell
Non cyclical consumer goods					buy (yr 3) ... sell (yr 9)
Beverages	2	1	6	19	
Food producers and processors	1	2	10	13	
Pharmaceuticals, health, personal care	1	1	10	20	
Tobacco	1	1	11	28	
Non cyclical services					buy (yr 3) ... sell (yr 9)
Food and drug retailers	1	1	10	5	
Telecommunications	2	3	15	25	
Utilities					buy (yr 3) ... sell (yr 9)
Electricity and other utilities	2	2	3	19	
Resources					buy (yr 5) ... sell (yr 7)
Mining	4	4	12	13	
Oil and Gas	3	1	11	9	
Basic industries					buy (yr 5) ... sell (yr 7)
Chemicals	4	5	1	3	
Construction, building materials	5	4	14	11	
General industrials					buy (yr 5) ... sell (yr 7)
Aerospace, defence	4	2	-4	10	
Electronic, electrical, engineering	4	5	-2	5	
Cyclical consumer goods					buy (yr 5) ... sell (yr 7)
Automobiles, household goods	4	4	11	-18	
Cyclical services					buy (yr 5) ... sell (yr 7)
General retailers	4	3	10	10	
Leisure and hotels	4	3	4	16	
Media and entertainment	4	3	13	12	
Support services	3	3	7	8	
Transport	3	3	2	15	
Information technology					buy (yr 5) ... sell (yr 7)
Information technology hardware	4	3	-14	-32	
Software and computer services	4	3	10	-6	
Financials					buy (yr 5) ... sell (yr 7)
Banks, speciality finance	5	1	9	n/a	
Insurance	3	4	5	n/a	
Life insurance	2	2	4	n/a	
Investment companies	4	3	n/a	n/a	
Real estate	5	3	n/a	n/a	
Market average			9	15	

*1 is the highest, 5 the lowest. Profit growth and margins are as at end of 2004.

We now look at each of the sectors in detail. The score for recession resistance and competitive advantage is 1 for highest and 5 for lowest, with an average of 3. Note that this does not score them as attractive sectors on valuation or technical analysis grounds since these change daily. The sector's capitalisation as a percentage of the UK stock market at the end of 2004 is also shown. This is also the date used for the profit and growth margins in the table.

4a. Non cyclical consumer goods

Beverages: recession resistance 2, competitive advantage 1. Percentage of stock market capitalisation 3%.

'Diageo. Based on the Latin word for day and the Greek word for world. Diageo captures what this business is all about – bringing pleasure to consumers every day around the world.'
The logic behind the new name for the merged Guinness and Grand Metropolitan.

Beverages is an attractive sector as it offers defensive growth. It is essentially a tried and tested, simple business, although changing tastes and fashion are important factors. There has been consolidation amongst the players, as economies of scale are significant so that products achieve critical mass, for example, in distribution networks.

Its resistance to recession is above average because beverages are low-ticket items and there is high compulsion to consume. People are reluctant to give up their tipple when they need cheering up in hard times. However, there will be some fall-off in demand and trading down to cheaper brands when consumers are forced to tighten their belts.

The sector has high international competitive advantage, driven by the power of leading brands, heavy advertising and global reach. This enables its claim on disposable income to remain steadfast. However, it is not all plain sailing as the market is mature and there is tough competition from overseas brands, as well as from supermarkets' own label drinks. Although the sector does supply own label, the margins tend to be lower. Other downsides include heavy 'sin' taxes and a trend towards a healthy lifestyle. Overseas developing markets are attractive as incomes rise and consumers can start to afford such high status products. Please also see leisure and hotels below.

The profit growth of the sector over the last five years was 6% per annum, compared to 9% for the stock market as a whole, and the 19% profit margin is above the stock market's 15%. The dominant player is the peculiarly named Diageo, with Allied Domecq a long way behind. Diageo is a gorilla and the world's number one seller of spirits with long-proven brands like Johnnie Walker, Smirnoff and Guinness. Market segments have been established with new products like alcopops. This has driven growth, although demand can be fickle and some new launches have failed. Both Diageo and Allied Domecq are exposed to US dollar weakness. The temptation for the gorillas has been to diversify to boost profit. This has resulted in mountainous goodwill and expensive failures, such as Diageo with Burger King and Scottish & Newcastle with Center Parc. The key, then, is to buy when the sector is cheap, as the share price will more likely be driven by a re-rating rather than profit growth. The niche players lack powerful brands and have less competitive advantage than the gorillas.

Food producers and processors: recession resistance 1, competitive advantage 2. Percentage of stock market capitalisation 2%.

Like beverages, food producers and processors is an attractive, defensive sector. It is a stable but mature market, with sales stimulated by flair and new product launches.

Demand is robust in a recession because the products are staples of life and are low-ticket items. Brands are important to achieve premium pricing and strong product differentiation, established over many years through reputation, value for money and advertising. Supermarkets' own brands are a threat and supplying this market has to be at keen prices and top quality. This is a tough space to occupy, as Northern Foods has found.

It has above average competitive advantage overall and is dominated by gorillas like Unilever and Cadbury Schweppes, which have significant economies of scale after extensive takeover activity but has resulted in high levels of goodwill. Nevertheless, there is strong competition from overseas giants like Nestlé, which also has been acquisitive. Generally, the space to occupy is selling the brand to the consumer and capturing that value, like Cadbury Schweppes, rather than being squeezed into producing commodity products like sandwiches and milk for supermarkets, like Geest and Dairy Crest. Such minor players struggle to pass on higher input costs to powerful supermarkets and have to resort to cost cutting. Nevertheless, gorillas can struggle in this regard too and Unilever has embarked on an expensive, five-year restructuring programme to reduce the 'noise' of having too many brands and to focus on the most promising 400. Likewise, Cadbury Schweppes has announced a somewhat similar restructuring programme. In such cases, share performance can be at the mercy of meeting restructuring targets.

The profit growth over the last five years was 10% per annum and the margin is 13%, which are both similar to the stock market as a whole. Niche players like Richmond Foods and Inter Link Foods have sound business models, in spite of supplying to powerful supermarkets, are growing fast and are more attractive than the gorillas. They both have low costs and differentiated products, with Richmond's Nestlé brands and Inter Link's customer relationships and new lines. Both have avoided the trap of being overly reliant on too few customers.

Pharmaceuticals, health, personal care: recession resistance 1, competitive advantage 1. Percentage of stock market capitalisation 9%.

'What good is health? You can't buy money with it.'
Charlie Munger, Vice President of Berkshire Hathaway.

Pharmaceuticals, health and personal care is the first of only three sectors to earn the maximum score for recession resistance and competitive advantage. The sector was riding high in the mid-1990s to the end of the decade, as the market was growing, new blockbuster drugs were launched, prices were increasing and regulatory approval times were falling. This lead to overvaluations based on the lure of defensive growth. This optimism then hit the realism of a high cost base, few new drugs and a weak pipeline, strong generic competition as important drugs came off patent, longer regulatory approval times, worsening economic conditions and opposition to prices from government and healthcare bodies. Visibility of earnings dropped sharply and emphasised the high operating risk. The next few years offer little respite from these problems so an investor should be wary in spite of the strong recession resistance and competitive advantage.

The strong recession resistance reflects the fact that drugs are 'must-have' products, are low-ticket items and typically free or subsidised for the end user. Therefore, demand and growth are never ending. Demographics favour the business, as the population is ageing, and drugs are much cheaper than hospital stays. It rides the tailwind of governments spending more on health and this is a main objective in some cases, such as in the UK. However, various health reforms over the years have played their part in holding down the cost of drugs. Personal care includes household products and the gorilla Reckitt Benckiser dominates this sub sector. It has an impressive list of brands, like Dettol, that helped to increase margins in this very defensive play. Warren Buffett likes this sort of company because it has a strong consumer franchise and is similar in this regard to Gillette, in which he has a large holding.

International competitive advantage is very good and the gorillas are GlaxoSmithKline, the fourth biggest UK company, and AstraZeneca. There has been significant consolidation to cut costs, an example being the £5 billion Amersham takeover, and the amount of goodwill on the balance sheets is significant. There are very high barriers to entry due to the massive economies of scale that are needed to fund the enormous research and development expenditure, trials and the long time it takes to bring a blockbuster to market. However, once this has been achieved, the company can enjoy that most wonderful of competitive advantages, a monopoly, for years and the super profits roll in. Eventually, the drug comes off patent, which lasts up to 20 years, and generic competition leads to price-cutting. It is a race, therefore, to bring out new products from a long pipeline more quickly than old ones lose patent protection and such a race has similarities to the oil sector. It is preferable to concentrate on a few blockbusters rather than be an average competitor in many products, as the development costs for each are comparable.

The profit growth over the last five years was 10% per annum, just above the market's 9%. The margin is an impressive 20%, five points above the overall stock market. Niche operators are more attractive than the gorillas, examples being Celsis, which provides contamination testing and Synergy Healthcare that offers sterilisation services.

Tobacco: recession resistance 1, competitive advantage 1. Percentage of stock market capitalisation 2%.

'We'll all be jockeying for position in Playboy and Penthouse.'
RJ Reynolds, on new tobacco advertising bans.

Tobacco is the second sector to score maximum points on the recession resistance and competitive advantage yardsticks. It is a unique product as it is highly addictive and is the only legal product sold that can be lethal if used in the manner intended. Advertising bans and smoking restrictions become ever tighter and tobacco is on the black list of ethical investors. The market is stable and there is no product obsolescence.

It is difficult to imagine a product that has a stronger resistance to recession. The addiction means that customers are hooked, so demand is extremely robust and insensitive to the high price charged. Although the developed world is a mature market, there is growth in the developing world, which feeds off rising living standards that increasingly enable such products to be bought. Young populations and per capita incomes are the most significant growth drivers.

It has very high international competitive advantage. This is a remarkable testament considering it is achieved by a commodity product where little value is added in production. It is strongly cash generative, creates value for shareholders and the cost of production is very low compared to the high selling price, which is mostly comprised of punitive taxation. There is an old saying: what other products are like tobacco that cost a penny to make and sell for a dollar? The high price encourages consumption by both legal and smuggled importing from low tax countries. Brands are important as consumers respond to status and health messages. The profitability of the sector has been undermined in the US due to price-cutting by generic brands. The PER is usually low and the yield generous, reflecting the dullish growth. The latter has been boosted by numerous takeovers and goodwill is material.

The profit growth over the last five years was 11% per annum, slightly above that of the market, but the profit margin is the highest at 28%. The strong cash flow encourages high, tax-efficient gearing. The risk of litigation is high and awards in the US are astronomical, from both the civil courts and the government, which aims to extract $280 billion in a settlement with tobacco companies. Litigation news has a major bearing on sector share prices and can provide buying opportunities. Therefore, it is important to avoid British American Tobacco, as it has US exposure, whereas Gallaher and Imperial Tobacco do not. The latter two are smaller players and takeover potential is good. This is a very popular sector in a bear market but is ignored in a raging bull market, when high growth is the mantra, so sell in the former and buy in the latter. Profit warnings are rare, which is a major advantage.

4b. Non cyclical services

'England is a nation of shopkeepers'.
Napoleon

Food and drug retailers: recession resistance 1, competitive advantage 1. Percentage of stock market capitalisation 2%.

Food and drug retailers is the last sector to earn maximum on recession resistance and competitive advantage ratings. Retailing is a straightforward but fickle business and a player can do well for years and then suddenly hit problems, such as Sainsbury's and Somerfield.

The recession resistance is excellent as the product is a necessity and low-ticket. However, hard-up customers will try to economise by consuming less and trading down to cheaper items. This could fit in well with a recent trend in supermarkets to segment the market by offering value, standard and premium versions of the same product. Own label products reinforce this search for value for money with higher quality and cheaper prices than brands. Defensive growth sectors are very attractive.

The competitive advantage is demonstrated by the juggernaut pace of the supermarkets that eat up the competition in whichever products they turn their attention to, including newspapers, wine, petrol, electronics, clothes, music, utilities and financial services. Tesco accounts for 12% of all retail spending. Although turning this flair internationally has not been a huge success, Tesco is now showing the way in Eastern Europe and the Far East after initial hiccups. The customer is transactional, meaning one-off, but this is offset by loyalty, convenience and pricing which lures them back. Supermarkets try hard to differentiate their products, like Tesco with its very sophisticated internet shopping designed to solve customers' problems, a powerful source of competitive advantage. Planning consent is very tight, competition is intense and price wars are a recurring threat. Bolt-on acquisitions, such as the battle for Safeway, have been one response and the entrance of mighty Wal-Mart with its takeover of Asda merely reinforced this point. Further consolidation is limited as the players are few and the competition authorities are vigilant. Tesco and others are seeking growth through mini supermarkets in the high street, garages and community shops and traditional butchers and greengrocers are rapidly disappearing. Food prices suffer deflation, especially since Wal-Mart arrived. The players are very powerful and have the all-important contact with millions of customers. They occupy an excellent position in the value chain and beats being a supermarket supplier. The sector has been investigated by the Competition Commission, which found there was a complicated monopoly but excess profits were not being earned.

The profit growth over the last five years was 10% per annum and was just above the market's 9%. The margin was 5%, 10 points below the overall stock market. Neither is surprising as this is a high volume, low-margin business in a mature market. Morrisons Supermarkets has an impressive 35 years of unbroken growth in pre-tax profits and is attractive, although it needs to digest Safeway successfully.

Telecommunications: recession resistance 2, competitive advantage 3. Percentage of stock market capitalisation 8%.

'NASDAQ stands for No Actual Sales, Dividends, Assets or Quality.'
Sean Corrigan, financial journalist.

Telecommunications is, in principle, an attractive sector and has been transmogrified in the last two decades, the starting point being the end of the General Post Office monopoly and the birth of the privatised British Telecom. Then the floodgates of competition were opened and new technology, such as fibre optics, mobile phones, 3G and the internet explosion excited speculators who blindly piled into the TMT boom in the late 1990s. The bust in 2000 was brutal with profit warnings, bankruptcies, collapsed share prices, horrendous debts and an economic and sector slowdown. The fabulously expensive 3G licences have proved to be largely worthless so far. The government thought it would raise £3 billion and the final bonanza was £22 billion, thanks to some clever gamesmanship on its part. These sums blew away even the most outlandish estimates from industry experts as the players lost the plot. Some survivors have been writing off that cost by the billion, both in the UK and overseas. MmO2, for example, lost £10 billion in 2003 due to write-offs, including £6 billion for 3G licences. Nevertheless, the chairman proudly claimed in the annual report, 'The past year has been a period of significant achievement'. The only participant making money out of 3G has been the government. Companies have been re-focusing and selling what have now been deemed to be non-core businesses, such as BT's Japanese investment. In short, the profitability of the sector was seriously undermined. Restructuring has been extensive, debt has now been tamed and cash flows are more respectable.

The recession resistance is above average but the fact that the product is 'must-have' is small comfort as the value is being captured not by shareholders but by consumers, who have largely been subsidised by the excesses of the TMT boom. The sector does have a decent tailwind in an increasing digital age but it will be years before the massive overcapacity ceases to be a problem. Further, demand will drop in a recession, especially by businesses that cut back or go bust. This particularly affects the alternative networks.

The competitive advantage is average, in spite of Vodafone, which is the third largest UK company and, as a world player, provides strong competition. It has £94 billion of goodwill yet to be written off its balance sheet and this is not far short of its £112 billion of equity. It has lost £43 billion of shareholders' equity, mostly in the last three years. Therefore, it has not added one penny of shareholder value so far and the share price has been dire since the TMT height. Other companies' attempts at being a world player have been unsuccessful, in part due to obstacles and muddled thinking, as in BT's case. The sector is still partly regulated, for example in high margin mobile phone calls that have been capped, which is something of a wild card threat to profitability. The myriad of resellers pushes prices ever lower and this murderous competition eats away at the market share of incumbents, like BT and Cable & Wireless, in both the home and business markets. Major growth drivers in the near future are thin on the ground. Increased internet usage, such as broadband, and advanced services, like 3G, games and picture sending, are opportunities. However, the internet is also a major threat due to its free telephony and videoing. Mobile phones are a saturated market since there are 42 million in the UK. However, they are taking business from landlines, which many customers see as redundant.

The profit growth over the last five years was 15% per annum, well above the market. The sector profit margin looks healthy at 25% but that is before the huge goodwill amortisation, which plunges the sector into a pre-tax loss. A niche player is more attractive than the gorillas and Telecom plus is a low-cost reseller of utilities that has a successful business model and is growing fast.

4c. Utilities

'If only Karl had made capital instead of writing about it.'
Jenny, wife of Karl Marx.

Electricity and other utilities: recession resistance 2, competitive advantage 2. Percentage of stock market capitalisation 4%.

Electricity and other utilities, being gas distribution and water, is the classic defensive sector. The best investment opportunities were in the early days after privatisation, when cost savings were easy and significant. The game is much harder today. They are commodity products and therefore consumers can shop around for the best deal based on price. Loyalty is low but switching is offset by inertia. In addition, some like the peace of mind that a big and respected brand name implies. The market is mature and low growth.

The sector should weather a recession well, as the products are necessities with little scope for cutting back. However, like telecommunications, it has felt the chill wind of competition since privatisation and some of the value added has been enjoyed by consumers, rather than the sector, as the regulators have made price cuts.

The sector is efficient and the competitive advantage is above average. There are millions of sticky customers and, as the product is generally a low-ticket item, savings from switching suppliers could be viewed as not worth the trouble. Starting with electricity, this is good news for incumbent gorillas like Scottish Power. The installed base can be cross-sold other services, which are higher margin, such as repairs and warranties, and tend to have high recurring revenue. The sector was unpopular in the TMT mania and has since recovered as investors sought refuge in what appears to be strong and predictable cash flows. This strategy may be flawed, as a higher equity risk premium is demanded as the regulators have undermined profitability. For example, a new wholesale electricity pool was imposed in 2001 that lead to a 40% fall in prices. It proved the death knell for British Energy and a quarter of capacity was removed. Some of this capacity is now coming back but energy prices should be bolstered in the longer term by lower output of gas and oil from the North Sea. The need for 15% of energy to be renewable by 2015 means substantial investment lies ahead. Therefore, what should be a safe but dull sector contains significant operating risk, given that prices fell a tenth in the last decade.

Water companies do not have competition but they are regulated. Prices have been allowed to rise in the latest review compared to that of 2000 when they fell 12%. Investment could more than double from the present £3 billion a year, as higher quality water is stipulated by the UK and European legislators. It is a unique sector in that the raw material falls like manna from heaven and typically is plentiful. Water consumption rose a third in the last decade due to improved living standards that feed into the likes of dishwashers and sprinklers for more elaborate gardens. The companies want to tap this increased demand with their push for metered water, whose price is increasing faster than non-metered supply. Centrica is the gorilla in gas distribution, which is a regulated market, and it has diversified into services, such as warranties.

There has been extensive corporate activity with mergers, de-mergers and takeovers plus foreign investors have played their part. There have been attempts to diversify the risk by branching out into new areas like waste disposal, tying up with other utilities and seeking growth overseas, such as in the US. The results have been very mixed.

The profit growth over the last five years was 3% per annum, compared to the market's 9%. This reflected electricity's minus 3% under performance, whereas the other utilities' growth was a healthier 6%, which reflects the maturity of the sector, but the shares have a generous yield. The sector profit margin is a robust 19%, compared to the market's 15%. Lack of profitable investment opportunities has lead to buy-backs, which lend support to share prices as the aim is to enhance earnings.

4d. Resources

Mining: recession resistance 4, competitive advantage 4. Percentage of stock market capitalisation 4%.

'A gold mine is a whole in the ground with a liar at the top.'
Mark Twain

Mining is not a very attractive sector as it has commodity products and control over its destiny is poor. It is essentially a simple activity. The ore is dug out of the ground, processed, shipped and sold. Therefore, the activity is easily replicated by competitors and does not add much value to the customer. The product includes iron, zinc, platinum, coal, gold, silver, nickel, tin and copper. Stockpiling can result in an overhang of supply that weakens prices. Some sectors do not generally suffer this problem, such as services.

Mining has below-average recession resistance, as it is heavily reliant on the economic cycle because demand will rise in a boom and fall in a recession. In the latter case, falling revenues quickly translate into losses because the cost of production is largely high and fixed. China's high growth is driving demand for vast amounts of raw materials, including iron, copper and nickel, and its fortunes have a direct bearing on the sector. It is a major low-cost producer of tin and zinc and can inundate the market.

The competitive advantage of UK-listed companies is below average because of high costs and the product is undifferentiated. Companies have to plan and invest years in advance, not knowing the terms of trade they will face when they are in production. This is because the prices of such commodity products are set by worldwide supply and demand over which they have no control. This is an unattractive proposition. It does have a modest tailwind in that the world population and real incomes steadily rise so demand will increase for basic goods, like cars and refrigerators, which need metal. However, there is no escaping the fact that sunrise industries, such as technology, use little metal, unlike the declining smokestack industries of yesterday. Negatives include political instability in some mining countries. South Africa has black empowerment pressures that would mean ceding significant ownership, as well as the threat of royalties. Geopolitical tensions can affect prices and there can be unexpected supply shortages or excesses. The prices are typically set in US dollars so there is a currency risk, given the slump in that currency.

The profit growth rate over the last five years was good at 12% per annum and the 13% margin is respectable. This performance reflects higher commodity prices and growing economies but it will nose dive in a recession. Cash generation is good. There has been sector consolidation and Lonmin and Antofagasta would be attractive bolt-on acquisitions. Anglo American and Rio Tinto are the gorillas, followed by BHP Billiton. They are dissimilar, in that they have exposure to some commodities more than others. Lonmin produces significant platinum whereas BHP Billiton has a major oil interest. The performance of individual shares will reflect the fortunes of these individual commodities. The sector should generally be avoided but if you do want to buy then the safest time is just when the economy has bottomed out after a recession. There are indications that the twenty-year bear market in commodities is ending, as some of them, such as gold, copper, nickel and platinum have been at multi-year highs.

Oil and gas: recession resistance 3, competitive advantage 1. Percentage of stock market capitalisation 12%.

'Behind every great fortune there lies a great crime.'
Honoré de Balzac, writer.

Oil and gas are similar to mining in that they are commodity products with prices set on the world stage, with a similar set of pros and cons. However, they do add great value to the customer. Oil has 4,000 uses, for example. Without them, the world economy would grind to a halt very quickly, as indeed it did back in the 1970s. Oil companies are often unpopular with the public.

The recession resistance is average because demand drops significantly in an economic slowdown. However, it will not collapse, as power is a necessity. This is in spite of oil products being expensive, as they are a natural target for high taxation. The long-term tailwind is set fair in an oil hungry world with ever increasing economic development. The industry has only replaced half of its reserves used up in production recently and, even if more is found, it is not being made any more. This suggests a long-term increase in real prices.

The international competitive advantage is highest. This is due, in large part, to historical and first mover advantages when the industry was being established, such as being the colonial power in oil producing countries. The Iraq war may have been 'won' for now but the vast majority of the 'black gold' lies in the Middle East. The religious and geopolitical tensions remain and further serious turbulence should be expected in the long-term. The OPEC cartel has the objective of achieving a steady but rewarding price for its output, which is 40% of the world total. Its influence has waned with squabbling and the unforgiving laws of supply and demand that confounded their previous unrealistic attempts at setting the price too high. Saudi Arabia remains the 'swing' producer, accounting for 30% of OPEC output and having a quarter of the world reserves. Some pundits maintain the 'deal' is their plentiful and reliable oil in exchange for security provided by the US, as evidenced by its two wars with Iraq. Oil production costs are rising and enormous, especially in inhospitable areas and in deepwater wells. There has been consolidation in the sector, for instance Exxon merging with Mobil. This may continue, although the remaining UK targets are rather small, except for BG, previously part of British Gas.

The profit growth over the last five years was 11% per annum, reflecting buoyant prices. The profit margin is low at 9%, which might be surprising for such a valuable commodity. However, it is a high volume, modest margin business with much of the value captured by taxation and the oil producing countries, combined with high costs. It is sensible to gain exposure to this economic lifeblood and the majors are BP and Shell, who are a whopping 9% of the stock market. They have strong balance sheets, are very cash generative, pay reliable dividends and their share prices have a low correlation, or beta, with the stock market. BP merged with Amoco and embarked on a risky Russian venture. Shell radically restructured to improve profitability but seriously blotted its copybook by fiddling its reserves. These are the safer plays as they are vertically integrated, so that they control the industry from initial drilling to selling in the petrol stations. Therefore, they do not have all their eggs in one basket and these 'upstream' and 'downstream' revenues mean a problem in one can be offset by good news in the other. Exploration and production companies are riskier. It is best to buy at the bottom of a recession. Another opportunity is when crude prices are the lowest for many years, as in 1999 when it fell to a bargain $10 a barrel, and sell when it peaks, as in 1981 when it hit $53 a barrel. Such extremes are likely to be abnormal, as the price will tend to revert to the norm, where the long run demand and supply are in equilibrium. The companies need $14 a barrel to break-even.

4e. Basic industries

Chemicals: recession resistance 4, competitive advantage 5. Percentage of stock market capitalisation 1%.

'Of all the mysteries of the stock exchange there is none so impenetrable as why there should be a buyer for everyone who seeks to sell.'
John Galbraith, economist and author of *The Great Crash*.

The chemicals sector does not appeal as it is old economy, with a disappointing past and its future profitability is doubtful. The number of products is enormous and they have almost universal applicability. They are largely commodities and this lack of added value limits the ability to command a decent price. Nevertheless, it is the third largest sector worldwide, with sales of £0.6 trillion. Like pharmaceuticals, it needs a pipeline of new products to sustain growth and replace those that have reached the end of their life cycle. This innovation does provide pockets of growth in a mature industry.

The recession resistance is below average as at is heavily dependent on the prosperity of manufacturing companies, which are in long-term decline, and is prone to the overall economic cycle. It also suffers from high capital costs and the resultant fixed depreciation means that costs are hard to rein in when the times are tough so losses ensue. The plant needs to be run at full capacity to cover the overhead, which is not an option if demand is weak.

The competitive advantage is the lowest. Although there are companies that add some value, such as BOC's speciality chemicals and gasses or Victrex's medical applications, the sector is subject to intense international competition and pricing pressures. Moreover, speciality products need higher levels of research and development, know-how and marketing, so the higher prices can be swallowed by increased costs. All raw materials and much of the output are priced in US dollars so there is currency risk. Overseas opportunities look poor with uninspiring Asian demand affecting margins and there is little promise in the US or Europe, where news flow is deteriorating. In short, the sector economics are unfavourable and they respond to, rather than are masters of, events. Excellent management is crucial in order to compete, given the sector's lack of tailwind.

The profit growth rate over the last five years was just 1% per annum and this was during prosperous times. The profit margin is a low 3%. The sector's stock market performance was good when there was an industrial based economy. This withered in the last two decades, leading to increasing underperformance. The cyclical industrial sector is typically much lower rated than its cyclical consumer counterpart, reflecting the greater risk in a downturn, particularly due to the high fixed cost and more extreme reduction in sales. A bellwether share is Imperial Chemical Industries, which has struggled to achieve stability. Even its name has an echo of a bygone era. Johnson Matthey and Yule Catto produce constituents of generic drugs, which is a growth area. The sector's share prices are volatile.

Construction, building materials: recession resistance 5, competitive advantage 4. Percentage of stock market capitalisation 3%.

The construction and building materials sector has unattractive economics because of its extreme cyclicality. All seems to be set fair at the moment but this is expected to change for the worse. The unwinding of the housing bubble will affect some sectors more than others but the construction and building materials sector will be in the front line. It is difficult to think of a sector that is harder hit in a recession, with the possible exception of banks.

The sector has the lowest recession resistance, as it is very heavily dependent on the economic cycle. In a recession, construction grinds to a halt due to lack of demand for commercial property as businesses contract. Even those businesses that remain prosperous tend to be cautious and cut back on such big-ticket items. Sector losses are then racked up as land banks and work in progress plummet in value and the heavy cost of plant and machinery thump the bottom line with depreciation. House building is similarly affected in a recession, as job losses and the fear of negative equity put activity in a deep freeze. Interest rates have been at a fifty-year low and this has inevitably lead to extreme reactions in the economy, such as the massive increase in house prices and borrowing. This has been aided and abetted by the lowest levels of unemployment for a generation and the unattractive alternative investments of the stock market or cash. The bend in the trend beckons, however, and the party will stop at some point. When interest rates return to the norm, there will be a severe recession and the unwinding of the housing bubble will be very painful.

The competitive advantage is below average as costs are high and product differentiation is fairly low, particularly in building materials. However, at least it has little exposure to international competition. Planning consent is hard to obtain and the consequent scarcity of land hinders activity considerably and increases cost. The government's ambition to increase dramatically the number of homes, particularly in the southeast, is a favourable tailwind. There has been consolidation in the sector, such as Wimpey buying the house building division of McAlpine, which is one way of increasing land banks. Contractors are riding the tailwind of private finance initiative work for government and this is likely to be recession resistant. The building material gorillas generate over half of sales from the US, so are heavily dependent on prospects there and the value of the dollar, neither of which is promising. However, they are benefiting from increased UK and European government spending on infrastructure.

The sector's profit growth rate over the last five years was 14% per annum. This was above the market as a whole, reflecting the benign economic conditions, but the profit margin is a modest 11%. The PER is typically low, even if profits are booming, because the quality of the earnings is poor as the market remembers the losses in previous recessions. Outperformance tends to happen when interest rates are stable or falling and they now appear to be on the rise. McAlpine has repositioned itself to focus on long-term support service, utility contracts and private finance initiatives. This will provide a cushion in a downturn, although one third of revenue is still exposed to commercial construction, a difficult market for some years and likely to deteriorate further. There are gains to be made in this very risky sector if it is bought when a recession has bottomed out.

4f. General industrials

Aerospace and defence: recession resistance 4, competitive advantage 2. Percentage of stock market capitalisation 1%.

'We might as well have a plague of frogs. We've had everything else.'

Harassed airline spokesman, reflecting on falling tourism after foot and mouth disease, the economic slowdown, September 11th terrorist attacks and the army guarding Heathrow from the threat of missile attack.

The aerospace and defence sector faces mixed fortunes. Civil aerospace is driven by general economic growth and rides the long-term tailwind of increased demand for air travel. This reflects the growing dominance of budget airlines, like easyJet, with its low fares compared to the high-ticket prices from the full service carriers. However, it is a very long-term business, as increased air traffic is often satisfied by taking planes out of mothballs rather than leading to an immediate increase in demand for new planes. Defence benefits from the heightened security concerns and the 'war on terrorism'. It is the more attractive sub sector, as government spending is more dependable in troubled economic times, although there are no companies solely reliant on this activity.

The recession resistance is below average for aerospace and average for defence. They are big-ticket items and there will be lower demand from the public, business and government when they need to rein in spending. However, due to the long time that contracts take to be completed, demand will not suddenly cease. The capital employed and fixed costs are significant and need high plant utilisation to cover the overhead. This can quickly lead to losses in a recession.

The international competitive advantage is above average. A yardstick for aerospace is the success of the European consortium Airbus, which overtook the only other major airline maker remaining in business, Boeing. Various companies, such as gorillas like BAE Systems, Smiths and Rolls-Royce, benefit from their involvement with Airbus. However, the US terrorist attacks on September 11th plunged the industry into its worst crisis for 40 years and illustrated the operating risk, as customers stayed away and planes were cancelled. The outlook for defence looked bleak back in the early 1990s when the cold war ended and military forces wondered if they would have a role. Since then, there have been two major Gulf wars and many minor conflicts, all overlaid with the growing menace of real or imagined terrorism. Annual US defence spending is planned to increase to $500 billion by 2011 and UK companies have good exposure to this, including BAE Systems and Smiths. Similarly, the UK is spending more and restructuring its forces to fight elusive enemies. Defence, therefore, is a long-term growth area, since the war on terrorism is unlikely to be no more winnable than the war on drugs.

The profit growth rate over the last five years for the sector was minus 4% per annum and the profit margin is 10%, reflecting the downturn after the US attacks. Prices are set in US dollars for civil aircraft so weakness in that currency is a risk. The preference should be for fast growing companies like Chemring, which is a world leader in decoy flares to counter enemy missiles. The number of suppliers to the aerospace manufacturers runs into thousands due to the myriad of components needed. Taking away this 'noise' by outsourcing to supply specialists provides an opportunity for the likes of Aero Inventory, which is also a play on Far East growth, and Umeco.

Electronic, electrical, engineering: recession resistance 4, competitive advantage 5. Percentage of stock market capitalisation 1%.

Electronic, electrical and engineering is an unattractive sector with high cost and low product differentiation. Electronic and electrical does add some value, such as precision instrumentation, advanced televisions and DVDs, but it is not world class and competition is intense. Engineering is predominantly old economy and will tend to follow manufacturing's future, which will continue to contract in size due to poor economics.

The recession resistance is lowest as it is a cyclical sector. It tends to be at the bottom of the value chain and the pain is passed down the line. The sector's control over its destiny is poor and currency swings can affect prospects. The woes are summed up by Invensys, which has been struggling for years with very poor sales, high gearing and selling off businesses.

The competitive advantage is low. Little value is added in the 'metal bashing' companies and sector competition is intense from low-cost overseas producers. At the higher end of the sector, such as electronics, the UK does not possess much competitive advantage compared to the Japanese or Americans. There has been some attempt at moving production to low-cost countries.

The growth rate over the last five years was minus 2% per annum and the profit margin is a low 5%. Although there are one or two companies that seem to have promise, like Minorplanet and NXT, the rewards tend to be elusive. Some engineering companies have come close to going bust in the trying times of the last few years and face rising costs and US dollar weakness. The sector is best avoided but is a geared play on economic recovery, given its cyclicality. They thus tend to outperform coming out of a recession.

4g. Cyclical consumer goods

Automobiles, household goods: recession resistance 4, competitive advantage 4. Percentage of stock market capitalisation 1%.

Automobile and household goods is a sector similar to electronic, electrical and engineering with poor economics and low recession resistance.

The recession resistance is below average as automobiles are big-ticket items and quick to be postponed in hard times so the sector is very prone to the economic cycle. The household goods sector comprises carpets, textiles, furniture and the like and is similarly unattractive, as it is dependent on a healthy housing market and economy.

The competitive advantage is also below average as it is exposed to the full rigour of international competition. The UK does have competitive advantage in automobiles, providing that the manufacturer is foreign: Honda, Nissan and Toyota lead the way, followed by European companies like BMW. The painful memories of the disaster that was British Leyland are still vivid. The sector has boiled down to selling the cars or providing components, neither of which adds much value and is subject to fierce competition. The UK is the world epicentre of Formula One racing cars, which implies that competitive advantage can be gained by specialised and highly talented small teams, although the companies concerned are not quoted. The household goods sector has poor economics since it adds little value and fights an uphill struggle against cheap imports.

The sector's five-year profit growth was 11% per annum but the profit margin is minus 18%. This poor performance has been under favourable economic conditions so one can only dread the results in a recession. The biggest company is GKN, which is dependent on new car sales and the health of the commercial and military aerospace markets. The sector should be avoided.

4h. Cyclical services

General retailers: recession resistance 4, competitive advantage 3. Percentage of stock market capitalisation 4%.

'He who does not smile should not open a shop.'
Chinese proverb

General retailers is one of the trickiest sectors. The customer is transactional, meaning one-off. Customer loyalty is all-important, therefore, to ensure that they return. Tactics include loyalty cards, developing brand awareness and generally focusing more on customer service than was the case a decade ago. The snag is that customers are fickle and sophisticated, so companies need to be alert to their changing tastes.

The recession resistance is below average because the sector is exposed to rising interest rates, consumers tightening their belts and most purchases can be postponed or abandoned. The cost of stores is high and fixed so losses stack up in a recession. Indeed, a major player like Next came near to collapse last time. Those selling low-ticket items, like discount clothes, should fare better in a recession compared to those selling expensive items like televisions. Even worse are those that are housing related, such as carpet sellers, as that market is dire in hard times.

Competitive advantage is average and the attempts to replicate UK success overseas have been a graveyard. This illustrates the point that retailing seems easy but in fact is much more difficult than it looks. It requires continuous marketing flair and a very keen sense of satisfying customers' changing fads and fashions. Competition is fierce, as consumers increasingly seek discounts and good value, compounded by alternative sources of supply, like the internet, which have empowered them with information. This can only be to the detriment of margins. Problems with retailing include: variations in seasonal weather; Christmas trading that is as crucial as it is unreliable; inappropriate expansion; widespread and growing discounting; and increased operating and property costs. Imported price deflation hits profits and this will worsen with the abolition of quotas and China waiting in the wings to take advantage. Retailers' ability to forecast demand is often poor, leading to warehouses full of unsold stock that will have to be discounted and will undermine regularly-priced goods. Traditional clothing operators, like Marks & Spencer, are being squeezed by 'brands with attitude', such as French Connection and Gap, and discounters, like Matalan and

Peacock. Demand is driven by disposable incomes and, although these have been rising, the boost given by equity withdrawal from rocketing house prices is one-off and the debt problems will come home to roost. Heavy government spending means tax increases are on going and bite into incomes. Companies like newsagent WHSmith are in a pickle, as juggernauts like Tesco invade their space.

The five-year profit growth was 10% per annum, reflecting the consumer boom. The profit margin is a low 10%, which is understandable in a high volume business. There has been considerable takeover activity that snapped up players like Debenhams, which has been partly driven by their attractive real estate. Niche operators are preferred, such as Merchant Retail, which sells a wide range of branded perfume at cut-prices.

Leisure and hotels: recession resistance 4, competitive advantage 3. Percentage of stock market capitalisation 2%.

Leisure and hotels is an attractive sector as it benefits from the one-third increase in real incomes each decade and most of this will be spent on services, like leisure. It rides the demographic tailwind of the prosperous young and elderly who spend time and money on leisure, sport and travel activities, such as pubs, restaurants, flying, fitness, hotels and art galleries. The services have to be constantly provided, often round the clock, as in the case of hotels, so it does not have the attractive business model of 'make once and sell many times'. Leisure is a play on property prices, as substantial premises are typically required and, if prices are set to increase, companies with freeholds will be preferred to those that rent and vice versa if property hits a bear market. Leisure is a good sector to scuttlebutt, being a retail business, as explained in chapter 7.

The recession resistance is below average as the sector will suffer in a recession when spending is mainly reserved for essentials. Consumers will be more price-conscious and make do with cheaper alternatives, such as a pizza instead of an expensive restaurant, or do without. Hotels, like Intercontinental and Hilton, have high overheads and employ large amounts of capital. They are to be particularly avoided in a recession, as the all-important business trade is cut back to the bone. The largest UK company is the US-based Carnival cruise line and its high-ticket items will be under pressure in hard times, especially as capacity continues to increase enormously. It also has high fixed costs. An old adage is that it is the third owner that makes money out of a golf course. It is built in the good times and capacity is greatly increased overall. Then the economy deteriorates and customers vanish, since such services are discretionary expenditure that can be cut. Eventually, the business has to be sold below cost. The second owner thinks he has a bargain but the losses mount even higher. He eventually sells in the teeth of a severe recession at a fire sale price to the third owner, who then enjoys the subsequent recovery. Fitness clubs are a classic example of this scenario, as evidenced by the trading problems of Holmes Place and its subsequent takeover.

The competitive advantage is average. On the plus side, the sector is largely immune from overseas substitution. Operators can have good pricing power if the service is local and the choice is limited, such as country pubs. Otherwise, competition can be intense. However, the UK has still much to learn about the service industry compared to the US, for example. There are bouts of consolidation in the leisure sector and its close counterpart, beverages. Mergers and takeovers amounted to £25 billion in the last decade and fostered giants like Scottish & Newcastle and Diageo. This is followed by bouts of disposals, when hard times or focus is prevalent. The former is a buying opportunity and the latter is a selling opportunity. The rationale for consolidation will be part justified by the benefits of synergy but these are elusive as outlets are stand-alone: there are 135,000 licensed premises, half being pubs. This makes economies of scale difficult, although buying larger volumes of food and drink should increase the discount negotiated. It is labour intensive and overheads are high. Customers are transactional, meaning one-off, so loyalty, brands and value for money are important to ensure repeat business. A replicable and successful rollout of a concept is a sound business model and problems with new outlets can be quickly remedied. However, leisure is a fashion business that can quickly grow cold. This increases risk and the ageless concepts are safer plays, especially since real innovation is rare in this very old business. Legislation can drive change, for example limiting the number of tied pubs that gorillas could own and the proposed relaxation of opening hours and gaming. Tenanted pubs are a better model than managed pubs, as the former have the 'owner's eye'. The weather can disrupt trading patterns and excellent management is crucial.

The five-year profit growth was only 4% per annum, reflecting the maturity of the industry, competition and the aftermath of September 11th terrorist attacks. The profit margin is average at 16%. Serious excess capacity and price-cutting have adversely affected the profitability of high street pubs and clubs, such as Luminar, and some have gone bust. Retrenchment is now the order of the day. Belhaven and Hardys & Hansons are attractive companies that are brewers and community pub operators. They have undervalued assets on the balance sheet, a differentiated product and a long track record of growing profits. In addition, Domino's Pizza is growing fast by rolling out a successful consumer franchise.

Media and entertainment: recession resistance 4, competitive advantage 3. Percentage of stock market capitalisation 4%.

'Don't tell my mother that I work in an advertising agency. She thinks I play the piano at a whore house.'
Jacques Seguela, title of his autobiography.

The media and entertainment sector has similarities to leisure and hotels above. Media is the 'M' in TMT and that mania lit a fire under the shares, which has long been extinguished. It does have a good tailwind with increased spending power and leisure time, with more distribution channels due to satellite television, digital radio and the internet. The problem is to make money out of them, with a bewildered consumer spoilt for choice, a deteriorating product and advertising expenditure spread thinly over so many channels. The brave new world of possibilities was a disaster for ITV Digital, which lost £1 billion by paying too much for second-rate football that drew a meagre audience. It is very difficult to be original because any book or film will be in one or more of only 36 possible formats, such as revenge, love, action and drama. There is no shortage of supply either of an increasingly undifferentiated product, with the UK launching a staggering 80,000 new books a year. When an original product does hit the market, it is seized by the public and quickly imitated by others if they can, examples being The Beatles, Sergio Leone's spaghetti westerns, Cats, British Sky Broadcasting or Stephen Hawking's *A Brief History of Time*.

The recession resistance is below average and companies like WPP find that marketing is an easy cost for companies to cut, as the benefit is ephemeral and probably pointless when demand is dead. The sector also relies on discretionary spending by consumers and this likewise comes under pressure in a down turn. Advertising has been dire for some time and the likes of Pearson have suffered. This can be blamed on geo-political problems like war. However, the reason is more likely to be a lead indicator that the economy faces hard times.

The competitive advantage is medium as, although the added value is considerable, the global leaders are the likes of Disney, AOL Time Warner and Sony. Nevertheless, the English language and historical reasons lend support to UK efforts and there are flagships with differentiated products, such as The Financial Times and The Economist. The operating cost tends to be high. The good news is that regulation is being relaxed but that is because of the bad news, namely increased competition. This situation is thus a two-edged sword and is similar to telecommunications in this regard. Foreign ownership will be allowed and the remaining terrestrial television companies have effectively consolidated down to just one gorilla to compete against the BBC, British Sky Broadcasting and cable. It has the formidable task of retaining its share of viewers. Radio deregulation is far reaching and consolidation is likely. Newspapers are becoming ever more turgid and have poor competitive advantage compared to internet content, which is free and instant. Elsewhere, the promise of children's characters has been uneven, although strong brands, like Hit Entertainment's Bob the Builder, have prospered. Copyrights are attractive as they endure for 50 years. The likes of Reuters depend on a healthy financial services sector but that is still licking its wounds after the bear market. Those companies that are internet based, such as Ingenta, lack robust business models and the likes of EMI are being undermined by the ability to download free music at sites like Kazaa. In other words, technology has enabled the consumer to capture a good chunk of the value added rather than the shareholders.

The profit growth over the last five years was a healthy 13% per annum and the profit margin is below average at 12%. This sector is best bought when a recession has bottomed out. The largest company is British Sky Broadcasting and, although it has an attractive business model with its 'must-have' premier football, its costs and operating risks are high. It faces a threat from the Freeview digital package, which is promoted by the BBC and others, and it has retained losses of £2 billion, not that this has stopped it from unwisely paying 'dividends', as discussed in chapter 8.

Support services: recession resistance 3, competitive advantage 3. Percentage of stock market capitalisation 3%.

Support services is an attractive sector on the whole as it benefits from the increasing trend of companies to concentrate on core activities and outsource peripheral tasks to experts. The sector covers a wide variety of activities, some with strong defensive characteristics and others that are very cyclical. Therefore, sector generalisation is less helpful than analysing each company on its merits.

The recession resistance is average overall. Those businesses that enjoy long-term contracts and recurring revenue are very attractive, as the control over profits is strong. For example, RAC and Homeserve have high recurring revenue from providing breakdown and repair cover, respectively, to a large number of customers, giving critical mass and a barrier to entry. Compass is the world's largest caterer and demand should be resilient in a recession, in spite of some reduction due to company failures and lack of expansion. Others ride the tailwind of increased public spending, like Connaught, which manages and repairs social and council housing, and Capita, which has high retention rates and a strong pipeline of contract bids. Private Finance Initiatives have provided very long-term contracts from governments for companies like John Laing and Capita. The projects include hospitals, roads, information technology, congestion charging and schools. These are recession resistant but there have been operating, pricing and political problems. These companies should deliver defensive growth, a most highly prized trait. The cyclical companies are unattractive, such as engineering consultancies like Atkins, which struggle to make money even in the good times. Recruitment consultancies, such as Michael Page and Hays, and plant hire, like Aggreko, are a rags to riches story depending on whether the economy is in a recession or not. They have high fixed costs that lead to losses when revenue dries up in hard times but outperform in a recovery. Support service companies that feed off the construction cycle include Serco and Jarvis.

The competitive advantage is average and the activities do demonstrably add value or the clients would otherwise perform the work in-house. Services are difficult to import so the sector is shielded from intense international competition. However, ways are being sought to lower cost, for example by using overseas call centres. Pricing pressures are ever present and many of the sub sectors are mature, which may encourage companies to seek growth from overseas expansion. There has been consolidation but there are still 180 quoted companies. Be wary of those with significant goodwill, like Capita and Tribal, as explained in chapter 8.

The five-year profit growth was 7% per annum and it tends to be a high volume, lower margin business, the latter being only 8%. The gorillas, like Rentokil Initial, have demonstrated how hard it is to maintain growth. Niche operators are to be preferred, like Homeserve, Connaught and MITIE.

Transport: recession resistance 3, competitive advantage 3. Percentage of stock market capitalisation 2%.

'An out-of-town visitor to New York was admiring the elegant vessels harboured off the Financial District; 'Those are the bankers' and brokers' yachts!' exclaimed the guide. 'But where are the customers' yachts?' questioned the naïve visitor in response.'
Fred Schwed, author of *Where Are The Customers' Yachts?*

The attractiveness of transport is average and is a major part of the economy, at about 15% of GDP, but only 2% of the stock market. The sector has largely been privatised, exceptions being the London Underground and the re-nationalised Railtrack, and this has increased competitiveness. There are various sub sectors, some of which operate worldwide: passenger transport (trains, buses, cars); logistics (overnight delivery); airlines; shipping; and infrastructure (railways, ports). All are subject to various degrees of legislation and regulation. Eurotunnel is a good £9 billion example of the sector risk, as the cost overruns were enormous and the interest and depreciation have been an anchor round its neck.

Its recession resistance is average as, although transport is a necessity, companies and consumers do cut back when the times are tough. Also, the amount of capital employed is prodigious, as are the resultant depreciation charges, so the costs are high. An indication of how demand can fall has been the reduction in first class business travel due to terrorism fears and resulted in British Airways stopping Concorde. Customers increasingly flock to low-cost carriers, which have impressive business models and strong management, like easyJet and Ryanair. This search for value for money in a largely undifferentiated product can be expected to intensify in a recession. Therefore, airlines are generally to be avoided. Sir Richard Branson said that the way to become a millionaire was to start as a billionaire and then buy an airline. Warren Buffett said that whenever he feels like buying shares in an airline he lies down in a dark room until the feeling goes away. Their experience reflects high fixed cost, transactional customers with fickle loyalty, intense competition and the price of fuel is outside the operators' control. Nevertheless, the demand for air travel has been growing steadily for decades and will continue with an increasingly affluent and mobile population. A safer way to feed off this megatrend is to invest in an airport, which is a low risk monopoly and has a 'toll bridge' business model, as a charge is made every time the facility is used. The biggest company in the sector is BAA, which also makes money from retailing. This airport operator is defensive and growth should come from the fifth terminal at Heathrow. However, it is regulated, although its last review was favourable. Avoid shipping companies like P&O, as the fixed costs and competition are high and demand is very cyclical, although it does have exposure to China's growth. Sector risk is compounded by the wild card that the all-important American traveller will evaporate in hard times or at the first sign of danger, such as terrorism and foot and mouth disease.

The competitive advantage is average as the value added is significant but costly to provide. The service is time sensitive and cannot easily be stored to meet demand on another day. For example, planes fly according to their schedule and not when they are full. This feature of the business fuels the desire for companies to operate at high capacity, encouraging last minute price-cutting that undermines the sector's profitability. International competition is intense for airline and ships. Parts of the business benefit from technology, such as booking through the internet that cuts out the travel agent. EasyJet takes a staggering 90% of bookings over the internet. Logistics has the tailwind of the trend to outsource and is faster growing than mature sectors like train operators. The desire to diversify into high growth areas has had some unfortunate results, an example being Stagecoach's ambitious acquisition of Coach USA. Competition within the UK is muted in some operations and often protected by regulation, such as train operators, although franchises can be lost. Indeed, various factors, such as lack of land, create potent but regulated monopolies, for example ports, airports and trains. First class management is crucial in transport, given the intense international competition, the dynamic and risky environment, and living up to the expectations of the regulator. However, the sector's fortunes largely depend on factors outside management's control, including the economy in general. It can suffer from piling on capacity in the good times with long lead times, only to face a down turn.

The five-year profit growth was a paltry 2% per annum but does reflect US terrorism and war. The profit margin is 15%, the same as the stock market as a whole. The ability to adjust profits by estimating future costs in some cases means that it is wise to examine cash flow closely. This is a sector to consider buying at the end of a recession.

4i. Information technology

Information technology hardware: recession resistance 4, competitive advantage 3. Percentage of stock market capitalisation 1%.

'To err is human, but to really foul things up requires a computer.'
Paul Ehrlich, scientist.

Information technology hardware ought to be an attractive sector, as it is the engine of the new economy, is very innovative and can add great value. Indeed, so popular was this sector in the TMT mania that it blew apart, leaving bombed out companies and bust business models. However, hardware tends to be a commodity product with intense international competition and high costs. The profit zone in information technology is in the software rather than the hardware. Personal computers have fallen in price by three quarters in the last four years yet the chip speed has quadrupled and is a classic 'bitch of a business', mollified by selling follow-on services like financing and warranties.

The recession resistance is below average. This must have been a surprise to all those pundits in the TMT mania who claimed that it was recession-proof. IT was thought to be a non-negotiable item and essential if a company wanted to compete. The product has since proved to be 'nice-to-have' rather than 'must-have'. Demand has been cut back to the bone and companies are tending to make do with their existing infrastructure. Generally, a killer application is found wanting, compared to the juggernaut products that drove earlier demand, such as servers and a personal computer on every desk.

The competitive advantage is average as the gorillas are American, and include Cisco, Hewlett Packard and Intel. UK latecomers like Marconi tried to capture a piece of the action but wasted a $4.5 billion fortune buying a US re-router at the top of the market and subsequently fell apart. ARM is a niche chipmaker but is struggling with increasing competition. Radstone Technology, however, has an excellent business model supplying rugged computer products and is analysed in appendix 1.

The last five years' profit growth was minus 14% per annum and the profit margin is minus 32%. As a sector, it almost ceased to exist and was well under 1% of the stock market before recovering somewhat. This might have been an opportunity for a contrarian but the snag is that many of these companies looked cheap after losing 80% or more of their value in the bear market, only to keep on falling. Security software company Baltimore Technologies, for example, was a FTSE 100 company as its shares raced to a peak of £137 and subsequently collapsed. The sector is risky and was detested after the mania. Rallies are likely to be hit by sellers anxious to redeem some of their lost fortune and so the sector should be in the doldrums for some time. There are much safer ways to make money.

Software and computer services: recession resistance 4, competitive advantage 3. Percentage of stock market capitalisation 1%.

'Who is your boss, really? In reality, 99% of the population works for Bill Gates.'
Linda Smith, comedian, on Microsoft.

Software and computer services has suffered a similar fate to information technology hardware above and it shares common characteristics. It is an attractive sector, in principle, as it has the advantage of 'make once and sell many times', often at very low cost. The example of Microsoft springs to mind as it dominates the market with its operating system and standard products like Windows, Excel and Word installed into millions of computers. These were initially created years ago and the marginal cost of production is miniscule.

The recession resistance is below average and please see the information technology hardware comments above. Again, there is a lack of a new killer application like Windows and recent products, such as XP, are more refinements rather than blockbusters. In the commercial market, there is promise from the likes of SurfControl with its internet filtering although there is US competition. Such products can pay for themselves in boosting productivity and provide a powerful incentive to buy, even in a recession.

The competitive advantage is also average, with US companies like Oracle dominating the industry. As a result, sector consolidation should continue and follows in the wake of the 2002 LogicaCMG merger. There are opportunities for niche UK players like iSOFT that cater for the health market. This feeds off the rapid increase in government spending and provides recession resistant, long-term contracts. Outsourcing is also a growth area supporting the likes of Xansa. Dicom has an attractive business model as it moves up the value chain away from hardware into software with its scanning technology. This is very cost effective and is being installed as standard in some machines. However, these are limited markets compared to Microsoft's, which has worldwide applicability and, in a sense, is unlimited. Low-cost countries, like India, are increasingly likely to make their presence felt, not only in software outsourcing but also in their own start up IT operations. The competitive advantage of distributors of hardware, such as Computacenter, is poor not only because little value is added but also because the commodity product is subject to relentless price deflation.

The last five years' profit growth was 10% per annum, just above the market's 9%, but the profit margin is minus 6%. The sector is risky as it suffers from the 'black box' syndrome, which means that the competitive advantage of the product is very difficult for an investor to second guess. Some do not even try, like Warren Buffett. Avoid companies that still have mountains of goodwill, in spite of previous write-offs in the sector that run into billions. Although this only confirms the painful destruction in shareholder value, it can lead to breached banking covenants and bankruptcy.

4j. Financials

Banks, speciality finance: recession resistance 5, competitive advantage 1. Percentage of stock market capitalisation 21%.

'Bank failures are caused by depositors who don't deposit enough money to cover losses due to mismanagement.'
Dan Quayle, the unforgettable US Vice President.

Banks and speciality finance is an attractive sector as it is essentially a simple business. It makes a turn on someone else's money and is easily scalable to accommodate increased volumes. It is a 'switchboard' business model, bringing together many depositors on the one side with many lenders on the other that need the bank to act as an intermediary, like a switchboard operator, with some of the money passing between the two sticking to this middleman. This is a powerful space to occupy that creates significant and enduring value, being a unique and essential business. Unsurprisingly, it is by far the largest sector, accounting for a fifth of the stock market capitalisation. There are few businesses that are as old and so the sector is mature. The banks' fortunes and loan growth track the wider economy and intense competition has put margins under pressure. The sector has also been affected by the deteriorating economy, as demand for financial products has been generally depressed, except for mortgages and consumer loans.

The overall recession resistance is the lowest because bad debts are a major problem. In the good times, there are reassuring words about how credit procedures have been tightened but the ability of the major clearing banks, like Barclays, to lose mountains of money due to company and consumer defaults is legendary. This also applies to losses from countries, examples being Russia and South America, whose defaults have cost billions. Banks have diversified into other businesses, like life insurance, but not all have been wise, such as those that bought estate agents at the top of the last property cycle. Banks receive a very bad press in hard times, as stories are run of unfortunate people with some implication that the bank is to blame rather than the borrower. Banks vie with oil as being the 'bad guys'. The time to buy is coming out of recession after hefty cost cutting, as they will make prodigious amounts of money in the good times ahead but this is not yet reflected in the price. This is not a sector to buy and hold.

Mortgage banks, on the other hand, have reasonably high recession resistance, as their loans are secured on housing. They will still suffer in a recession, as house prices revert to the norm, and then the conservatism, or lack if it, of lending and use of mortgage indemnity insurance will be revealed. In the last recession, the latter was very important, as many customers paid premiums to insurance companies to cover the risk of defaulting on the loan. As a result, the canny mortgage banks suffered much lower bad debts than would otherwise have been the case and cost the insurance companies a fortune. Interest margins are a wafer thin 2%.

Speciality finance has low recession resistance as bad debts and low volumes become painful. Their competitive advantage is only average. The sector includes brokers, lenders and derivatives traders. Banks and financial companies are the cornerstone of confidence in an economy and the authorities would be loath to see the failure of a significant player, which provides reassurance to investors. When disaster strikes, such as in the UK secondary banking system in the 1970s or US Savings and Loans in the 1980s, then the bailout is usually swift. Asset managers are geared plays on the stock market, as their commissions rise with increased prices and volumes traded.

The international competitive advantage is the highest, in stark contrast to the recession resistance rating, as the UK has benefited from its history, language and time zone. Such strong competitive advantage may seem odd since banking is a commodity product but the business has millions of sticky customers, who are often under-informed. This produces recurring revenue, durable fee income and the installed client base, where the real value lies, can be cross-sold higher margin products like life insurance. However, there is no shortage of competition and margins are under pressure. The sector is not renowned for low costs, although some lead the way, like Northern Rock, and are preferred. There have been takeovers for decades, notably Midland, National Westminster, Bank of Scotland and Abbey, and the remaining players are few. The mortgage banks are tempting, small, bolt-on acquisitions and Alliance & Leicester and Bradford & Bingley are leading candidates. However, the very strict regulatory environment is hostile and further mega consolidation amongst UK players is unlikely, although foreign bids may well succeed. The high cost of regulation reinforces the high barriers to entry. New entrants, such as Egg and Standard Life, have not been a material threat.

The profit growth over the last five years was 9% per annum, the same as the market, which is what you would expect in the good times. Return on capital averages a healthy 15%, with Lloyds TSB way out in front. Balance sheets are strong, with excess capitalisation of £9 billion. HSBC and Standard Chartered have high Asian exposure, which may be considered a shrewd play on Far East growth, although the operating and currency risk is higher than mainstream western banks like HBOS. The London Stock Exchange is a listed company whose fortunes reflect trading volumes. It is a takeover target, is regulated and has had to reduce its fees. A niche operator like Broadcastle is attractive, which has moved away from the increasingly risky consumer towards lower risk lending, like invoice discounting. Doorstep providers, like Cattles and Provident Financial, and pawnbrokers Albemarle & Bond, are high margin, recession resistant businesses. The former two have recorded an increase in earnings per share every year for a decade, as noted in chapter 1, section 5.d. Avoid sexy stories that rely on 'black boxes', such as derivative traders.

Insurance: recession resistance 3, competitive advantage 4. Percentage of stock market capitalisation 1%.

'There are things worse than death. Have you ever spent an evening with an insurance salesman?'
Woody Allen

General insurance covers a wide variety of risks from oil platforms to household contents in the commercial and consumer markets. It is not an attractive sector, as it is a commodity product and underwriting profits are difficult to make on a consistent basis in this volatile business. Instead, profits are usually made from investing the cash flow from premiums but this is no easy task with low interest rates and a bear market.

The recession resistance is average, as customers will shop around when the times are tough, but is offset by their tendency to stick with the exiting provider. More importantly, insurance has its own business cycle, epitomised by capacity rushing in when premiums harden and this excess leads to cut pricing and underwriting losses. Capacity then withdraws and rates harden once more and the cycle is repeated. If you are tempted to buy, then wait until the bottom of this cycle has been reached and rates harden.

The competitive advantage is below average, as intense competition puts pressure on margins. The contract is typically for a year to cover assets such as houses, contents and cars and, although there is inertia, customers are price-conscious and look for the best deal. Loyalty is low and new entrants from the likes the internet and supermarkets have increased capacity. Reinsurance is to be particularly avoided, as the liabilities are 'long tail', meaning that they are unknowable for years hence and there is no control over claims. Please see chapter 2.7g for more detail. The backbone of Warren Buffett's success has been to invest the cash float from premiums until the claims are paid and so, in expert hands, there are ways to make a profit. Unlimited liability, as with Lloyds of London, is the epitome of foolishness, as so many names found out in the 1990s when the market was rocked by scandal.

The profit growth over the last five years was 5% per annum, not helped in the least by the massive losses arising from terrorism in the US. This resulted in rates hardening dramatically but they are now showing signs of softening. The operating risk is demonstrated by the gorilla Royal & Sun Alliance, whose share price fell 90% in a few years. A better space to occupy is that of a broker earning risk-free commissions on the premiums, thus piggybacking on their growth.

Life insurance: recession resistance 2, competitive advantage 2. Percentage of stock market capitalisation 3%.

Life insurance, in contrast to general insurance above, is an attractive sector. It has very little to do with life insurance and more to do with savings products, such as pensions, bonds and with-profits policies. It rides the tailwind of increased prosperity and a desire to save for retirement in a tax-efficient manner.

The recession resistance is above average as there is no other consumer business where contracts are so long, except for mortgage loans. Therefore, the premiums roll in, come rain or shine, and the control over revenue is excellent. Consequently, operating profits are very robust. However, life insurance companies have significant exposure to the stock market, both in terms of the life funds and their own reserves, and this can materially affect pre-tax profits, although this is reversed when the stock market recovers. These are exceptional items and the sector has become a geared play on the stock market, as their share prices have been rising or falling much more than the market as a whole. This is in spite of the companies drastically cutting their exposure to the stock market and increasing their liquidity. A bear stock market also undermines the customer's confidence in savings products. Some of the smaller players closed their books to new business in the three-year bear market up to 2003.

The competitive advantage is above average as the product is very difficult to evaluate by the customer. The charges have the attraction that no bill is presented to him but they are quietly deducted from his pot of money. This minimises consumer resistance. In addition, the benefits are paid years hence, so the customer finds it very difficult to make an informed decision about changing companies and there are exit costs. The customer is therefore very sticky. The installed base can be cross-sold high margin products. Trust is an all-important feature and this has been undermined by the collapse of Equitable Life and pensions mis-selling. The market is mature and new sales are not easy, needing high commission payments to motivate salesmen. Growth may come from overseas and Prudential is looking to Asia. The barriers to entry are high due to regulatory and capital requirements. Although overseas competition is muted, local competition is intense and other financial institutions, such as banks and supermarkets, have added new capacity. It is not a low-cost business, as overheads and new business commissions are significant. Hence, there is reluctance by life companies to embrace calls for low-margin products available for small savers.

The pre-tax profit growth over the last five years was 4% per annum, principally reflecting the bear market. The regulator is very obliging in these difficult times and would be loath to see a life insurer go under, Equitable Life not withstanding. Share prices were undermined by 'fears over solvency' banded around by the press, which does not mean the company is going to go bankrupt but, instead, determines its ability to sell new business. Therefore, at the bottom of a bear market, such uninformed scare-mongering creates a buying opportunity, as share prices become unrealistically low. Friends Provident would make a tempting bolt-on acquisition for one of the gorillas like Prudential. Life insurance accounts are extremely difficult to analyse, even for the experts, as 'embedded value' profits are endlessly adjusted and an investor is in the hands of the actuaries, who thankfully are generally very clever and conservative. This is a prime sector to buy with confidence when the stock market has finally bottomed out.

Real estate: recession resistance 5, competitive advantage 3. Percentage of stock market capitalisation 2%.

'Nearly all of us made promises we can't keep on account of the turn in Wall Street. I promised my wife a rope of pearls. I can't get the pearls but I've the rope - and I'm thinking of using it myself.'
Eddie Cantor, author, on the great crash of 1929.

Real estate does have its attractions but needs to be handled with care. Please see the comments under construction and building materials, as they also apply here.

The recession resistance is the lowest because it is a big-ticket item and is badly affected by hard times. Demand is very elastic and customers either have no need for increased space in a recession, or none at all, if they go bankrupt. Unfortunately, supply is very inelastic, as projects take years. Therefore, it is not easily withdrawn and this is why, with depressed demand and supply trying to find a buyer, real estate prices can fall so dramatically. The sector is characterised by frenzied activity in the boom times and much of that capacity hits the market just when demand is weak, causing major problems. Companies often have high gearing and then bankruptcy looms, such as with Canary Wharf back in the 1990s. This is one sector where it is crucial to have a very clear idea of what happens next in the economic cycle and it is sensitive to interest rates.

The competitive advantage is average. The obvious point to make is that they do not make real estate any more. This rarity value provides a good tailwind, underpinned by a growing economy over the long run, but land bank and development costs are high. Also, planning restrictions are formidable.

Real estate companies generally sell at a discount to net assets and when this discount is very high there is potentially a greater margin of safety. This is one to buy when a recession is well and truly over, as the sector then outperforms. Exposure to real estate can be gained by investing in other sectors, such as food and general retailing and leisure companies, and can thus provide safer exposure.

Conclusion

An objective way to assess those sectors that have international competitive advantage is to see which ones have the highest market capitalisation. This is a winner's league of prosperity and investors should gain exposure to them. They are in order: banks, oil and gas, pharmaceuticals and telecommunications. Together, they account for half of the market and there is a large gap down to the next highest capitalisations, which are electricity and utilities, mining and media and entertainment.

CHAPTER 5

Growth at a reasonable price

'It's far better to buy a wonderful company at a fair price, than a fair company at a wonderful price'.
Warren Buffett

We have seen how important it is to consider both the business model of the company and the competitive advantage of the sector, and how they fare in the economic cycle. The next step is now to analyse shares that have made it thus far in the sieving process. The objective for the investor is to have control over the share and choose those that offer growth at a reasonable price. This provides a margin of safety to minimise the risk that is inherent in investing. Overpriced shares can easily be de-rated and are a sitting duck if there is a profit warning. There are many books on this subject, such as Benjamin Graham's *The Intelligent Investor* and Jim Slater's *Beyond The Zulu Principle*. The statistics below are easy to evaluate using REFS, or Really Essential Financial Statistics, which was developed by Jim Slater. REFS also allows companies to be sieved using various criteria, such as growth rates and profit margins, and the whole market can be searched for the best opportunities.

1. Growth statistics

The following four growth statistics help to see the future, as they estimate a company's financial progress over the next 12 months.

Price earnings ratio

The price earnings ratio (PER) is usually regarded as the most important measure of a share, as it represents the number of years that the earnings per share (EPS) will repay your investment. Thus, a PER of 10 means that over 10 years the earnings will equal the cost of the share. The PER can be for the last set of results but it is more useful to look forward over the next 12 months, based on broker forecasts. Be wary of buying any share on a high PER, as all the good news is likely to be in the price and it can be very exposed if there is bad news flow or if there is a de-rating in the share or in the overall market. A PER of 10 or less is a good target and up to 15 is also acceptable, as long as the story is very good. The margin of safety is eroded if it is above 15 and it was difficult to find low PERs in the stock market mania that ended in 2000. Indeed, PERs of 70 and higher were common. That was a clear sell signal. Look at the PER over the last few years and see if the forecast PER is in the lower range, as it implies a reasonable entry point. When a sector becomes 'hot', other sectors may become neglected and that is often where value and opportunity lies. For example, in the TMT mania, solid sectors, like mortgage banks and tobacco, were very cheap and subsequently rebounded strongly when there was a flight to safety.

Growth in earnings per share

'Earnings are the engine that drives the share price.'
Jim Slater

The brokers' forecast growth rate in earnings per share (EPS) over the next 12 months is a vital tool. Ideally, this should be in the mid teens to the high twenties. Beyond that and the growth rate is unlikely to be sustainable. Increases in broker forecasts can be an important share price driver. Also, be alert for forecasts which are accelerating over the next two years, as this demonstrates that the pace of growth is escalating. This improves the margin of safety and implies the competitive advantage is strengthening. Look at the past growth in earnings and the aim is for this to be increasing with no erratic years where they fell significantly or losses were incurred.

There should ideally be three or more broker forecasts to provide a consensus view. A single forecast is less reliable and the house broker's forecast should be taken with a pinch of salt, as there is a potential conflict of interest since they are paid by the company. On the other hand, it is reasonable to expect that it is closer to the company than the other brokers so the forecast may be more incisive. The forecasts should not be widely different or materially reduced recently. Forecasts are not a panacea and can swiftly be overtaken by profit warnings. However, they are better than flying blind. It is because they are unreliable that this book emphasises additional investment analysis tools, namely company and sector business models, the economic cycle, growth at a reasonable price, technical analysis and scuttlebutting. These provide the real margin of safety.

PEG

The PEG system was popularised by Jim Slater and is simply the PER divided by the growth rate in EPS. Therefore, a PER of eight divided by a growth rate in EPS of 16 produces a PEG of 0.5. A PEG of 0.6 or under is attractive for a growth company. A value company is chosen for attributes, such as a high dividend and asset backing, and PEGs of under 1.0 can be considered. The PEG is awarded if there are four years of growth, so there could be three years of historic growth and one year of forecast growth. House builders need five years of growth in EPS to qualify for a PEG due to their cyclicality. An investor is spoilt for choice in a booming economy, as PEGs will be plentiful. A bear market results in many companies having an interruption in profit growth and so fewer qualify for a PEG. However, the principle is still valid and calculating a PEG ratio for the next 12 months is a useful yardstick even if the four requisite years of growth are absent.

Dividends

'Dividends are for wimps' is the mantra in a raging bull market. They take on much greater importance in a bear market, as they will be the only return available when share prices are falling. It is worth bearing in mind the importance of dividends, since they provide two-thirds of the return on the stock market, with the other third from capital gains, and the payment is a constraint on management's actions. They are loath to cut dividends and it is important that the forecast yield is at least equal to the overall market. The forecast dividend cover, likewise, should match or beat that of the stock market, which is about 1.6. Look at the growth in dividend over the last few years and beware if it has been cut. Aim for a cover of at least two so that there is still room to maintain the dividend should there be a fall in profits. There is more on the subject of dividends in chapter 8.

The following three growth statistics are historical and based on the last annual report. This detracts from their usefulness, as they are not forward looking over the next 12 months, unlike PER, growth rate, PEG and dividend above, but they are nonetheless vital.

Profit margin

The profit margin is crucial. This can be the gross or net pre-tax profit as a percentage of turnover. Ideally, a share should have a net pre-tax profit margin of at least 10% and ideally nearer 20%. It should be near the top of its sector and above that of the overall market's profit margin, which was 15% in the sector analysis in chapter 4. A company may look attractive on a PEG basis but if it is in a low-margin business, like car distribution, then the operating risk is high. A small reduction in turnover or increase in costs can lead to the margin being eliminated and losses being incurred. A high margin is a good indicator of strong competitive advantage. The trend in the margin over the last few years should ideally be rising.

Return on capital employed

The return on capital employed (ROCE) measures how much value the company is adding and should be compared to the cost of capital. The latter is not easy to know but, as a rule of thumb, take the bank rate and add an equity risk premium to provide a floor. Thus, if the bank rate is 5% and a reasonable equity risk premium is, say, 4%, then you should seek a ROCE of at least 9%. A ROCE in the high teens or more is desirable. The measure is flawed, however, because some companies, like steel, use prodigious amounts of capital, whereas others, such as advertising agencies, use human capital rather than financial capital and the former is not on the balance sheet. Therefore, a very high ROCE may not mean an excellent business, just that very little capital is employed. Generally, prefer companies that use capital sparingly. Look at the ROCE for the sector, as this provides a telling yardstick, and the aim should be for the company's ROCE to be towards the top of its sector. It is thus being compared to its peers. ROCE should be increasing over the last few years.

2. Value statistics

The following six value statistics are all historical numbers, rather than being forward-looking, and are based on the last annual report. They are value, rather than growth statistics, and focus on assets and income.

Gearing

Gearing is covered in chapter 1, under economics of the company, 3a. Gearing is the amount borrowed by a company and is tax efficient, as the interest payments are allowed against corporation tax, unlike dividends. The drawback is that the interest payments are a prior charge on profits and cannot be waived, unlike dividends, and the company can go bust if it is unable to pay the interest. Therefore, some gearing can be beneficial but too much increases the overall risk. The optimal point varies according to the company but under 50% is desirable. However, the amount of interest cover is crucial and there is a good margin of safety if it is over, say, five. It is essential that the company has a sound business model and control over its revenue streams so that the interest can be paid. Erratic cash flows can be a death knell. Also, be very wary of companies with over 50% gearing and entering a recession. Gearing is one of the prime reasons why companies collapse.

Net cash per share

Net cash per share is a useful measure, as it is the war chest available for dividends, investment, share buy-backs and to weather a downturn. Too much cash implies that the company is not employing it properly, as it should be invested in the business. Alternatively, it can be returned to shareholders via dividends or share buy-backs. The latter can be a share price driver, as this increases demand for the shares and should enhance EPS. Many TMT companies after the 2000 crash had a very high percentage of cash per share, presenting attractive takeover targets. Consider the 'cash burn' from loss-making companies and whether new funding will be forthcoming when the cash runs out.

Price to cash flow

Price to cash flow (PCF) shows how much a share is returning as cash each year. If the PCF is 10, then the price is 10 times the cash flow or the cash flow yield is 10% of the price. The aim should be for the cash flow yield to be well into the teens or above, giving a PCF of under 10. Cash flow is a useful but flawed measure, as explained in chapter 8. The problem is that cash flow is affected by a variety of factors, such as temporary increases or decreases in debtors and creditors, so one year's number may look good or bad but may not be a true and fair view of how the business is performing. A trend is much more helpful, as consistently poor cash flow over years can be a sign of creative accounting.

Price to book value and tangible book value

'When you buy a stock for its book value, you have to have a detailed understanding of what those assets really are. At Penn Central, tunnels through mountains and useless rail cars counted as assets.'
Peter Lynch

Price to book value (PBV) and tangible book value (PTBV) are useful measures because they show how much the share is backed by assets. In theory, these could be sold and the cash returned to shareholders. They are also usually a benchmark of value in the event of a takeover bid. Consider PTBV rather than PBV, as the latter includes intangible assets, being primarily goodwill and whose value is uncertain, as explained in chapter 8. A PTBV of one or less is attractive, as the share is fully backed by tangible assets. Extremely low PTBVs are available in the market, for example Hardys & Hansons, which has undervalued assets on its balance sheet. The price of a share is, in theory, the discounted net present value of all future dividends and is, therefore, not based on net assets. Therefore, PTBV should be seen as additional margin of safety rather than a prime determinant of the share price.

Price to research ratio

The price to research ratio (PRR) compares the proportion of the share price that is spent on research. For example, if 2.5 pence per share is spent on research and the share price is 10 pence, then the PRR is four. A PRR under 10 is considered attractive and the lower the number the better, with the caveat that an investor will not easily know if the research is money well spent and adding value to the company. PRR is not applicable to companies that do not carry out research or disclose it.

Price to sales ratio

The price to sales ratio (PSR) measures the proportion of the share price that is represented by sales. A low PSR indicates that the share price represents a high level of sales and may indicate that it is undervalued. A small increase in the margin on these high sales can thus lead to a significant boost in profits. Turnover per share should be on a rising trend over the last few years. PRR and PSR are particularly used to analyse technology companies where EPS can be notoriously volatile or non-existent.

Conclusion on growth and value statistics

Value statistics are more limited as they are historical but are helpful as a back up to good growth statistics. Be wary of choosing shares wholly or mainly based on value statistics, as that value could take years to emerge in an increased share price, if ever.

3. Further considerations

Depreciation

Depreciation is a prior charge in the profit and loss account and will be there come rain or shine. Be wary if the depreciation is material in relation to the pre-tax profit. Ideally, it should be well under a fifth of pre-tax profit so the company has a margin of safety. Profits would then have to drop significantly before such fixed costs bite.

FRS 3 and normalised pre-tax profit

In an age of spin, the board will steer you to a normalised pre-tax profit that has the 'nasty bits' excluded rather than to the FRS 3 pre-tax number that is in the audited profit and loss account. For example, the Vodafone chairman said 2004 was 'another highly successful year for your company, with an excellent overall operating performance generating further substantial growth in profits and cash flows'. This is quite an astonishing claim from the third largest company in the UK, considering the operating loss was £4 billion and the FRS 3 after tax loss was £9 billion. He did not elaborate on what the profits were but he may have been referring to a normalised pre-tax profit of £10 billion, which excludes amortisation of goodwill and exceptional items, such as gains and loses on disposals. If an item truly is exceptional, then consider the normalised profit but always include goodwill amortisation.

Be wary of a company that every year has significantly lower FRS 3 profits than normalised, as this implies the exceptionals are recurring items and really are operating costs. There could be large goodwill amortisation, which is a fixed and prior charge just like depreciation. Investors should try not to be forgiving of the nasty bits and take the view that the board has responsibility for the operations of the company and must take full responsibility for any destruction of shareholder value, however caused. The tax rate and capital expenditure are worth evaluating and examine them for the last five years to see if there are any unusual blips. Trends rather than individual year are more helpful.

Profits and established business

Companies should be profitable and been established long enough to have a track record. Loss-making companies or start-ups should be avoided. This is not to say that there are not good opportunities amongst them but the risk is much higher, as performance is less certain. One such opportunity can arise when a company changes from making losses to profits. The market then looks it in a different light and can use valuation yardsticks such as the PER. It can thus be compared to peers and boosted by evidence of a turnaround to a brighter future. The share price gain can be handsome but, to repeat, this is a higher risk proposition.

Size

The size of company should be significant, say over £20 million, so the share can have reasonable liquidity. This is essential in order to buy and, more importantly, to sell the share so that an investor does not become locked in. In addition, the spread between the buy and sell price generally narrows as the company capitalisation increases. Larger companies tend to be better run both in terms of corporate governance and management expertise.

4. Trading

'Sometimes the hardest thing to do is to actually pick up the phone and buy or sell that share.'
David Wash, former deputy editor of *Investing for Growth* newsletter.

Buying and selling is fully discussed in chapter 6 on technical analysis, in chapter 9 on axioms and briefly included here for completeness.

Buying

Buying is easier for an investor to do than selling, although today is always the worst time to buy a share from a psychological viewpoint. If a share has met the strict criteria laid down in this book, then go ahead and buy. Do not be put off by a recent lower price, as that is no longer relevant and, in any case, may signify lack of support in the market. What is relevant is the expectation that the price will rise from here. By all means, monitor the share and choose the moment to buy, especially if it is over-bought and a correction is anticipated. Be aware of the normal market size of trades in the share and the number of market makers, as it is very important to be able to buy and sell unhindered. Take great care to avoid being stuck in a falling share that cannot be traded due to its illiquidity.

Selling

Selling is one of the hardest investment decisions. If a share falls in price, the hope is that it will recover but, if it is sold now, then an unnecessary loss will be realised. One way to take out the emotion is to set a stop loss of, say, 20% and strongly consider selling if this is triggered. A wider stop loss may be preferred for more illiquid shares, as they can be more volatile. Many shares in a portfolio may have the stop loss breached if there is a sudden market wash-out. Nevertheless, the principle still holds and selling them will prevent suffering further falls. It is worth remembering that a stop loss at 20% means that the next share you buy has to rise from 80 to 100 to make good this loss, a rise of 25%. Without a stop loss, hanging on to a share which falls 50% in value means that the next share has to double from 50 to 100 to make good the loss.

Sell when the story changes. If the reason why a share is bought no longer holds then the share should be sold. For example, if there was a promised roll out of a consumer franchise, such as a restaurant chain, of 25 new outlets a years and this has now been scaled back to say 10, then the story has changed and the share should be earmarked for disposal.

Sell when there is a better opportunity. Investors should constantly be on the look out for upgrading the quality and prospects of a portfolio and selling a share for a better one is the way to achieve this. Do not be tempted to continually add shares to the portfolio but keep the number steady at around a dozen shares spread across at least five sectors. If you want to add a share to your portfolio then do so on condition that an existing share is sold.

Set a price that you would sell any share in the portfolio. Monitor the shares and when the pre-set level is reached strongly consider selling in the light of prospects. Do not be greedy and, when you have achieved your goal, sell, even if the prospects look good. Do not try to squeeze the last bit of performance from a share but instead leave something for the next investor.

CHAPTER 6

Technical analysis

1. A useful tool to improve performance

'Keep your technical systems simple. Complicated systems breed confusion; simplicity breeds elegance.'
Dennis Gartman, trader.

This book is primarily about the fundamentals of a company, with particular emphasis on business models, sector competitive advantage and the wider economic backdrop. It is not a book about technical analysis but, nevertheless, the fundamental approach can gain extra performance if some simple technical analysis is borne in mind. This chapter looks at this world and some of the tools which supplement fundamental criteria. The one-minute guide to this chapter is to buy shares that are rising and sell shares that are falling, bearing in mind the fundamentals. Also, the relative strength of a share is a good proxy for technical analysis and is easy to use, as it is a single number to consider rather than numerous lines on a graph.

Technical analysts, or chartists, study the share price graph. They ignore the fundamentals of a share, such as its competitive advantage and growth rate, as they assume that that this is all known to the market and is reflected in the price. They believe future performance can be forecast by looking at patterns that have indicated success in the past. For example, a fundamental investor might have thought that Marks & Spencer was a buy in 2000 when the price was 190 pence, reasoning that the net asset value was 220 pence and so was cheap. The point is that the market knows that too. Therefore, a fundamental investor may think he is being smart with some shrewd information but, in fact, the market has already discounted it and it is reflected in the chart.

The problem with fundamental investors is that they can become convinced that they are right about a share and the market is wrong. It is, unfortunately, very expensive to argue with the market. Dennis Gartman expressed this as follows: 'The market is the sum total of the wisdom and the ignorance of all of those who deal in it; and we dare not argue with the market's wisdom'. Technical analysis can take out the emotion by objectively telling an investor it is time to buy, sell or do nothing. Chartists emphasise that you should be dispassionate about shares and never fall in love with them, as that clouds judgement, and they are definitely not in love with you.

Sometimes the stock picker is right but he needs a very powerful argument to hold or buy a share that the market dislikes. It is therefore risky. It is generally better to have a strong feeling about a share and have the market momentum behind you. That is why a fundamentalist approach is powerful when combined with technical analysis, so an investor has the best of both worlds. Neither is sufficient on its own.

Note that technical analysis applies to any graph and, in addition to shares, it can be used on sectors, funds, currencies, commodities, bonds and stock market indices. One rule of technical analysis is that shares are never too expensive to buy or too cheap to sell.

2. A chartist's view

a. The trend

'Buy low, sell high'. This advice seems obvious, but investors always ignore it. The demand curve for investment assets is like that for a luxury good-the higher the price, the greater the demand.'
Edward Chancellor, author of *Devil Take the Hindmost*.

Economics states that a price will be established where demand and supply are equal and the product will be sold. Normally, if the price rises then demand will drop and vice versa. This rule is sometimes reversed and increased prices can lead to increased, not reduced, demand when the emotional public take part and logic is replaced by greed and fear. It is a peculiarity of human behaviour that the demand for products, such as shares, which seem to promise a change in wealth, are subject to violent swings. This is not true demand in the sense of wanting to consume the product but the coveted asset is, instead, a store of wealth, which is to be maximised and then sold to a greater fool. Speculators extrapolate the past and think that price rises will continue so they buy more, not less, as the price rises. Houses are an example of demand increasing as prices rise because they become items of speculation to increase wealth, rather than places in which to live. Likewise, speculators extrapolate in a bear market and, thinking that prices will continue to fall, the result is that lower prices lead to lower demand.

Share trading is not determined, therefore, by existing prices but on expectations, resulting in the stock market producing trends rather than stability. When the trend is established, it will continue because the speculation increases until eventually it runs its course. This allows manias to flourish and it becomes a game of outwitting the enemy and anticipating what it will do under various scenarios. An understanding of this can be gained by looking at the master strategists of war, such as Napoleon or Sun Tzu in *The Art of War*.

The trend is your friend

'Trying to sell an illiquid stock in a down market brings to mind the galley slaves in Ben-Hur, chained to their bench while the ship sinks.'
Ralph Wanger

The key principle is the 'trend is your friend until the bend' in the share price chart. Investors should thus follow the line of least resistance, buying shares in an up trend and selling those in a down trend. Do not attempt to sell at the top or buy at the bottom. This cannot be done except by occasional fluke. For example, a speculator could have tried to catch the bottom of Marconi at any time from its height of £12 in the TMT mania as it spiralled downwards. Indeed, some may have thought it must be a raging buy at £2 because it was so recently 'worth' £12. The share carried on down to a penny. Instead, wait until the market has bottomed out and there is sustained recovery. Picking bottoms is foolhardy because a share in an established down trend will likely continue in that down trend for an unknown period and you will be dragged down with it. Let that fate befall the existing, hapless shareholders and do not volunteer to suffer their fate.

A typical scenario

A typical scenario is as follows. The trend starts but is not initially spotted. Buying then begins and reinforces the trend. The trend holds true and is confirmation to those testing the market. Confidence grows and the public jumps on the bandwagon. Prices then become far out of kilter with any valuation yardstick. Eventually, all that want to buy are in the market and, with no more demand, prices falter. This is the reversal point and it is unknowable because it depends on the actions and minds of the many. The same reinforcing process now happens in reverse with many sellers but few buyers. The trend has been your friend on the way up when speculators bought and vice versa on the way down. The long-term investor seeks value and will buy when prices are cheap. Thus, they will tend to be successful because they buy around the bottom before the trend is fully established. However, they do need to take profits when the party is over.

Trend examples

'Investment results largely depend on how one behaves near the top and near the bottom.'
John Maynard Keynes, economist and renowned investor.

There are up trends, down trends and sideways trends. Two points are needed for a trend line and a third confirms it. The trend line is shown in the line below.

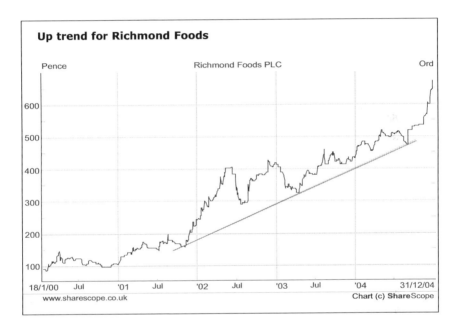

Note that in the up trend chart for Richmond Foods, the share price is making higher highs and higher lows, keeping the trend intact. Falls in the price are soon reversed. Buying on such a retrenchment is a wise strategy. The chart may start to increase in steepness in an up trend and further lines can be drawn confirming that the shorter-term trend lines are increasing.

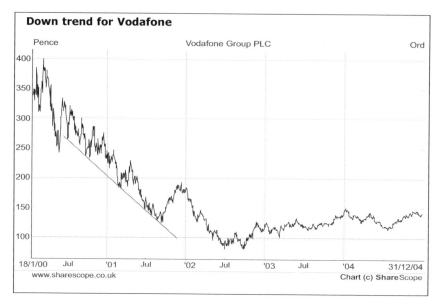

In the down trend chart for Vodafone, the share price is making lower lows and lower highs, also keeping the trend intact. Rallies in the price soon fail and new lows are reached. Buying on a rally and hoping the down trend is over is not a wise strategy.

The sideways trend in the Tesco chart below is a market for a trader who attempts to profit by buying near the bottom support line and selling at the top resistance line, since there is no real direction in the overall share.

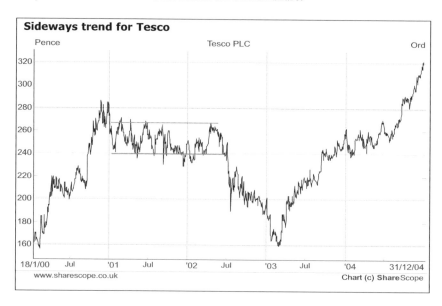

b. Support and resistance

'A picture is worth a thousand words.'
Fred Barnard, advertiser.

The market has a memory and is illustrated in the Tesco chart above. There are three groups of sellers when the price hits the upper resistance line at 270 for the second time. There are those that bought previously at the lower support line at 240 and want to realise the profit, those that previously bought at 270 and want to get their money back, and those that did not sell before at 270 but now can. These sellers cap the price and provide a resistance level at 270.

There are three groups of buyers when the share price then falls back again to 240. The first is investors who bought at 240 previously, then sold at 270 and want to repeat the profitable experience. The second is investors who previously sold at 240, then saw the price zoom up to 270 and now want to buy at 240, as they anticipate the share will go back to 270. The third is investors that did not buy at 240 but can now do so. These three groups buy at 240 and this becomes a support level.

The price holds at 240 but the rallies begin to fail as the buyers fade away. The price then falls through the 240 support, as all the investors at that level have already bought, and the price drops to 230. This is a good point to put your stop loss, as it should be placed just below the support level. The price rises to 240 again for the last time. This triggers selling because those that bought at 240 have a chance to get their money back and they take advantage of the opportunity. The rally fails, therefore, and the price drifts south again. Once the 240 support level is breached, it then turns into a resistance level. Note that the share makes numerous bottoms at around 240. This is bearish, as another attempt to fall through 240 is eventually successful as investors lose confidence in the share's ability to perform. The price then quickly drops below 200.

When a share breaks out above its resistance level, which is 270 in the example, this brings in waves of buyers who anticipate making a profit. All the existing holders are in profit so there is no forced selling to get their stake back and the share can carry on rising. Conversely, when a share gets into a down trend, any rally is hit by waves of sellers taking advantage of the now higher prices to get out. The down trend then continues.

A support level can be made by reference to previous lows and a resistance level by reference to previous highs. These are 230 and 270, respectively, in the above example. They can also be set by round numbers, e.g. buyers emerge when the FTSE 100 falls to 4,000. The levels can also be because of retrenchment of previous moves. A share can often bounce ahead of the support level as buyers are eagerly waiting in the wings and buy a little too early before it hits the support level. Very strong support is shown when a share has a steep 'V', as the reversal in the share is sudden. Where support levels are broken, especially over a long time frame, it is a very strong indicator that you should get out or short the shares. A sound strategy is to add to a winning share that is channelling upwards by buying when it bounces back up from its support line.

When a share hits a double top, or numerous tops, as at 270 above, the implication is that it is having difficulty breaking out as the sellers have the upper hand. This is a very strong sell signal and is definitely not the time to buy. Every failure to break out is a warning. If a break out is achieved, then buy quite early on to capture most of the up trend but not too soon, as you seek confirmation that the breakout is real. Continue to buy as successive breakouts are achieved. Never do the opposite and average down when support levels are successively broken, as that just reinforces investment failure. The trend here is a deadly enemy.

c. Moving averages

A moving average smoothes out the share price over a number of days by using an average value and provides a clearer view of the trend. It thus cuts out the 'noise' of a wiggly share price line. The moving average will be below the share price when a share is in an up trend and will be above the share price when a share is in a down trend.

At some point, the moving average will cross the price line and this provides a trading signal. However, the snag is that the moving average may not be firmly established if the share trades sideways and you can be bounced in and out of a share frequently. A shorter moving average, such as 80 days, will generate an earlier signal than a longer moving average, such as 200 days, but the tendency to be bounced in and out is greater. Conversely, a longer moving average will generate fewer false signals but the signal will be later and much of the price action may already have happened.

Moving averages are very good in trending markets as they keep investors in an up trend and out in a down trend market. As with trend, support and resistance lines, they do not work well when the markets are moving sideways, so do not use this system blindly.

The Telecom plus share price bottoms out and then enters a steep up trend: the moving average is below the price.

The Marconi share price tops out and then enters a steep down trend: the moving average is above the price.

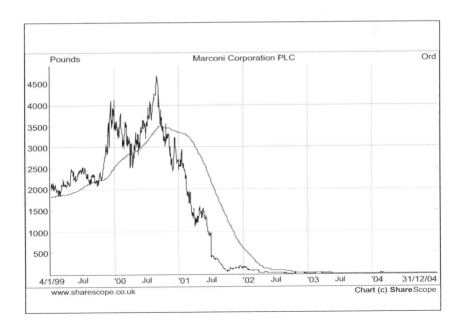

Using two moving averages

'Buying on the dips would be a great strategy if we only knew what point on the dip was lowest.'
Todd Jaycox, consultant.

Using two moving averages is ideal, as the shorter one of, say, 80 days will be closer to the price performance while the longer one of, say, 200 days helps to cut down on false signals. In an up trend, the price line will be on top, followed by the short-term moving average and then the long-term moving average. The converse is true with a share in a down trend. The trading signal comes when the short-term moving average crosses the long-term and is a golden cross.

If the short-term moving average, shown as dark grey, rises through the long-term moving average, shown as light grey, which is also moving up, then that signals a buy. This golden cross is marked circled below for RIT Capital Partners at 415. Buying at 415 would capture the run in the price all the way up to 700 with a good margin of safety.

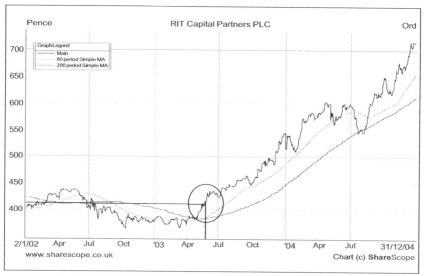

If the short-term moving average, shown as dark grey, falls through the long-term moving average, shown as light grey, which is also moving down, then that signals a sell. This golden cross is below for the FTSE 100 index at 6,400. Selling at 6,400 would avoid the pain of the bear market that fell to 3,280 by March 2003.

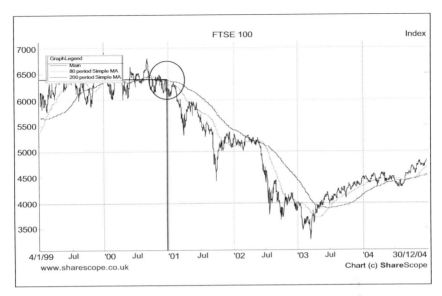

The problem with golden crosses is that there is a lag and the price could be much higher or lower by the time the golden cross occurs. Some chartists use trend-line analysis and support and resistance lines because of this, as they are similar ideas to moving averages but trigger earlier signals. More of the price action can be captured but it does increase the risk of a false signal. As can be seen in the charts above, the sell and buy signals come when the share price has risen some good way off the bottom with the buy and has fallen some good way off its peak in the case of the sell.

Health check

A quick look at a share portfolio can reveal its health just by checking whether all the moving averages are below the share price, so that they are all in healthy and established up trends. If the moving averages are below the share price then consider selling. Technical analysis can be used for short- and medium-term charts but tend to be more reliable over the longer term. For example, if a share hits a 10-year low then this is typically more significant than hitting a one-year low.

d. Relative strength

'My philosophy is to float like a jellyfish and let the market push me where it wants to go.'
Stuart Walton, in *Stock Market Wizards*.

There is strong evidence that technical analysis works. James O'Shaughnessy's book *What Works on Wall Street* looked at share selection methods for the 40 years up to 1994. It showed that good relative strength of the share compared to the market was a golden thread that ran though the best share selection methods. Conversely, shares with very low relative strength had extremely poor results. If a share rises by 20% and the market remains the same then the relative strength is 20% and this is the outperformance. If the share fell 20% instead, then the relative performance would be minus 20%. Relative strength numbers are widely available, such as on the Yahoo Finance website for each company or in REFS. Relative strength is useful as it is one, easily understood number and does encapsulate the above technical analysis. Therefore, if the latter does not appeal then you can use relative strength instead as a good proxy.

If you want to buy a share then always check that is has good relative strength. If it does not, then you would be wise to re-consider. Be very wary of buying a share with poor relative strength. Instead, it is a candidate for selling or shorting (i.e. selling a share you do not own). Relative strength should be positive for the last one, three and twelve months. If the trend in the share is about to end then this is likely to be evident in the last one and three months, so it is important to pay particular attention to recent relative strength. Strong recent relative strength can be a powerful share price driver as this may herald the start of a strong up trend. Relative strength is very useful in a bull market but remember it is a relative measure. Therefore, in a bear market, you could have a share with good relative strength yet is still losing money, albeit one that it is losing less than the market as a whole. The key objective in a bear market is still to make a real return or at least preserve capital. Lastly, the above analysis also applies to sector relative strength and, if this is strong, it provides a favourable tailwind for the shares in that sector and can be a powerful share price driver.

Such is the importance of relative strength that it provides an excellent first sieve of all the shares in the market. After all, if strong relative strength is a pre-requisite then all the shares which fail to qualify can be dismissed without further ado. One approach to select those that are in multi-year up trends is to flick quickly through the charts of the 1,900 shares in the market in the monthly book edition of REFS. This does not take long and should boil the population down to the best 30 candidates or so for further sieving. Note that relative strength here measures a share against the overall market. It is not the same as the popular relative strength indicator, or RSI, which measures the relative upward movement of a share versus its average downward movement.

e. Investment strategy

'My basic advice is don't lose money.'
Jim Rogers, co-founder of the Quantum Fund with George Soros and author of *Investment Biker*.

The market trend is of utmost importance because most investors only gain in a strong bull market. At all other times one needs the skill and techniques to take the money from others who have the same objective. Other critical factors include psychology and risk and are discussed in chapter 9. Basic technical analysis does provide an edge but is less significant than these factors.

Markets take time to reach their highs and lows and they do not go suddenly from a top to a bottom or vice versa. This gives time for investors to buy and sell safely. Run profits and quickly cut losses. You should always use stop losses. Trends provide an opportunity since history tends to repeat itself. Amateurs buy ignorantly but most investors use fundamentals, such as the Marks & Spencer example where they would consider buying as it traded below net asset value. The more that people use a system, such as technical analysis, the less useful it becomes, as not everyone can make money by adopting the same approach. Although it is likely that only a minority of investors do use technical analysis, there are enough of them to introduce an element of the outcome becoming self-fulfilling.

Be an active investor and examine your portfolio at least once a month but avoid day trading. Investors can long or short a security, using such instruments as contracts for difference or futures contracts. Markets can be cloudy at times and very difficult to read, so there is a time to trade and a time to leave alone until the picture is clearer. Generally, only about 3% of shares have good charts that look interesting enough to trade for an investor using basic technical analysis. It makes sense to buy in the strongest sectors as a starting point and avoid the weakest ones.

Trends, moving averages and support and resistance levels are very helpful in timing the purchase and sale of shares. However, some technical analysts believe other tools are less useful, such as triangles, Elliott Wave, volumes and candles.

This is because more is not necessarily better and using too many tools, some of which are esoteric, can indicate overwhelming buy or sell signals. The snag is that there is often one indicator that does not work or is overlooked. As a result, they believe technical analysis should be kept to basics using the KISS principle (Keep It Simple, Stupid). A basic level of technical analysis is appropriate in the context of this book, as there are five other weapons to deploy and that all takes time. Therefore, simple but effective technical analysis may be more appropriate than a long, detailed, and possibly ineffective, analysis that could hold up decision-making.

Technical analysis does not work well in a raging bull market, like the TMT mania, as the price line becomes too steep. Moving averages will lag too far behind the price action and much of it will be lost when the share price eventually falls. In such circumstances, the best approach is to run a tight stop loss system and thus lock in profits.

Conclusion

Technical analysis is a useful aid in timing the trading in shares that have been selected on fundamental criteria. The trend is your friend until the bend. This can be spotted by looking at support and resistance lines. If the price breaks down through a support line, the share should, prima facie, be sold. If the price breaks up through a resistance line, it should, prima facie, be bought. Moving averages are a similar idea, and lead to fewer false signals, but less of the price action will be captured. If the short-term moving average passes up through the long-term moving average, then that is a strong buy signal. If the short-term moving average falls through the long-term moving average then that is a strong sell signal. The relative strength of a share is a good proxy for technical analysis, is easy to use and there is strong empirical evidence that it is an essential tool for outperformance. Lastly, this chapter is aimed at investments over the medium-term rather than the short-term. There is a great difference of emphasis required when moving from the one to the other. Successful medium-term investing methods can be useless over the short-term and vice versa.

Resources

Sharescope charting software is inexpensive and good enough for professionals. For example, it can sieve the market for golden crosses. Portfolio Advantage and Updata are good but more expensive. Many websites are useful for charting. ADVFN.co.uk provides much free information including excellent charts, although they cannot be printed out. It has two very good bulletin boards, one of which is free. Bigcharts.com is free and has better charts than ADVFN but are small. However, they are extremely flexible, such as for drawing trend lines, and can magnify any time period. Stockcharts.com has free technical analysis educational guidance in addition to charts, many of which are free. Yahoo.com is another useful free site. Investtech.com provides a brief commentary on each share to interpret the chart, although these are computer-generated and can be rather general. Contact details are included in the further information at the end of the book.

CHAPTER 7

First-hand experience of the product: scuttlebutting

'Reading the printed financial records about a company is never enough to justify an investment. One of the major steps in prudent investment must be to find out about a company's affairs from those who have some direct familiarity with them.'

Philip Fisher, author of *Common Stocks and Uncommon Profits*.

Definition of scuttlebutting

The term 'scuttlebutt' describes the chatting that would take place round the scuttlebutt, the name of a water barrel or butt on a ship. In investing terms, it means assessing a company by testing it for yourself through empirical observation. Philip Fisher brought this method to prominence and suggested talking to company employees, suppliers, customers, company management and knowledgeable people within the industry. This way you can try to assess the real company and its strengths and weaknesses. This can involve much work and not everybody will be willing to discuss the company so it does have limitations.

Sectors to scuttlebutt

Scuttlebutting can be carried out more easily in some sectors than others and are principally those with consumer products that can be readily accessed and tested. Visiting retail outlets and discussing the business with the staff is often a very good source of information. Scuttlebutting is less useful when the product is more technical and sold to businesses. Suitable sectors include: telecommunications; insurance and life insurance; media and entertainment; banks; some support services such as estate agents; general retailers; transport; real estate; food and drug retailers; leisure and hotels; utilities; tobacco; food producers and processors; beverages; and some information technology software and hardware that is consumer-orientated, rather than business-orientated.

Asking management

The people most knowledgeable about a company are its management. There are several ways to gain access to them and ask questions.

1. AGM

Management may normally be reluctant to spend time answering investors' questions but a prime time to quiz them is at the AGM. After the formalities of the meeting, there is usually some refreshment and the directors can mingle freely. However, if an investor asks a pertinent question and is fobbed off with a 'reassuring' but unconvincing answer then do not be surprised. Your question has, in fact, been answered and the shares should be avoided. Most people gain an impression of what someone is like very quickly and a chat with a number of directors should enable an assessment as to whether they are honest, trustworthy and capable. Also, assess them when they make their presentations and see if they have a tendency to 'spin' the company's progress. Unfortunately, this is very likely to be the case, as evidenced by the fact that almost all companies employ financial public relations firms to interface with the City and investors. Indeed, if you find one that does not, like Morrisons Supermarkets, then that is a point in its favour. Even so, an investor should try to see if the directors are presenting a true and fair view.

2. Calling the company

Calling the company can be tried. Management are likely to be very busy so the response an investor receives may be limited. However, many companies can be helpful and answer investor's questions, although they will not divulge price-sensitive information. You can get a feel of a company just by how long it takes to answer the phone, whether the employees are helpful and if calls are promptly returned.

3. Investment conferences

There are a many investment and business conferences every year and there will be presentations made by companies to investors. Obviously, these are public relations exercises but, nevertheless, it is an easy way to gain an understanding. The companies will often have stands around the conference hall with senior management available all day, so this can be a useful opportunity to obtain information. Indeed, by their very presence, the company is making a statement that they are interested in encouraging people to invest and are likely to be shareholder-friendly.

Broker research

'Investing without research is like playing poker without looking at the cards.'
Peter Lynch

Broker research is scuttlebutting by proxy, as investors can gain insight into the company via analysts. The research notes are often worth their weight in gold, as the analysts should have met and talked with management at length and over some years. They want to keep their jobs so they may not always provide a true and fair view about all the company's prospects. This is particularly the case if it is the house broker, who might have a conflict of interest, since it provides research and an opinion about a company which is paying them. However, the actual wording used in a broker note can be indicative and it always useful to see what is not included. For example, if management is regarded as strong and respected in the city this point will usually be made and there should be some evidence to back up this assertion, such as track records. If the broker note is silent about management's capabilities then that can be a telling sign. Generally, broker research is extremely useful for a SWOT analysis (strengths, weaknesses, opportunities and threats).

This research is provided as a matter of course to institutions and the financial press. It is not normally available to the public, although a company might be willing to give an investor a copy. However, it can be bought and Reuters has a comprehensive collection from 50 sources at reuters.co.uk under research reports. Prices are typically in the £8 to £20 range. This is a small investment to make if thousands of pounds are at stake. Ask the company, public relations firm or the brokers which are the best notes and also seek the latest and lengthiest. Another source is Investorease, which contains extensive narrative for several years for all companies, including summaries of brokers' views where applicable. Investors Chronicle features brokers' views for some companies.

Competitors

Competitors can be a useful source of information and can be quite revealing. The higher up the management ladder you go then the cagier the answer is likely to be and very often the person on the shop floor can be helpful. Bear in mind that competitors may have an axe to grind and their opinions may lack objectivity.

Independent research

Independent research is worth noting from consumer organisations, such as Which? and JD Power. There are numerous surveys carried out into cars, holidays, financial services, retailers, electronic goods, etc. and the winners and losers can be telling. For example, car companies like Ford, Vauxhall, Citroën and Peugeot are typically at the bottom of the pile and the Japanese are at the top. This information is useful in deciding which companies can benefit from a tailwind, such as car distributors and components suppliers. MyTravel is the renamed Airtours and has not scored well. This should have been a sell sign before its share price collapsed. Criticism of retailers and selling tactics of utility companies are also pointers. This research provides good copy for the press and, to make life easy, an investor can absorb the information that way without the need to look at the original research.

Investors' clubs

It is hard to be a solitary investor, as the chief enemy is looking back at you in the mirror. It is wise to seek the counsel of others and an investment club can be a useful source of pooling information and dividing work if sharing out a project, such as analysing a company. A good starting point would be SIGnet, which is The Serious Investor Groups network with 700 members who meet in 20 regions. UK Shareholders Association (UKSA) seeks to empower individual shareholders and Proshare promotes wider share ownership and financial education. Their contact details are at the back of this book.

Networking

It is frequently the case that the answer you want is but one person away from someone you know. People are often very happy to pass investors down a chain of connections. Other sources of information can come from networks of friends, neighbours, and family plus work and social contacts.

The internet

The internet is constantly expanding and contains eight billion 'surface' pages searchable through Google, for example, plus perhaps 500 billion more contained in the little known 'deep web'. More information on the latter is at brightplanet.com and a deep web search engine is completeplanet.com. The internet has a wealth of information that can be very helpful and the speed of access quickens the analytical process. The bulletin boards in financial websites, such as ADVFN and Hemscott, have messages posted and these can be accessed for an individual company. Much of the comment is, admittedly, poor or from share 'rampers' but some of it can be useful. For instance, there can be comments from people who have tried the company's products, as well as from current or past employees who give feedback. Given that the bulletin boards are nationwide, the coverage can be far in excess of what a single individual can achieve. In addition, you can post and ask a specific question, such as what is the trading at a new outlet? For example, one retailer that was selling direct had over 200 bulletin posts, containing information about working conditions, customer satisfaction and sales volumes.

Trying the product

Trying the product can be very helpful. If you have a complaint, does the company try to fob you off or do they really try to make amends? Dissatisfied customers are unlikely to return, especially if complaints are unresolved. Is your supermarket always out of the products that you want, especially so-called specials? Do the employees then irritate you by saying that they are victims of their own success? Do you leave the store thinking that was money well spent or unhappy at what you have bought? What do friends and family have to say? The snag is whether your experience is mirrored at other outlets and whether the City shares your conclusions about the company. In other words, you need to feel that the information you have gained is applicable to the whole company and that eventually the market will recognise it.

Scuttlebutting examples

'Never underestimate the power of an irate customer.'
Joel Ross, management guru.

Here are some scuttlebutting examples. Late on the last Saturday afternoon before Christmas in 1998, a local Marks & Spencer store was practically deserted. It should have been thronging with last minute shoppers. Had they all done their shopping and already gone home? Were they waiting for the sales to start instead? Then there was one significant director's share sale and the company issued a profit warning on 14th January 1999, saying that there had been a slump in Christmas sales. The news stunned analysts and the shares fell 13%. An investor that saw the dearth of customers could have sold well in advance.

The following companies have not been identified, as they are based on personal experiences and confidences. A manager of a pub, that was part of a chain, revealed at a conference that the mangers were 'prima donnas' and were not working as a team. He had dumbed-down its highly-rated menu and the days of trying to find an empty table had gone. Such poor management was unlikely to have the ability to create shareholder value. However, the net asset per share was far in excess of the share price and a takeover was a strong possibility. This duly happened at a substantial premium. A visit to another pub chain in the country in winter showed that the food was poor and there were no other customers. That chain bombed.

A visit to a pizza chain's new outlet showed that the waiting list at the weekend was a staggering five weeks and persisted even during the week, normally a quiet period. This may have been because of lack of competition, because it was new and being tried out or because the product was good value for money. The shares were nonetheless struggling. However, a revisit confirmed that the queues had died away with curiosity satisfied. Several managers had left in a matter of weeks and the staff were overworked, demoralised and underpaid. The food was tedious. Nevertheless, the roll out of outlets has been successful thus far.

At another pizza chain, a waiter mentioned that they were mostly students and the company was keen to retain them by keeping their jobs open after their holidays to provide continuity. They were polite, intelligent, friendly and provided a youthful air. They are a valuable asset, as they are the interface with the customer. Food retailing typically has high turnover of casual staff. That chain has continued to prosper.

A holiday company is ideal for scuttlebutting and bad service is quickly unearthed. In one company, the experience was so poor that the customer service department should have been renamed 'customer disservice' department and, clearly, the shares were to be avoided. Indeed, it subsequently ran into serious trouble and the shares plummeted.

A roll-out of a retail chain is easy to scuttlebutt and a visit to one revealed that the CEO was behind one of the counters on Christmas Eve, helping the customers, gaining shop floor feedback and boosting staff morale. No ivory tower and power meetings here but evidence of a CEO who was prepared to get his hands dirty. That chain has continued to expand.

A visit to a nightclub chain showed that, in the west end of London at least, a round of four drinks was a mighty £28 and that customers were well-heeled and thought nothing of it. This meant that pricing pressure was not an issue and the margins were excellent. That chain has experienced mixed fortunes because some regional outlets have significant pricing pressures.

A glance through newspapers and magazines shows the amount of advertising and that is a comment on not only their circulation but is a litmus test of the health of the economy. Job advertisements are another key indicator. Many publications state their ABC circulation, which is audited, and rises or falls are an easy check on the economic pulse.

Transport is straightforward to scuttlebutt, such as comparing and contrasting a flight with a low-cost carrier, compared to a national flagship. Trains are in a class of their own for consumer dissatisfaction and performance levels can easily be assessed.

One supermarket was emphasising its organic produce but a visit revealed that it was expensive and was not being bought, probably because its customers were from a very cost-conscious segment. What else might management mis-handle if it had so misjudged this? It issued a profit warning. A visit to a new store at another chain clearly demonstrated they were streets ahead in design, product choice and display and it was a pleasure to shop there. It has gone from strength to strength.

A minor food producer entered into what looked like an advantageous contract with a blue chip company. This augmented its production for supermarkets and its own minor brands. Visits to outlets showed the product was good, new lines were being added and customers were happily buying. The company's profits continued to grow.

Two discount clothes stores showed that one was fairly empty with 'me-too' stock and prices. The other was packed with shoppers who were pulling stock off the shelves, as they were selling very cheap, end-of-line stock in a price conscious part of the country. The former was going downhill until it was revitalised with a bolt-on acquisition. The latter was unexpectedly overwhelmed with accounting irregularities and taken over.

Internet operations are easy to scuttlebutt. One drinks chain that offered internet sales made life easy with e-mailed promotions. An order was placed and executed flawlessly. The delivery was on time and the employee was a credit to the company. The customer saved money and did not even have to leave his house. That chain is making strong progress. A non-internet competitor would not match the price and did not deliver, so did not win the business.

Property is easy to scuttlebutt and it is useful to keep an eye on projects which have foundered in past recessions, such as hotels, golf courses, business parks and housing developments. In a boom, these long abandoned projects are dusted off and rushed to market where any old thing sells at a high price. What is noticeable is that some particularly unpleasant ones are being developed that could not get off the ground even in previous booms, suggesting this mania is more extreme than before. It is a strong clue that the bust will be similarly extreme.

Visiting the premises

'One 1'.

Number plate on a university vice chancellor's car.

Visiting the premises is very useful. A retail outlet is a public place and can be visited easily. Company premises are private and are more difficult. Nevertheless, you might visit them by arranging a meeting with the investor relations department, if they have one, or just ask if you can go. The response can be revealing in itself.

Some companies have costly, palatial head offices that appear to be an ego trip for management. One institutional investor always visits the offices of a prospective company and counts the number of Porsches in the car park. Others have a spartan approach to life, such as Warren Buffett who runs his Berkshire Hathaway empire from a tiny head office. He does have a corporate jet, however! A utility reseller has a low-cost business model and its very head modest office is in keeping with that. The board has a large stake in the business and presumably they think of their own money being spent. One entertainment chain held its AGM in a themed marquee in a stately home. In the meantime, toilet seats had fallen off in an outlet and the walls and bar were badly scuffed. This seemed like management were enjoying themselves, instead of attending to the efficient running of the business. It has not survived.

One fund management group has splendid, opulent premises. They provide an uplifting work environment and the building is likely to be a good investment. Crucially, do they bring in customers and professional contacts that want to deal with such an organisation? Probably yes, so the grandeur may not be self-indulgence. At another group, the fund manager would hold court for hours after the AGM, answering all sorts of questions and giving a tremendous download on a whole range of investment topics that you would gladly pay to hear. That fund was worth buying just for the exposure to his brains and experience. It was reaffirmation that investors' money was in safe hands. By contrast, others treat the AGM perfunctorily, offering little fund manager contact.

Which director?

'Always tell the truth. That way you don't have to remember anything.'
Mark Twain

If you have the opportunity to speak to any member of the board, then the best one is typically the finance director. He will usually have the most complete and accurate picture, as he is responsible for the entire financial operation. He will be highly trained, intelligent and hard working and been used to the concept of true and fair when he cut his teeth in the auditing profession. Once working outside the profession for a company, he will have carried on providing a true and fair view of the company's performance to the board and, hopefully, the same to shareholders in the audited annual accounts. An institute of accountants regulates him so he will have professional integrity to bear in mind. He will be disinclined to run the risk of being reported to the institute and perhaps struck off. In other words, you are more likely to get a better answer from the finance director than any other director. The next best bet is the CEO but they can have a salesman's optimism or be 'colourful characters', without the professional restraints of the finance director. Often, they have a weaker grasp of operations and sometimes are plain wrong. Finance directors are not a panacea, however, as they can sometimes be 'economical with the truth' and occasionally they lie blatantly, although this is very much the exception rather than the rule.

A list of sample questions to the finance director might include the following. Please see chapters 1 and 2 for a more detailed explanation of some of these terms.

Checklist of sample questions to ask the finance director

Business model

What is the business model, how has it changed and what plans, if any, are there to change it?

Customers

Are customers glued to you?
Does the company improve the economics of the customer's business?
Why should a customer deal with you rather than a competitor?
How many customers do you have?

What is the percentage of turnover from the top five and ten customers?
Are there recurring and long-term revenues and what is their percentage
of turnover?
How big is the order book as a percentage of turnover?
Are customers locked in and, if so, are they happy to be so?
Why are contracts not renewed, why do customers not return and why are
new sales pitches lost?
How many sales pitches turn into contracts?
What is the contract renewal rate?
Are contracts lumpy?
How will demand fare in a recession?
Are customers long-term or transactional?
Is there resistance to a sales model, e.g. buy versus rent?
Do they have superior channels to market, i.e. how do they sell: clicks and
mortar?

Competition

What is the competition for each product in the UK and overseas?
How do you compete: price, service, unique selling point?
Is the competition intensifying?
Whom do you most fear?

People

Is there an emphasis on training staff, especially sales and customer care?
Is there a board member dedicated to customers?
How well do the board members and senior management know the
customers, pay site visits and obtain feedback?
What is his shareholding in the company and changes thereto?
What does he feel about the share price?
When and why did he join the company?
Who would he like to work for if not this company?

Product

Do you have a superior or must-have product?
Do you have patents?
Do you have a differentiated product – e.g. is it perceived as offering better
value?

What is the percentage of the overall market for each product?

Which of the products has greatest potential and why?

What are the margins in each product and trend compared to competitors?

When is the revenue recognised? This is particularly relevant to software companies.

Sector

Who has the power in the sector? Is it the supplier, producer, distributor or customer? How much power does your firm have? Is it changing?

What are the sector economics and are they changing?

What effect does technology have on your business – inputs, production, distribution and channels to market?

What special problems are there in your business and the sector?

Is there takeover potential?

What is the policy towards acquisitions?

What are the biggest threats to your company and the sector?

What are the barriers to entry and exit?

Conclusion

Scuttlebutting is not a panacea but it is a good check. If you are keen to buy but have poor scuttlebutting then that is a warning sign. You should be keen to buy and have positive scuttlebutting. The opposite is true if you want to sell. Scuttlebutting can provide a unique insight into the company before the market wakes up to the positive or negative story.

CHAPTER 8

Accounting for growth

'Company accounting is a jungle with many species of animal – some benign, some carnivorous – and its own rules. Anyone who believes this is an exaggeration should read one of the entertaining studies of the securities industry, most notably Liar's Poker.'
Terry Smith, *Accounting For Growth*

There is a tremendous amount of spinning in reporting company results. This is unlikely to lessen in an age where moral standards have dropped alarmingly at all levels of authority and society. There has been widespread adoption of base, rather than higher, values and greed is endemic. It is difficult to think of any part of the 'Establishment' that stands in higher regard than it did two decades ago, as each segment has blotted its copy book in turn, like politicians, or become marginalised, such as the church. Businessmen live in this 'brave new world' and bring this lack of values with them to their work. Remnants of the 'old school' are rare, although they are discernable in some companies like Hardys & Hansons and Morrisons Supermarkets. The old concepts of 'my word is my bond' and settling deals on a handshake have long gone. 'Caveat emptor', meaning let the buyer beware, is now the watchword. The directors' motivation is simple. They are selling their performance and the company's prospects to the reader and, with huge share options at stake, they have an added conflict of interest in putting on the rosiest gloss possible. Therefore, investors are right to be suspicious of not taking part in a mug's game and the utmost caution is needed.

Terry Smith's book in 1992 *Accounting For Growth* opened the lid on how companies resorted to various tricks to increase their profits and is still a classic today. The backlash from companies was so intense that he sought alternative employment, which indicates that it hit upon the truth, rather than being an academic exercise. The areas he covered were: pre-acquisition write-downs; disposals; deferred consideration; extraordinary and exceptional items; off balance sheet finance; contingent liabilities; capitalisation of costs; brands; depreciation; convertibles; pension funds; and currency mismatching. This chapter examines five further areas that should be understood before buying any share. They are broker forecasts, cash flow, dividends, goodwill and share options.

1. Broker forecasts – every one a buy or hold

The TMT mania, in particular, showed that broker forecasts were widely wrong, both in the expected earnings and in their buy, hold or sell recommendations. Forecasts are the essence of valuing a share but their integrity is undermined, due to brokers having potential conflicts of interest.

Importance of forecasts

Broker forecasts are an essential tool in valuing shares, such as the PEG system, popularised by guru Jim Slater. Since the PEG is the price earnings ratio divided by the earnings growth rate, any error in the latter renders the PEG unreliable. However, in spite of profit forecasts often being inaccurate, some guidance is better than none. Why are forecasts sometimes suspect?

Every one a buy or hold

Typically, the FTSE 100 companies' consensus broker forecasts do not contain a single sell recommendation. Instead, half the shares are usually rated buys with the rest as a hold. Similarly, the NASDAQ 100 in December 2000, before the full pain of the bear market was yet to be felt, had only three holds and all the rest were a buy or accumulate. Not a single share was rated a sell, which was ridiculous since the laws of probability would suggest a more equal spread of buys, holds and sells, with perhaps a third in each category. The NASDAQ 100 subsequently collapsed by four-fifths. Amazingly, Yahoo was still rated a buy after losing a staggering 84% of its value in 2000, only to lose a further 39% in 2001. Therefore, a realist could interpret 'broker-speak' by treating a strong buy as a buy, a buy as a hold and a hold as a sell.

Conflict of interest

'Enron: strong buy.'
Four analysts continued this recommendation until a few days before the fraudulent Enron collapsed. The four banks that employed them received huge fees from Enron as they were involved in selling $25 billion of its securities and advised on numerous lucrative takeovers.

Why do brokers recommend either buying or holding but not selling? One likely reason is a conflict of interest. The broker forecasts tend to be run as a loss-leader by the investment banks that produce them, as forecasts are generally freely available to clients or at a modest cost. Instead, a lucrative business for investment banks is the secondary profit zone of huge fees from companies for finance work, such as takeovers, new issues of shares, diversification advice and mergers. Thus, the forecasts tend to be biased in the companies' favour because they can open the door to selling these high-margin, follow-on services. Naturally, the investment bank does not wish to upset an existing or potential client so it will be more inclined to accept a rosy view of prospects and will be very reluctant to issue a sell note. Unsurprisingly, a study found that 20% of US companies admitted that negative research would lead to no business being awarded to the investment bank. That 20% figure is likely to be much higher in reality.

Lack of objectivity

Management should know what their results are likely to be, based on daily developments and board meetings in their company. Brokers, by contrast, do not have access to such confidential information and rely on management to assist with their research. Thus, the forecasts can be very much what the management wants and sometimes they simply tell the brokers what the forecast should be, or 'guide' them in the required direction.

Is this lack of broker objectivity a problem? It can be if management have their interests at the forefront of their minds, rather than those of the shareholders. For example, some management have the short-term share price movement as a priority. This applies more to those who have an 'employee' eye to running the business. Their motivation may be to maximise their share options and remuneration. This is much more common with large companies in the FTSE 350. In contrast, 'owner' managers of smaller companies often have large shareholdings and may have built up the company over many years. Their objective should be to create long-term value and they are maybe less concerned about short-term price movements. Therefore, for some 'employee' management, there is a natural tendency to wish to present the prospects in as rosy a light as possible for as long as possible. A warning that profits will fall short of the forecasts will unfortunately restore reality in the end, of course. However, reality can be obscured by 'smoke and mirrors' accounting, such as for goodwill, and this is examined in this chapter. Further, it is not unheard of for directors to sell shares just before a profit warning and thus benefit from an unrealistic forecast out there in the market beforehand.

Broker reputations

Some company directors have scratched their heads at independently-produced broker forecasts, admitting that they have very little idea about their results and so how could the broker forecast be meaningful? Other forecasts are simply the extrapolation of the past into the future. The reputation of brokers is enhanced or reduced over time, depending on their forecasting track record. Consequently, some broker forecasts are well respected and others are not. Therefore, the credibility of a forecast can be enhanced, or otherwise, depending on who issues it. Therefore, it is important to consider the broker's reputation.

Time for a change

One healthy development is that the broking arm of HSBC recognised that it was unrealistic to issue constantly upbeat forecasts and it said in 2001 that it would issue as many sell recommendations as buy recommendations. This is an important first step in producing forecasts which are more even-handed and, hopefully, will be followed by other brokers, now held up in an unfavourable light. In addition, there are moves in the US and the UK to ensure there are more effective 'Chinese walls' between the brokers and the investment bankers, following large fines. Finally, stricter regulation might result in more objective and useful forecasts.

Conclusion

Single forecasts have limitations, so investors should use databases like REFS or Yahoo Finance to see the various forecasts from competing brokers and the consensus view. This is a guide for investors to form their own judgements. For example, is the house broker's forecast more favourable than the consensus? Forecasts are largely 'guesstimates' but they are better than flying blind. It is precisely because of this notorious unreliability that it is essential to use the techniques outlined in this book to achieve an adequate margin of safety when investing. The starting point is to consider the soundness of the business model and resultant competitive advantage of the company and its sector.

2. Cash flow – a flawed investment tool

'My accountant says that I did this at a very bad time. My stocks are down. I'm cash poor, or something. I've got no cash flow. I'm not liquid. Something is not flowing. I don't know, but those people have got a language of their own.'
Woody Allen, from the film 'Manhattan'.

Cash is the lifeblood of any business. It is needed to pay for factors of production, such as labour, plus reinvestment, dividends, taxes, etc. It has been seized upon by some as a panacea for assessing a company, with the thinking that if the cash flow is good then the business is attractive. Although cash flow is a useful tool, it is flawed. Forecast growth in earnings per share (EPS) and the PER are more appropriate numbers to find out whether a share offers growth at a reasonable price.

What is cash flow?

Firstly, operating cash flow is calculated by taking the operating profit for the period and adjusting for various 'non-cash' items. These include depreciation, amortisation of goodwill and changes in debtors and stock. Depreciation, for example, is an estimate of the amount that an asset has fallen in value but no cash has actually been paid relating to this item in the current period. That cash was paid years ago when the asset was originally bought. Secondly, operating cash flow is then adjusted for such items as tax paid, capital expenditure, dividends and loans to arrive at the amount that the net cash of the company has increased or decreased in the year. The easiest and most effective way to check cash flow is to compare operating profit with operating cash flow and any significant difference may be an indication of accounting for growth.

The case for cash flow

Proponents of cash flow like to rely on this tool and ignore EPS. They point to the saying that accounts are an opinion but cash is fact. Cash is difficult to falsify, which is reassuring at a time when accounts are mistrusted after the creative accounting at Enron and other fiascos. Profits are easily manipulated by methods of accounting for growth. Cash flow fans also like to examine the operating cash flow return on capital employed, compared to the risk-free return from a bank deposit or alternative risk investments, such as a company in the same sector.

Operating cash flow can be adjusted to include or exclude a number of items, such as interest, capital expenditure and tax.

Similarly, capital employed can be adjusted to assess management's stewardship. An example might be to increase property assets that have not been revalued for years, as in the case of Hardys & Hansons. However, cash return on capital employed is not a panacea, as companies use different amounts of capital. Nevertheless, it could be a useful guide when comparing similar companies in the same sector. For example, Ultimate Leisure has one of the highest returns on capital in the bar and clubs sector, in spite of the fact that its estate is largely freehold and thus uses more capital compared to competitors who rent. These are all reasonable points to make in support of cash flow but it needs to be treated with caution, as explained below.

Problems with cash flow

a. a muddle

The main problem with cash flow is that it combines profit and loss and balance sheet items. The former increases shareholders' equity but not the latter. For example, a profit of £1 million increases shareholders' equity by that amount. If there is a £1 million increase in a balance sheet item, such as creditors, then this does not affect shareholders' equity, as it will merely be offset by an increase in another asset, such as debtors. There is no change to shareholders' equity therefore. An investor should thus be very interested in the profit and loss account but less interested in the balance sheet. Cash flow unfortunately draws on both these items, only one of which increases equity, namely the profit and loss account.

b. lack of interpretation

Take an example of a company that, on the face of it, has good cash flow. Suppose this arose because there was an increase in creditors. There is typically inadequate analysis of this number in the accounts so there is no way of assessing the significance of this increase. It may indeed be a bad sign, in that the company is strapped for cash and having problems in paying its bills. Alternatively, the increase could be for purely normal business reasons, such as a seasonal increase in stocks. Therefore, it is very difficult, if not impossible, to interpret adequately whether the increase in creditors is a concern or not. Therefore, although an investor can see the constituents of cash flow, he is not much wiser.

c. looking backwards

Cash flow is an historical number, as it is contained in the accounts that have been published by the company. An investor is primarily concerned with what will happen in the future, rather than what has happened in the past, and, for this reason, forecast EPS are more helpful than cash flow.

d. difficult to understand

Some companies have simple business models and the cash flow is easy to understand and can give an accurate picture. Other companies are not particularly clear, usually due to reasons like restructuring, goodwill, acquisitions and the effects of currency movements. Cash flow is difficult to interpret at the best of times and such companies do not lend themselves to easy cash flow analysis. If a company is complicated then this is one reason to consider avoiding it.

e. good cash flow can be bad

A company that has poor prospects may nevertheless have good cash flow. Assume that it cannot find attractive projects in which to invest and, as a result, the cash flow appears to be strong. It is a strength arising out of weakness. Manufacturing companies often have good cash flow because they tend to have high depreciation charges which are added back to profit to produce the cash flow number. Conversely, building companies tend to have poor cash flow as they invest cash in their land banks. Therefore, the company may be unattractive in spite of its seemingly strong cash flow and vice versa. Fortunately, a look at the forecast growth in profits should alert an investor to this anomaly. Conversely, a company that is growing strongly because it is opening new outlets may consume significant cash and be tapping the stock market for yet more. Again, the forecast growth in profits should be a reassurance. Therefore, cash flow on its own can be a misleading measure of the attractiveness of a company.

The solution

Cash flow per share should ideally be in excess of earnings per share, so that the profit is really being turned into cash. If it is not, then find out why. If it just seems to be due to a normal increase in creditors or reduction in debtors, for example, then this should not be a problem. It is more useful to check the cash flow trend over a number of years rather than just one year, as this will tend to highlight any accounting for growth. If the company consistently fails to turn EPS into cash then the share may well be avoided.

Another measure is the price to cash flow (PCF). This is merely the cash produced per share, say 10 pence, as a percentage of the price, say 100 pence. The PCF is 10, which means that 10% of the market capitalisation is being turned into cash. A very high and persistent PCF of say 20% or above is a good indication that the share is attractive. However, recognise that the cash flow number has the flaws mentioned above and an investor should examine why the cash flow is good.

Conclusion

The conclusion is that investors should assess a company by considering the growth rate of EPS and the PER, although cash flow should always be examined. Do not necessarily dismiss a company if the cash flow is less than EPS or turns negative. Examine the reason and if it looks to be in the normal course of business then it may not be a worry. Cash flow on its own should not be the tail that wags the dog.

3. Dividends – to be or not to be?

'The most important thing in communications is to hear what is not being said.'
Peter Drucker, management guru.

Dividends are now valuable

The bear market that started in 2000 caused much pain to shareholders' net worth and many portfolios halved in value. However, the return from a share is also determined by the dividends paid and they account for two thirds of the total return, capital gains representing the remaining third. They are hard cash in the hand that can be spent and they should be uppermost in investors' minds. The perspective has turned full circle from the TMT mania, when rocketing share prices were the prime objective and dividends were unimportant. Indeed, dividends could have been frowned upon as that money could have been used to grow the 'wonderful' businesses that were driving the new economy. Not any more. The stock market yield is normally around 4% over the longer term, compared to just 2% in 2000 at the height of the mania.

Dividends paid out of capital

However, accounting for growth is still with us and the disease has infected dividends. This is surprising, perhaps, as the payment of a dividend looks like a simple enough transaction. The problem arises when the dividend is not paid out of profits but effectively out of capital. The accounting profession and company law state that dividends can only be paid out of profits. If they were paid out of capital then that would represent a reduction in the amount available to pay creditors. The capital is intended to be preserved and is a quid pro quo for the limited liability that companies enjoy. A court order is required to reduce capital in the normal course of affairs for that very reason. It is startling, therefore, that companies are effectively reducing their capital by paying dividends. Not only does such a dividend mislead shareholders but they also have to pay income tax on what is, in essence, their own capital. The capital will be run down because of the dividend and will need to be replenished at some stage. This is achieved through endless new rights issues which effectively fund these 'dividends'. The usual suspects over the decades both here and in the US have included the oil, chemical, automobile, utility, telecommunication and railway sectors.

An example

Suppose that some subsidiaries in a group make losses which exceed the profits made by the other subsidiaries. Taken as a whole, the consolidated profit and loss account will show a loss. Since the group has thus destroyed shareholder value in the year, there are no profits to pay a dividend. However, the profitable subsidiaries can pay a dividend to the parent, who in turn can pay a dividend to shareholders. The losses incurred elsewhere in the group are simply ignored. This practice is possible because dividends are paid by individual companies, rather than the group as a whole.

A dividend can, however, be legitimately paid out of retained profits in the balance sheet, even if there is a loss in the current year. If there are retained losses and there is a loss in the current year then any 'dividend' is a most unwise repayment of capital. Unfortunately, this is exactly what does happen. If there is a profit in the current year and retained losses from prior years, no dividend should be paid until the shareholders' equity has been restored to its original yardstick, as stipulated in the Companies Act 1980. Again, paying dividends in such circumstances is not uncommon.

Red flag

'When managements take the low road in aspects that are visible, it is likely they are following a similar path behind the scenes. There is seldom just one cockroach in the kitchen.'
Warren Buffett

As always, an investor is looking for clues about how a company is run. The complete picture is only known to the directors and, hopefully, the auditors and they are not telling. Therefore, if you see a company whose actions raise a red flag in your mind it is a warning sign that it might be racy in other areas that you cannot judge, due to your lack of information. Neither is paying dividends out of capital confined to smaller and less well-run companies, as blue chips are equally guilty. At a time when corporate governance is at the fore, this is both surprising and disappointing, as one would expect these stalwarts of the economy to set high standards. Such shares should be avoided.

Why does it persist?

Why does this dividend practice persist? The answer is that it suits the main parties to the transaction. The individual shareholder is hardly going to complain that he has received a dividend and he may be reluctant to look too closely as to how it was justified. He is just glad to be receiving some cash. Institutional investors do not seem inclined to stop this foolishness, which they could, given their power. One supposes that they are acting like the other shareholders, being grateful for the cash and not too inclined to ask questions which might stop its flow. Maybe they believe in 'new accounting' for a 'new economy' where common sense is an outdated concept.

Management has every incentive to protect the dividend at all cost. After all, they can spin the company's performance as much as they like but a dividend adds credibility to their story that they are doing a good job. It deflects worries if the group as a whole is loss-making. The dividend is a powerful signal to the markets and a cut is a testament to the fact that the company's prospects have declined. That could be awkward when remuneration and share options are so hotly debated.

The auditors, of course, see the ploy but they do not have the power to force management to take action. Their job is to express an opinion on the accounts as presented to them by the directors. Paying dividends in this way out of capital may not break the letter of the law or accounting standards, although they are certainly against their spirit, so therefore the accounts can receive an unqualified opinion.

Examples of companies paying dividends out of capital

Here are some examples of FTSE 100 companies that are paying dividends effectively out of capital, rather than profits, since their capital is impaired by retained losses.

£m	Profit and loss account		Balance sheet	
	pre-tax profit (loss)	dividend	retained loss	equity
Compass	370	200	-2,005	2,482
EMAP	144	60	-378	285
ICI	359	86	-658	721
Imperial Tobacco	688	362	-919	118
Rexam	5	84	-652	803
Rentokil Initial	397	110	-715	619
Vodafone	-5,047	1,378	-43,014	111,924
Total	**-3,084**	**2,280**	**-48,341**	**116,952**

Figures are from results to 2004.

The worst culprit is Vodafone, which made a current year loss as well as having retained losses. These companies made a total loss of £3,084 million and yet paid 'dividends' of £2,280 million. This increased the retained losses to £48,341 million, which shrank the shareholders' equity accordingly to £116,952 million. Thus, £2,280 million of capital was returned to shareholders in the form of a highly-taxed dividend.

Conclusion

If a company is paying dividends and has no retained earnings in the balance sheet, it is effectively returning capital to investors in the form of a taxable income stream. This is a contravention of the Companies Act 1980 and is even more reprehensible if there is a current year loss. This is deeply unattractive, racy accounting.

4. Goodwill = Badwill

'I am pleased with the overall fourth quarter performance. We will run each of our businesses as well or better than before.'

Richard Parsons, CEO of AOL Time Warner, after announcing a 2002 goodwill write-off of $100 billion, a world record and equivalent to Bulgaria's GNP.

What is goodwill?

Goodwill is an intangible asset that cannot be touched or counted. It may provide a competitive advantage, such as a strong brand, reputation, high employee morale, distribution channels, access to factors of production, technical expertise and loyal customers. The significance of goodwill has grown as companies rely more on brainpower in today's service-dominated economy and less on tangible assets, which were crucial in the smoke stack industries of yesterday.

Goodwill is both intangible and not separately identifiable and that means its economic life is very difficult, if not impossible, to determine. The calculation for recording it in the accounts is simple. Goodwill is merely the difference between the consideration paid for a business and its net assets, being the value of its tangible assets less liabilities. Therefore, if the consideration is £1 million and the net assets are £100,000, then the goodwill is £900,000 for accounting purposes.

Bull market

The bull market lasted for 18 years from 1982 to 2000 and was epitomised by fancy company valuations, as PERs increased to stratospheric levels. Many companies used their overpriced paper to buy other companies in a takeover bonanza. The acquisitions resulted in mountains of goodwill of such dubious value that a more apt description might be 'badwill'. It provided an ideal way of accounting for growth and the bear market has exposed this fallacy, the consequences of which have often been dire.

Accounting treatment

Unfortunately, putting a realistic economic value on goodwill is all but impossible, so it cannot be revalued each year. Consequently, there is no way to assess any diminution in value that should be written off in the profit and loss account. Goodwill has always been an intractable accounting problem. The accountancy profession adopted a simple approach to this problem, until 2005, by writing off the cost, in the same manner as depreciating tangible assets, like cars and computers. This was a reasonable and conservative approach, as the assumption is that this intangible asset withers over time. The write-off period was a maximum of 20 years. This was intended to apply to exceptional circumstances and, in the vast majority of cases, the write-off period was to be much less, say 10 years. Needless to say, directors overwhelmingly adopted 20 years so the maximum become the norm. This has the effect, of course, of minimising the amortisation cost each year in the profit and loss account.

Many companies did not amortise goodwill at all, as they maintained that its value had not diminished. These included: Diageo; Dixons; Kelda; Reckitt Benckiser; Rentokil Initial; and Sage. Companies that wrote goodwill off more than the maximum of 20 years included Alliance UniChem, Boots, Cadbury Schweppes, Kingfisher and Lloyds TSB. These companies had £19 billion of goodwill, being two-thirds of their £29 billion of equity. Their goodwill amortisation averaged just 1%. If the goodwill were to be written off over 20 years, then this would rise to 5% and increase their amortisation cost of £167 million by a further £760 million. This is not a conservative way to run a company. Rentokil Initial has the dubious distinction of appearing here and in the list above of companies paying dividends out of capital.

The accounting treatment changed in 2005 and now directors need only to write down goodwill if they assess that its value has fallen. This is a deeply unwelcome development. Since the assessment is all but impossible to prove or disprove, the temptation will be for directors to maintain that the goodwill has not been impaired and therefore no write-off is applicable. Thus, the goodwill will sit there as a soft asset on the balance sheet for years to come, until, that is, the day of reckoning. This accounting policy will make goodwill all the more important and controversial in future. Profits will be overstated and investors should make an adjustment by deducting a notional amortisation of goodwill to arrive at a realistic profit and PER. It would be reasonable for this notional amortisation to write off goodwill over 10 years and thus investors should deduct 10% of goodwill from profit.

Directors adopt accounting policies which account for growth because they have conflicts of interest. They want to maximise the price of the share so that this boosts share options and supports their generous remuneration. In addition, the average tenure of a FTSE 100 CEO is but a brief two years. The temptation is to minimise costs over that tenure and thus maximise profits in the short-term and leave successors to worry about all that unamortised goodwill on the balance sheet. If share options were eliminated this would at least remove one important conflict. The assumed objective in standard economic theory is that companies strive for long-term profit maximisation. The reality is that short-term profits tend to be maximised, often by accounting for growth.

Reality of acquisitions

'When it comes to the pricing of financial assets, perceptions count. Reality is of lesser consequence'
Charles Babbin, author of *Investment Secrets of the Masters*.

The reality of an acquisition is that one company is buying another company's income stream. That comes at a cost and this is the price paid for the acquisition. The acquirer will write-off the net tangible assets of the acquiree, such as plant and machinery, as depreciation. The goodwill amortisation is also a cost of benefiting from the acquiree's income stream. To see why amortisation of goodwill is necessary, assume that an advertising agency is bought. Its goodwill is represented by a creative workforce and existing contracts with customers. Over time, the workforce will leave and customers come and go. Over the next decade very little may remain of the company that was acquired, as it will have changed into something new. Therefore, it is inappropriate that the original goodwill should remain on the balance sheet. This would be even more the case after 20 years, which is a very long time in such a dynamic business.

The litmus test of a successful acquisition is whether it increases EPS, after taking into account the amortisation of that goodwill. However, there have been far too many cases of huge amounts of badwill lumped on the balance sheet that have not increased EPS but instead cost shareholders a fortune.

Look at the bottom line

The directors are keen to emphasise the profit and EPS before the irritating cost of goodwill amortisation. Consequently, the results in the directors' report can look quite different from the bottom line in the profit and loss account. To add to the confusion, there are usually four EPS numbers to ponder: basic and diluted by options, both before and after goodwill and any exceptional items. The true test of whether the company has added value is diluted EPS after amortisation and exceptional items.

A good example of putting 'spin' on results is Vodafone, mentioned before in chapter 5.3, where the chairman said 2004 was 'another highly successful year for your company, with an excellent overall operating performance generating further substantial growth in profits and cash flows'. This comment presumably related to a 'normalised' pre-tax profit of £10 billion. However, the goodwill amortisation was a staggering £15 billion and the loss was £9 billion after tax. Make no mistake, Vodafone destroyed shareholder value by this £9 billion loss, taking the retained loss to an eye-popping £43 billion, hardly an excellent result. Such spin may give a true view but it is not a fair view, i.e. all the facts presented on an equal footing. True and fair, then, are not the same thing. The auditor's opinion is that the accounts show a true and fair view and, therefore, are the best place to assess the company's performance rather than the glowing testament in the directors' report.

Amortisation is akin to depreciation

The market generally seems content to ignore amortisation, as it is interpreted as a non-cash item. This is foolish thinking, as it does not similarly ignore depreciation, which is also a non-cash item. Depreciation and amortisation are essentially the same animal. They account for an asset being used up in production and need to be measured. It is true that writing them off is a non-cash item in the current accounting period. However, they were cash outflows in a previous accounting period and will be so again if an acquisition is made or if fixed assets are bought. Ignoring amortisation for purposes of analysing cash flow may be a useful exercise but it should not be ignored when considering if shareholders' wealth has increased. Neither does it make any difference if the acquisition that caused the goodwill was paid for in cash or shares of the acquirer. The latter are a cash equivalent as the shares could have been sold in the open market for cash.

Goodwill threatens share prices

Writing off huge amounts of worthless goodwill is not an academic exercise. Banking covenants will specify that there must be a set amount of net assets backing the loans. If the goodwill is written off and the net assets fall below the covenant, then the company faces collapse if banks call in the loans. This is what happened to Marconi when it wrote off £5 billion of goodwill, following the unwise purchase of US telecommunications equipment companies in the TMT mania. In addition, goodwill amortisation reduces profit and thus restricts dividends. This should have an adverse effect on the shares, the value of which is the net present value of all future dividends.

Examples of companies with significant goodwill write-offs

Many of the worst culprits that have loaded the balance sheet with worthless goodwill have either gone bust or been relegated to small company status, losing the majority of their share value. These include Marconi, Baltimore Technologies and NSB Retail Systems. However, the issue is still present. Here are some examples of FTSE 100 companies and the impact of substantial goodwill write-offs.

£m	Pre-tax profit (loss)	Goodwill amortisation in P&L a/c	Share-holders' equity	Balance sheet goodwill remaining
Abbey	-984	1,202	5,644	376
BAE Systems	-616	615	5,410	6,417
Cable & Wireless	-6,373	2,851	2,149	-2
Granada	-378	287	1,641	1,305
mmO2	-10,203	10,108	10,066	7,582
Royal & Sun Alliance	-1,022	738	3,043	306
Reuters	-493	309	506	418
Shire Pharmaceuticals	-526	753	2,747	1,900
Vodafone	-6,028	15,723	128,671	108,085
Sub total	-26,623	32,586	159,877	126,37
Other	78,262	7,994	389,176	144,913
Total	**51,639**	**40,580**	**549,053**	**271,300**

Figures are from results to 2003.

This table emphasises the significance of goodwill on results to 2003, which was a notable period for write-offs. Just these nine companies wrote off £33 billion of goodwill and that far exceeded their combined pre-tax loss of £27 billion. What is more, there remained a staggering £127 billion of goodwill yet to write-off. The market value of the FTSE 100 was then £1 trillion. Its equity was £549 billion in the table above and half of that is goodwill at £271 billion, which is alarming as it is a soft asset. The total goodwill amortisation of the FTSE 100 companies was £41 billion and represented three quarters of pre-tax profit of just £52 billion. These examples pale into insignificance compared to some US companies that lost the plot, such as AOL Time Warner and JDS Uniphase, which wrote off $100 billion and $47 billion of goodwill, respectively.

The following FTSE 100 companies have immaterial or no goodwill: Alliance & Leicester; BAA; British Land; BHP Billiton; Cable & Wireless (after huge write-offs); Land Securities; Legal & General; Liberty International; Mitchells & Butlers; Marks & Spencer; Morrison Supermarkets; Northern Rock; Next; and Schroders. This list is a good hunting ground for the following reasons, which have been highlighted in previous chapters: Alliance & Leicester (takeover candidate); BAA (monopoly and toll bridge model); Morrisons Supermarkets (35 years of profit growth); and Northern Rock (takeover candidate and low-cost business model).

Conclusion

In the bull market to 2000, the tendency was to ignore the accounting 'nasty bits' and concentrate on rocketing share prices. Companies were valued according to such esoteric factors as website 'hits' or by comparison to other absurdly over-hyped companies. Profits were for wimps and Warren Buffet was accused of having lost the plot in the technology-free zone of rural Omaha. The markets have subsequently reverted towards the norm, as they always do. Goodwill has been a major part in the farce, which is still being played out. The recommendation is to be very wary of companies that have material amounts of goodwill in view of the pain they can inflict. Also, avoid companies that do not write it off conservatively. The easiest way to solve a problem is to avoid it in the first place so consider investing in companies that have immaterial goodwill.

5. Share options – no free lunch

'There is nothing more short-term than a 60 year old CEO holding a fistful of share options.'

Professor Gary Hamel, author of *Competing For The Future.*

Irresistible appeal

Share options have become a nearly universal feature in company accounts and are a material item. Their appeal was irresistible to directors because they looked like a 'free lunch', as they can greatly increase their remuneration but avoided the tiresome business of recording it as a cost in the profit and loss account. There are very few companies that do not have directors' share options but examples include Hitachi Credit, Hardys & Hansons and Telecom plus. However, the accounting changed from 2005 and the cost of share options will be included as an expense in the profit and loss account. This is very good news, as previously this was a scandalous way of accounting for growth and vast fortunes have been made by directors at the expense of shareholders. Few heeded the Association of British Insurers' corporate governance guidelines that the total number of options should not exceed 10% of the share capital over a decade, or more than 3% in any year.

It will be interesting to see the effect of including share options as an expense. The cost of share options has been enormous and has been calculated as 15% of the top 100 US companies' pre-tax profit. Some directors have enriched themselves by hundreds of millions of dollars, which is ludicrous. Directors should be fairly rewarded, not founding dynasties at the shareholders' expense. Microsoft has decided to scrap share options and this is a material development. If it had expensed options in 2002, profits would have fallen by a third from $7.8 billion to $5.3 billion. The 1998 profits of the largest US companies would have fallen two thirds if options were expensed. Similarly, a tenth of FTSE 100 companies' EPS would drop by half and the EPS of a third of them would fall by 10%. Shareholders are in revolt and companies such as GlaxoSmithKline, HSBC, Selfridges, Boots, Reed Elsevier and Mark & Spencer have felt their wrath. UK CEOs are the second highest-paid in the world after the US, earning more than £500,000 a year on average.

Changing the rules

'An executive who hedges his share options is a little bit like the captain of a ship who sees an iceberg up ahead and heads for his lifeboat without waking the sleeping passengers.'
Louis Lavelle, compensation consultant.

What also adds insult to injury is any attempt to re-price options after the shares have fallen dramatically in price. This has been the case in the US, rather than the UK, and was evident after the TMT bubble burst. A variation on this is to issue a chunk of new options when a share price falls after some bad news flow, like a profit warning or the September 11th terrorist attacks. This is hardly a sign that the directors are equally sharing in the company's fortunes but rather demonstrates that they are profiting from its misfortunes and their own incompetence. The Association of British Insurers states that options should not be granted at a discount to the current share price. This does not stop some companies from doing so, such as Lloyds TSB, and such transgressors should be avoided.

What further adds insult to injury is that usually the directors cash in their options rather than hanging on to the shares, which would align their interests more closely with those of shareholders. In effect, this is a warning sign that the directors do not have much faith in the company. True, the directors may wish to spread their risk and not want their remuneration and wealth to derive too much from one company, since if it failed they would lose both their job and the value of their shares. Nevertheless, the majority of shares could be retained and selling them en mass is not a reassuring sign.

Conclusion

Now that share options are expensed then, hopefully, the practice will lose its attraction and wither on the vine. The directors should have a material holding in a company and a mutuality of interest with the other shareholders. They should acquire their shares in the same way as shareholders, namely by handing over hard-earned cash rather than freeloading. An investor should avoid companies which have excessive share options.

CHAPTER 9

Investment axioms

'There is nothing we receive with so much reluctance as advice.'
Joseph Addison, poet.

Investment axioms, or rules, are very helpful as they examine the minds of gurus who have vast experience of being successful investors. Some axioms are the trademark of a single or select number of gurus, whereas others are widely shared. Sometimes they are contradictory. The lessons to be learned should be invaluable. They generally support the ideas in this book and, where they do not, it recognises that investors have different systems. For example, a few gurus pay little heed to the macroeconomic view or technical analysis. The investment world is a broad church and accommodates the whole range of investment styles, so select those that most appeal to you. There are many ways to make a profit, depending on such aspects as attitude to risk, skill, experience, time, financial objectives and personal characteristics. The first two axioms are arguably the most important: cut losses and run profits, and the trend is your friend until the bend.

The distilled wisdom of 35 gurus

'Great stocks are extremely hard to find. If they weren't, then everyone would own them.'
Philip Fisher

The distilled wisdom of 35 gurus with an estimated 1,000 years of the very best experience has been summarised. This approach is different as it is an amalgamation of gurus' ideas on each topic rather than each guru's individual philosophy. This is likely to be more powerful, as this collective wisdom reinforces the credibility of the axiom. The gurus include: Anthony Bolton; Warren Buffett; Phillip Carret; David Dreman; Stanley Druckenmiller; Philip Fisher; John Galbraith; Dennis Gartman; Benjamin Graham; Stanley Kroll; Leonard Licht; Jesse Livermore; Peter Lynch; Michael Moule; John Neff; William O'Neil; Thomas Rowe Price; Jim Rogers; the Rothschilds; Ian Rushbrook; Ed Seykota; Jim Slater; James O'Shaughnessy; George Soros; Michael Steinhardt; Nils Taube; Sir John Templeton; Larry Tisch; and Ralph Wanger.

Some gurus share common personal characteristics and it is likely that these contributed to their success. These characteristics have included the following in several cases. They had an early tragedy, such as the death of a parent, and many were poor as a child. They know the bitter experience of a crash that has wiped out the family coffers and made them aware of the threat of disaster. Their natural innocence and naivety were eliminated early and thoroughly. They have a strong craving to be financially secure and this drives them hard. They prefer to live modestly, even after being successful, probably reflecting the saying that 'the dumbest thing you can do with money is to spend it'. They are important philanthropists with charitable foundations. Being loners allows them to think independently and go against the herd instinct. They trade their own money and are convinced that they will succeed in the long-term. Many have found a system, have remained loyal to it and are disciplined with an unyielding approach to controlling risk. They are very serious traders and, although decisive, they are not particularly academic. In short, they love their job.

1. Cut losses and run profits

'Some people automatically sell the winners and hold on to their losers, which is about as sensible as pulling out the flowers and watering the weeds.'
Peter Lynch

Cut losses and run profits is simply the best advice that the gurus offer, as it is imperative not to incur large losses. This also reinforces the second best piece of advice that 'the trend is your friend', as discussed in the next axiom and in chapter 6. A share that has risen will be in an up trend and run the profits. A share that has fallen will be in some down trend and should be earmarked for cutting. Selling a winning investment and hanging on to a losing one is a cardinal sin. Cutting losses recognises that mistakes are often made and action must be taken swiftly, decisively and objectively. This is a rare gift and, to be a winner, learn how to lose and do not be afraid to take a loss. Profits take care of themselves but losses never do, especially in a bear market. The key is not to lose money so avoid the big losses.

Cutting losses is difficult because of ego, as investors do not like to admit they made a mistake. The pain of a loss is much more than the pleasure of a gain. There is the problem at what point to cut the loss, i.e. 10%, 20%. This is subjective but it easier and preferable to take a small loss rather than a large one. Also, should the loss be absolute or in relation to the market? If the market falls 10% and the share falls 10%, does that mean the loss should be cut? An investor must try to minimise absolute losses, so if a share has fallen by the predetermined amount it should be cut, notwithstanding what happened to the rest of the market. There is the fear of regret that the cut position will then turn into a winner. This does hurt but such sudden reversals do not happen often. It feels wrong to abandon an investment but this is less painful with practice. Accept small losses cheerfully and expect to experience several while awaiting a large gain. Automatic stop losses can remove emotion. Stop monitoring the share once it has been sold, as it is no longer a relevant investment and, if it does recover, then unhelpful and stultifying regret may take hold. However, you might want to monitor the share if you want to re-invest later. Learn how to lose and thus avoid hostile feelings.

It is a great mistake to average down by buying more of a losing investment, rather than cutting it. Instead, consider if you would purchase it now on its own merits rather than because you hold the dud anyway. If the conclusion is no, then do not average down and, if it is yes, beware you are not kidding yourself. The very idea itself can be a comfortable but dangerous reason for avoiding decisive action.

Running profits also needs discipline. Hold winners for the longer term, i.e. three to five years, providing that the story does not change or if it hits your profit target and is sold. Do what is right, not comfortable, so avoid the temptation of selling sure winners and resist the urge to take the cash now. Many people trade well with good timing but they make little profit because they go in and out of the market. The big profit is made by remaining invested in a bull market until it falters. You never go poor by taking profits but neither do you grow rich by making small profits in a bull market. Many get doubts or become impatient and do not give their investments sufficient time to prove themselves. The market does not beat them as they beat themselves. It is not difficult to be right about the markets but to have excellent timing and remain invested is very rare. It is the major move in the market that is important and trying to trade in and out can be a grave mistake. It is far more important to spend time considering when the bend in the market trend is going to happen than worrying about individual shares. The bull market ends before there is a general drop in the index and is evidenced by some shares starting to come off their highs.

2. The trend is your friend until the bend

'The trend is your friend most of the way, trend followers only get hurt at inflection points, where the trend changes.'
George Soros, billionaire trader and philanthropist.

The chapter on technical analysis also covers this subject. For some, a trend following or momentum approach can work amazingly well, compared to any other trading system. Wait until a major trend is clearly established and the broader the market trend the better. The real inside reason is unknown but you should climb on board by following the line of least resistance by buying an up trend and selling a down trend. The trend usually continues in the same direction and, by following it, an investor will not 'buck the markets', in the words of Margaret Thatcher. Do not be necessarily discouraged by the price, as a share is rarely too expensive to buy or too cheap to sell, although they may well look that way at the time.

Buy after a rise, even though you missed part of it, because catching the mid-range, broad momentum is fine. If you buy on the first correction of an up trend, then again on the next correction you buy less and carry on doing this. You have restricted the amount bought near what may be the top. This tests the market and verifies its strength so that if there is a loss, even briefly, then you know the timing was premature. You may thus incur a small loss but the main firepower is ready when the time is right. Therefore, do not be afraid of buying a rising market so that each purchase is at a higher price and profitable each time. As you buy more, you can raise the stop loss so that profit is locked in if the trend reverses. You should be going with the flow of the market and thus, for a share in an up trend, there will be other buyers out there and thus buying should not be too easy for you. Be wary if it is too easy, as it means that the sellers have the upper hand. The reverse is the case for a falling share, as there will be other sellers out there too and thus selling should not be too easy. This strategy does not make a few, big, high-risk gains but numerous, small, low-risk gains. Maximise the amount of gains, not the number of wins. Being right is more important than being a genius, so aim to ride the trend. Arguing with the markets can be very expensive. Being a trend follower means being bullish in a bull market and bearish in a bear market, the opposite of a contrarian.

Selling a share when it hits its peak would be a pure and unrealistic fluke. Instead, an investor can sell before the top or wait until the market weakens and there is no bounce back, thus selling shares that are in a down trend. This means forgoing a very elusive and difficult part of the profit that was available at the top but you will get out near the top, easily bagging most of the profit. Many investors have no fear and do not recognise that unrealised gains can disappear, as they never become a profit until you sell. Down trends can also be used for shorting, although this should be left to experienced investors.

Bottom fishing for bombed out shares, before an up trend is established, is a high-risk gamble. That does not stop amateurs, speculators and stock pickers from trying. They want to squeeze the last percentage of profit from a trade and are reluctant to buy if a share moves up a little. However, if they overcome their reluctance and buy, then the results are often good, which is unsurprising as the trend is more established. Bottom fishing takes a special feel for the market and if an investor just does not have this then it should be avoided.

Avoid guessing the breakout in a sideways trading market. Establish your limits in either direction and when the market moves through one of them then trade and ride the trend. This is much safer, as you trade from a position of knowledge, now that the direction is established rather than guessing.

A few gurus disagree and suggest forgetting about technical analysis. They may have been unable to find anyone who makes consistent profits and point to institutions which have poured fortunes into technical analysis 'black boxes' only to discard them. Other gurus are more forgiving and recognise that a chart can be a useful forecasting tool in the hands of an expert. The average technical analyst erroneously thinks that is all he needs to know about investing.

3. Avoiding shares

'I avoid fads like the plague.'
Philip Carret, described by Warren Buffett as the person with the best long-term investment record.

Avoid popular shares, fad industries or anything that is 'hot'. If you buy what everyone else is buying you will not enjoy a superior return. If you buy when everyone thinks a popular share is cheap, it is probably overvalued, since all the growth and good news is in the price. Glamour shares are the same and are overpriced. This also applies to shares receiving short bursts of enthusiasm. The best shares are often odd, uncomfortable, obscure and seem more risky. The best insurance is to check that very little has been written about it for a good while, nor are there recent broker reports. Never follow speculative crazes and often the best time to buy a security is when nobody else wants it.

To buy greedily when others are selling in despair and to sell determinedly when others are stampeding to buy requires great nerve and self-confidence but offers the highest return. Not everyone can outperform the market and if investors jump on a bandwagon of a share selection methodology or a way of evaluating the market then these tools will cease to work, just when the winning formula seems guaranteed. Once a country, sector or type of share is pursued by the masses, there will be a boom and the subsequent bust may be long-lasting. For those with an appetite for risk, booms can be ridden with momentum investing on 'the trend is your friend' basis but stop losses are essential. A buy and hold strategy will be very painful.

One way to spot a bubble is to watch the multitude of new funds launched to chase the far receding bandwagon. Also, there will be glowing and reassuring articles in the media. Another pointer is if a company's price jumps on news that it proposes to enter the hot area, for example anything with Net or .com in the name during the TMT mania.

Avoid official growth shares, as they tend to be overpriced. Hot new issues will not do well and avoid turnaround loss makers. Avoid quirky products that are difficult to understand, expensive to run and have uncertain value, such as derivatives and tax efficient investments. Avoid venture capital, as this is a high-risk area where bankruptcies are frequent and amateur outsiders will play second fiddle to the professional insiders, who may have conflicts of interest. Warren Buffett, for example, says why take such an unproven risk, with promoters getting fat fees when, in a recession, you can pick up superb companies selling for less than net assets? Avoid blue chip companies in dying industries, such as metal bashing and chemicals, because they are cyclical with poor economics. Their size seems to promise safety but they deliver death by a thousand cuts.

4. Consensus

Disregard the consensus opinion, as it is probably wrong, and think matters through for yourself. The media relentlessly emphasises that the majority is right and so it can feel unnerving to hold a contrarian view, which can undermine your determination. Be alert to this, unlike amateurs who are ignorant of it, especially during manias. It is more often the case that reality has dawned on the few rather than the many. However, do not be stubborn and just do the opposite of the majority for the sake of it but have an objective mind which constantly questions their influence instead of acquiescing to it.

5. Diversifying risk

'In my 70 years of looking at markets, I have known a lot of people who went bankrupt, many of them because they ignored the need for diversification.'
Sir John Templeton

It is important not to have all the investment eggs in one basket, so diversifying by country, asset class, sector and company increases the margin of safety, since the future is uncertain. Investing worldwide greatly increases the choice of finding the best opportunities compared to just your own country. Currency considerations do increase the risk of investing worldwide, however, and investing in a fund is a sensible approach rather than an investor buying individual shares. Countries should be avoided which discourage investments, such as those with left wing governments, depreciating currencies, high taxation and inflation. Instead, choose those that are stable, flexible and responding to international competitive advantage and lend support to business. Spread a single asset class, such as cash, shares and gold, across a number of accounts in case of default or fraud. Bonds do not preserve capital and shares are much better over the long-term.

6. Do not own a zoo

'If you have a harem of forty women, you never get to know any of them very well.'
Warren Buffett

Always invest significant amounts and avoid over-diversification. Large stakes can really make a difference but small ones will not, as they will be drowned out by other small under-performers. You also spread your time too thinly with many holdings and inertia is the result. Twelve holdings is a good size for a portfolio and will diversify 90% of the risk. Spread them across at least five sectors and be very knowledgeable about a few shares. Aggressively monitor your investments, especially any that are struggling, since change is ever present. There are no shares that you can just buy and forget. Avoid having long-term investments, where you pay no heed to performance as it is held for its dividend. Such investors are lazy and are the real risk-takers. Also, high yields are often a sign of trouble rather than opportunity.

7. Economic cycle

'Buy when most people including experts are overly pessimistic, and sell when they are actively optimistic.'
Benjamin Graham, author of *The Intelligent Investor*.

Please see chapter 3 for more detail. Invest from a top-down macro level by taking into consideration the economic cycle, interest rates and currencies to give country weightings and then choose the shares. Thus, an investor can then take advantage of the economic cycle and the mistakes of others. You can make exceptional profits by buying growth shares in a market wash-out, so time the market by raising cash at the end of a bull market and sell high beta shares, as they are more volatile than the index. Identify cyclical sectors and invest at the correct moment. The best time to buy is in the depths of a recession, rather than when the consensus says the outlook is encouraging, because bull markets begin when the clouds appear darkest. Buy those shares with the biggest prospective rebound and sell after the rebound.

Avoid the losing years and invest heavily in a few, really good years. There is nothing wrong with being out of the market in order to preserve capital, as it is your choice whether to participate or not. Spot the broad and most important megatrends in social, political and economic factors and buy shares that ride those trends. Some gurus do not take into account macroeconomics or try to time the market, as they are long-term investors. Others trade opportunistically, profiting from the public's emotions.

8. Fear and greed

'The market, like the Lord, helps those who help themselves. But, unlike the Lord, the market does not forgive those who know not what they do.'
Warren Buffett.

Fear induces pessimism and greed induces optimism. They are the raw emotions that fuel the stock market, as fear causes the bear market and greed causes the bull market. Be most afraid when there is no fear. Conversely, fear and pessimism of others greatly reduce the risk of investing. The best time to buy is when pessimism is at its greatest and the best time to sell is when optimism reigns supreme. The surest and greatest profit opportunity is when the masses are panicked into selling. They buy during a boom and sell in a bust, so there can be no value in the former, only in the latter. If you can spot a bandwagon then it is too late. To be contrarian and buy at the bottom is easier said than done, as bottom fishing is a risky strategy. This is because the bottom will only be proven in hindsight. Those who have a great fear of the market make the best traders. However, long-term investors should not be pessimistic too frequently, as shares rise in line with the long-term growth in the economy. Have the thought of what you can lose uppermost in your mind rather than what you can gain. Consider gearing up on crises, such as war, a government coup, terrorism and economic turbulence.

Greed and optimism greatly increase the risk of investing. You expect the best but need the self-assurance to deal with the worst. Do not trade if you are just merely optimistic. Optimists tend to assume 'if' is 'will', so keep hope and lucky thoughts out of your investments but, instead, be realistic about losing. Many amateurs are unrealistic and are wiped out. The professional is not optimistic but confident due to employing pessimism constructively. Assume a dire situation is exactly that, rather than kid yourself. We naturally prefer being optimistic rather than pessimistic, as it is a psychological boost. Therefore, there are more bulls than bears. Optimists also make better press, as the media likes to sell its wares and the public likes to hear positive stories. Therefore, beware the media's partiality that also infects broker forecasts and recommendations. When optimism is most abundant, it is least helpful, whereas when pessimism is most abundant it is very helpful. This is because bull markets are born on pessimism, grow on scepticism, mature on optimism and die on euphoria.

Greed means demanding more than you should expect. Determine at the outset what profit you expect from a trade and you should sell when that point is reached. As the trades are profitably concluded, the subsequent ones become starting points again, rather than ending points, and you have moved away from what was originally expected. Eventually, it may be very hard to sell out for the anticipated profit, as you are expecting too much. Set a sell price on all your shares and thus determine the end of the trade, rather than having it determined for you because of forced selling or a takeover. If a trade has no set ending then the share may wallow aimlessly in the portfolio. There will be times when shares take off but you do not know when or for how long so sell, locking in a decent profit.

9. Funds

'Why look for the needle in the haystack? Buy the haystack!'
John Bogle, founder of Vanguard Funds.

Investing in a fund may be a more effective and cheaper way of running a portfolio than buying shares directly, if you have a modest amount to invest. A good fund typically has an annual charge of 1% and choose three or four with superior management. How big the portfolio has to be for it to be worth managing yourself is a subjective matter. If you have a major flaw in your investment style then the answer should be never. Even if you are an average trader, you should quit. Recognise that 85% of funds do not even manage to match, let alone beat, the index so a start is to consider an index tracker so that you are at least in the top 15%. However, the larger the portfolio the more is the tendency to own individual shares. Avoid funds of funds as you pay two management fees with no real increase in diversification.

There is a good probability of losing money at the end of a bull market because very few investors, even experienced fund managers, can tear themselves away from a bandwagon. Fund managers that do well in a boom often do not preserve capital in a bear market. They may be young and have not experienced one before, or do not possess a sound methodology. They may have a mandate to remain almost fully invested in shares and this can be a noose round the investor's neck. Others may be content to lose money, as long as it is in line with the index. Few will stick their necks out and go into cash, hedge funds or other assets in a bear market. In other words, you should choose an all-weather fund, not just one that is suitable for a bull market, so look closely at the performance in the last bear market. Look at shares the best fund managers are buying and selling as good for pointers to buy individual shares.

10. Flexible

'Whoever desires constant success must change his conduct with the times.'
Machiavelli

A flexible investment strategy is vital, as the markets are continually changing. Industries regularly die and new ones are born, so be aware of trends. Expect and react to developments and downturns. Change strategy and selection methods as opportunities arise and be prepared to move between different asset classes.

These perform well at various stages of the economic cycle and the move should be from shares and property at the top, to cash then bonds, as explained in chapter 3. Be aware that no single asset class is suitable for all time.

Valuation yardsticks change, such as yield and PER, and these have to be re-evaluated. The problem with the majority of investment systems is that they may seem beguilingly easy. However, any system must be constantly revised when the rules no longer work and consider the future rather than the past. Whenever possible, try to remember the KISS principle – Keep It Simple, Stupid. If you have a greater understanding than other investors, you have an edge. Start with a small investment and, if it is successful, build up a larger position as the markets develop trends and these become more established and predictable. Prices always fluctuate for a reason but that may not become apparent for weeks, if at all. However, you have to act now.

If a share does not succeed then you should sell and invest elsewhere. Perseverance is considered noble but should be used sparingly when investing. Do not pursue a share out of bloody-mindedness or from a desire for vengeance if it does not do what you want. Concentrate on making the same profit elsewhere and do not take it personally.

11. Future

'If you can look into the seeds of time, and say which will grow and which will not.'
William Shakespeare, from *Macbeth*.

People crave to know the future, especially about money matters. Awkwardly, this future depends on the behaviour of millions of people, based on the emotions of fear and greed, and the result is unknowable. Therefore, be very wary of 'experts', such as economists or stock market players, who say they know what will happen. They are often simply mistaken, spout the consensus or extrapolate the past to the future and cannot see the bend in the trend. They will point out the few times they are correct but conveniently forget the many occasions they were wrong. Also, some experts' influence is such that they move the market with their prediction, so it is hardly surprising that it becomes a reality.

12. Instinct

'Never flinch – make up your own mind and do it.'
Margaret Thatcher

People often have an instinct or sixth sense about an investment. Such intuition is a feeling based on subconscious, prior experience and observation or on a natural inclination of knowing what is right. You feel it, sometimes very powerfully. It may not be explainable but, over time, you know that it exists and whether it can be relied upon or not, although this is difficult. The instinct is likely to be well founded if it is based on something about which you are knowledgeable. Its credibility is greatly reinforced if the outcome is the opposite of what you hope will happen and vice versa. Gurus have attributed part of their success to following instinct and were sorry when it was ignored. Some investors likewise refuse to follow instinct and want hard evidence and numbers to justify decisions. Others rely on instinct too heavily and are gambling.

13. Investor qualities

The gurus have a good deal of advice about the qualities an investor needs to be successful. Peter Lynch's view is: 'The list of qualities ought to include patience, self-reliance, common sense, a tolerance for pain, open-mindedness, detachment, persistence, humility, flexibility, a willingness to do independent research, an equal willingness to admit to mistakes, and the ability to ignore general panic'. An investor has to be constantly on his guard against the many expensive enemies within himself. Investing is often counter-intuitive so that the required action seems to be the opposite of common sense. For example, under 'the trend is your friend' principle, simple but incorrect logic might suggest that a share that has fallen and is 'cheaper' is a better buy than one that has risen.

Invest rather than speculate and the difference between them is patience, which means investing for the long haul, rather than trying to make short-term but risky profits. Wait for the right opportunity and only act when you know what you are doing, based on solid homework. Many investors feel the constant need to do something and thus forgo this advantage. You only have to make a few correct decisions in your life and not make too many wrong decisions. Do not try to guess short-term price movements, because if you are too market-conscious and do not know the facts you will tend to sell shares constantly as they go down. Never buy a share unless you would be happy if the market was closed for 10 years. Never fall in love with a share, as it certainly does not love you. Neither does the share know what price you paid or what is your target. Do not succumb to a temptation, such as buying a new issue, which you know from bitter experience has been hard to resist, yet has always proved to be painful.

Do not be arrogant, as you risk losing control, but, instead, understand your limitations. If an investor thinks he knows all the answers then he is over confident and will usually lose. However, a veteran investor will seek answers to new situations. Think independently but you have to be right, as well as a contrarian, who is defined as someone who bought what looked like cheap steel shares every year and lost money. Have the security and self-confidence that comes from knowledge without being rash or headstrong. If you lack confidence, fear will drive you out at the bottom. Try experimenting with a fantasy portfolio before starting trading but this is not the same as investing real money.

Beating the index is harder than it looks but just one lucky or shrewd investment can yield more than all the others will ever make. There is no substitute for hard and constant work in the stock market, otherwise you lose. Stay nimble, respond to events and avoid risk rather than remain dogmatic to ideas formulated a long time ago.

14. Management

Managers should be obsessive about running the business for the benefit of shareholders rather than for themselves, as symbolised by such extravagance as palatial offices. Avoid managers who make acquisitions to expand their own empire. It is preferable to have mediocre management in a good business than excellent management struggling with a bad business. Spotting good management is not easy but it will show up in sustained and superior profits over the years.

15. Margin of safety

'The ultimate risk is not taking a risk.'
Sir James Goldsmith

Investing using proven fundamental methods leads to preservation of capital and a reasonable return. Speculation is using any other method. All investments other than cash put capital at some risk. An investor should aim to maximise the anticipated gain and minimise any loss. This is best achieved by building in a margin of safety. This can be contrasted to speculating at the top of a mania when greed banishes any such idea. The margin of safety concept was laid down by Benjamin Graham, the father of investing, and subsequent advocates like Warren Buffett. Such investing is prudent and systematic, focusing on buying growth at a reasonable price in sturdy, profitable companies, with low debt and a good track record. A share might be selling for less than the net assets, for example, or have an attractive dividend with ample cover. Always buy value, as major discrepancies between the market and intrinsic value of a share do not exist indefinitely. This approach can be successful and is suitable for an average investor. It should lead to a well-diversified portfolio that comfortably outperforms the index over the long period.

Cautious investors may be attracted to methods like pound cost averaging or investing via funds and brokers. Attempting to buy at the bottom and sell at the top of the market is speculation and will fail. Instead, you should buy below fair value and sell above it. Investors buy shares at sensible prices, whereas speculators anticipate market fluctuations. You should not be deterred from buying even if you anticipate the market bottom has not been reached, as that may never happen or may be years hence. However, do not buy if the market is over valued and never buy a share just because it has increased in price. An ideal company is one that can re-invest profits at 15% or more, rather than paying out taxed dividends.

Speculation is buying badly run companies with unattractive economics, or average companies at a high price when the economy is rosy. Avoid companies with unsustainable growth rates but, instead, be cautious in forecasting future growth. The public regards the stock market as speculation in a bear market and a sell but as a solid investment during a bull market and a buy. It should be doing the exact opposite and is a peculiar version of the laws of supply and demand in that as the price goes up so does demand. This is because further increases are anticipated that will increase one's wealth. This phenomenon is true in all manias, as people extrapolate the past into the future and expect the trend to continue but without regard to the underlying value of the share. The bubble bursts when the lack of value becomes apparent to the majority and they sell. Similarly, the bear market ends when the value becomes blatant to the majority and they start to buy. The market is inefficient because the herd mentality is driven by fear and greed. Buy value in individual shares rather than the market as a whole because such shares can still rise in a bear market and also outperform in a bull market.

16. Making mistakes

'Experience is the name everyone gives to their mistakes.'
Oscar Wilde

The reality is that you will make mistakes in investing and make them all the time. It is important to recognise this and, when it happens, sell. The only alternative is not to be in the market at all and that would be a grave error. In the beginning, you will make the same basic mistakes as the naive speculator but you will go up the learning curve eventually. This will generate self-confidence and you will learn from a mistake so that you are less inclined to repeat it. Losses are a very good experience for understanding what not to do because pain is a powerful teacher. Also, partial victories can teach you as much as defeats. Do not be angry with yourself for making mistakes or try to rectify the matter by resorting to risky speculation.

17. Outperforming

'Wall street professionals know that acting on 'inside' tips will break a man more quickly than famine, pestilence, crop failure, political readjustments, or what may be called normal accidents.'
Jesse Livermore, *Reminiscences of a Stock Operator*.

Outperforming the market is hard and depends on time, an open mind and good judgement. More expertise is needed when investing in shares than in other asset classes, such as bonds or property. The task is not only to outperform the public but also the professionals working in institutions that dominate the market, which is in a constant state of flux. Shares are much more volatile than the businesses they represent. Therefore, investors need new weapons and tactics to succeed.

It is essential to carry out adequate research or seek the advice of very good professional analysts. They are unlikely to include stockbrokers, who are primarily salesman and often want the masses to buy shares they need to sell. The public foolishly and lazily likes to invest in tips. Beware of anonymous or subjective tips where there may be a conflict of interest and ignore those from friends, especially if they claim to be close to the company. Media tipsters can be expensive, as they usually do much worse than the market and are primarily financial journalists rather than stock market experts. Always read the annual report before you buy.

18. Order out of chaos

People like to understand and control their environment and, in the stock market, they seek order where there is randomness. Investors seek a winning system but the task is usually futile. For example, punters think they are geniuses in a bull market, whereas they are just winning by being there and riding short-term luck, which is the predominant reason for success. Institutions have squandered fortunes searching for a perfect system and have enjoyed precious little success. In some cases, like Long Term Capital Management in the US in 1998, such a system ended in catastrophic failure.

Likewise, history may appear to repeat itself, thus tantalisingly allowing the future to be foretold, but it does so either only occasionally or unreliably. For example, just because yields have never been below a certain level before is a perilous basis for thinking they will not do so in the future. A chartist thinks he can foresee the future out of historical price movements but they are random. Some investors see a cause and effect where none exists and it is just a co-incidence, an example being 'sell in May and go away and do not come back until St. Leger day'. A speculator is a gambler by nature who attributes a win to skill but it was more likely due to chance, over which there is no control.

19. Selling

'Sell on any first profit warning.'
Nicola Horlick, 'superwoman' fund manager.

When to sell is a favourite question for investors. Fortunately, the gurus have much to say on the matter. This should be read in conjunction with the above paragraphs on cutting losses and running profits, plus 'the trend is your friend'.

Sell a share when you find a much better alternative, even if the existing one is still good value. That way you constantly upgrade the quality of your portfolio. If you have held a dud share for a long time, do not hesitate to sell it for a better opportunity and ignore any later regrets, which can happen even if you hang on to it, as the wait could be never-ending. The dud owes you nothing and do not hold on because of sentiments like loyalty or loving the share. Do not be panicked into selling in a market crash and, if there are no better alternatives, maintain your exiting holdings. Recessions can create a perplexing backdrop and some sectors, such as general insurance, have separate cycles of their own. Avoid shares where poor liquidity may make it impossible to sell.

The time to sell a share is when: earnings growth is coming to an end; there is a decline in the return on capital; all the good news is in the price; everything still looks glowing; everyone else is euphoric; it is fully or over valued and no longer offers the upside; the story changes, such as the loss of a contract or talented director. Consider selling half when a share doubles and thus take out your cost and let the rest run for free. Alternatively, perhaps sell either if the share has risen 50% or after two years, whichever happens first. Sell 100% if the bull market has peaked or if the share seems to be collapsing.

The greater the price fall, the greater is the resistance to sell, as a higher price was recently available. Therefore, it is important to operate a stop loss system to lock in profits and avoid huge losses. This can take various forms, such as selling when the share has retreated 20% from the height since you held it, regardless if that means a profit or a loss. A share should be sold after any profit warning, as they tend to come in threes. Temporary company problems are often long-lasting. Do not try to catch the final and elusive bit of profit but sell before the top, leaving the last 10% for the next investor. Give up trying to catch the first or last 10%, as these are the most expensive 10%s in the world. Fortunes have been made by buying when the share price is in an established up trend and selling before it peaks. This may seem like buying too late and selling to early but it does capture the broad momentum of the run. Greedy people lose, as they hang on too long after the peak.

Take into account whether you want to sell in order to increase the proportion of cash held. It may be inadvisable to be more than 50% liquid, regardless of how bearish you are, as markets can bounce back strongly and, if you are mostly in cash, it is difficult to catch these good days. If you analysed correctly you should be reluctant to sell, although all shares have a price when they should be sold. However, you should sell if your analysis was wrong. Do not sell just because the share is highly-rated, if you think you can foresee a market drop or because it has gone up significantly.

20. Strategy

'The best time to invest is when you have the money. This is because history suggests it is not timing which matters, but time.'
Sir John Templeton

Decide and concentrate on a strategy, which should be in keeping with an investor's characteristics, such as experience, skill, temperament and time. There are various strategies, such as value versus growth shares, and they should reflect your priorities, for example yields, volatility and taxation. Write out your strategy and do not deviate, as whims are expensive. Note the reasons for buying a share and decide accordingly, without necessarily consulting others. Invest for maximum total return of dividends plus capital gains after taxes and inflation. Read and re-read the best books on investment regularly.

A defensive investor might split his portfolio equally into good quality equities and bonds purchased at reasonable prices. If equities rise to 60% of the portfolio, then sell 10%, and if they fall to 40%, buy 10%, thus selling in bull markets and buying in bear markets. Buy companies that are big, well known, soundly financed and have a good dividend history. Do not overpay, so buy shares on a PER of around 15 or under and this avoids official, trendy growth shares. Out of favour, large companies on a low PER can offer better value.

An aggressive investor might also split his portfolio equally into good quality equities and bonds purchased at reasonable prices. The aim is also to buy cheap markets and sell expensive markets, although this needs a certain skill. Buy growth shares very selectively. They usually have a high PER so beware paying too much, as the growth will eventually revert to the norm. Purchasing shares with a prospective PER of 20 or more increases the level of risk and they are very exposed if there is a profit warning. The evidence is that growth shares do not beat value shares and are riskier. However, large profits are available to those that buy early into the growth story and are knowledgeable about the business. Buy shares that meet your testing criteria, such as recovery opportunities, which should be unlike those of the masses.

One strategy is to select unpopular companies which are not too large but do have a good history and growth at a reasonable price. Another approach is to sieve the market down to a small number and choose the most promising opportunities.

21. This time it is different

'Markets can remain irrational longer than you can remain solvent.'
John Maynard Keynes

'The five most expensive words you will hear are 'this time it is different' ', said the guru Sir John Templeton. These words are used to justify a mania. However, markets have not fundamentally changed over the centuries because they are rooted in psychology and the pitiless laws of supply and demand. The lure of speculation is ever present. The past is being repeated today and will happen again. The trick is to understand why, when and how it happens.

People have been and always will be naïve, so will repeat past mistakes. They are sucked into a boom, convinced by 'this time it is different' argument, and buy near or at the top. They tend to hang on when the crash happens, thinking the market will recover. Despondently, they sell at the bottom. There are those who, by luck or judgement, do buy before the boom but they do not sell, also thinking that the subsequent bust is not a crash but a correction. They may even average down. They also eventually sell at the bottom and the fabulous unrealised gains available at the top are never realised. Some investors should realise their limitations and not manage their own money.

22. Trading

'Soros has taught me that when you have tremendous conviction on a trade, you have to go for the jugular.'
Stanley Druckenmiller, Soros Fund Management.

Keeping firm control over your emotions is the main ingredient to successful trading rather than cleverness. Winners know they are accountable for their performance, whereas losers think they are not and blame the market instead. It is to be expected to make some losses but if this becomes a losing streak then reduce your trading to allow the winning style to return. Alternatively, withdraw from the market for a while and even sell winning positions, as they might turn sour. You are likely to fail if your response is to try to recoup the loss. Be patient with winning shares but very impatient with losing shares.

Preset a price that you would sell because, if not, you are tempting the market to force you out at the bottom in a panic. The initial thought in a bear market is you will sell when you re-coup the cost. Then prices fall further and the thought is to sell on an initial rally. Eventually, the losses cannot be tolerated any more and the desperate cry is just sell at any price. Be as determined to make additional gains as the first gain and disregard the feeling that additions to your wealth mean progressively less to you. Alternatively, one way to remain objective is not to regard the money as real at all. View it as being unimportant and do not trade for the money itself but think about it as a game or intellectual exercise. This will reduce fear and increase your patience.

CONCLUSION

This book sets out six tools to choose shares that outperform. In summary, the business model methodology ascertains whether the company and its sector have strong competitive advantage. This results from low-cost activities/and or doing something different from the competition which adds value to the customer, who is then prepared to pay a premium price. Thus, costs are minimised and revenues are maximised, as is profit, which is the difference between the two. The company is then analysed according to how it will perform in the economic cycle; whether it offers growth at a reasonable price; and if the technical analysis and scuttlebutting are positive. These tools can be wrapped up in a simple table, as set out below, to rate a company's attractiveness overall, using some sample scores.

Company scoring using all six tools

Tool	Score*
Company business model	2
Sector business model	1
Economic cycle	3
Growth at a reasonable price	2
Technical analysis	1
Scuttlebutting	4
Overall score	2

* 1 is highest, 5 is lowest.

Examples of actual company business models scores are given in appendix 1 and 2 for Radstone Technology and Microsoft, which score 2.0 and 2.2 respectively. Next, a company might score the maximum 1 for its sector business model, if it had, inter alia, high barriers to entry and sticky customers. It fares less well, say, against the backdrop of the current stage of the economic cycle, as its recession resistance is only average, so scores 3 on this count. It is attractive, as it offers good growth in profits at a reasonable price, scoring 2 on this measure. The share price is in a strong uptrend, that looks set to continue, and scores the maximum 1 for technical analysis. Scuttlebutting proves to be limited and only scores 4. In this example, the overall score is 2 and the company is a candidate for buying.

Obviously, the scoring is subjective but it should be relatively straightforward to form a gut feeling about a company. To make it easier, an investor can express the scores of 1 to 5 in the following broad terms: very good, good, average, poor, and very poor. Such an exercise would be a very useful aid to decision-making, so that an investor can conclude that a company scores 2, or 'good', in this example. Equally important is to stay well clear of companies that score 4 or 5. The most likely time for there to be a good choice of companies scoring the maximum 1 overall should be at the end of a recession, when the green shoots of recovery are evident. Consequently, such an ideal buying opportunity can be expected to reap the greatest rewards. Lastly, always bear in mind the investment axioms of the gurus and profit from their wisdom.

APPENDIX

1. Example of a company's business model: Radstone Technology

2. How Microsoft triumphed because of its business model

Appendix 1. Example of a company's business model: Radstone Technology

Radstone Technology has a very strong business model and is a prime example of the methodology in this book. This is why it has been chosen and it was not based on its valuation at the time of writing, since this constantly changes. The first part is an analysis of its business model. This is followed by scoring the company in the table of 64 business models, as laid out in chapter 1, and the table is at the end of this appendix. The result is that it scores two out of five, which is very good. It is unlikely that any company could score one, the highest mark. It is practically impossible to find a company that scores top in all of the attributes set out in this book. The vast majority of companies score a lowly four or five and should be avoided.

Analysis of Radstone's business model

Radstone is a market leader in rugged, high-performance computer systems for the defence sector. It reinvented itself in the late 1990s, necessitated by a move in the US away from customisation to off-the-shelf procurement. It had to re-engineer its products but it provided an opportunity to use lower cost components. It is now a niche company and glued to long-term customers. This results in very strong competitive advantage and pricing power, given its differentiated, 'must-have' product. Almost half of group sales are from the US and a third from the UK. There are two divisions. The embedded computer division is three quarters of turnover but contributed 90% of 2004 profit. It is one of the two niche market leaders in the world that design and make proprietary rugged electronics for the military, including tanks, ships, submarines, aircraft and missile systems. The products range from single boards to complete boxed systems.

The electronic manufacturing division is a quarter of turnover and contributed 10% of 2004 profit. It specialises in outsourcing the manufacture of low volume, high complexity electronic circuits for third parties and also supplies Radstone's rugged computer division. It is a niche market and too small for the gorillas.

The business model

a) Embedded computer

The embedded computer market is fragmented and worth £300 million. Radstone has a 10% share and the growth prospects are substantial. Armed forces need rugged systems which can withstand the extreme temperatures, pressures, vibrations and stresses of combat. Radstone provides a 'must-have', comparatively low-cost product. This provides pricing power since it is foolish to risk the loss of lives and an extremely valuable military asset by using inferior components for marginal savings. It does not compete on price and the customer's requirements are in order of preference: performance; support in the design and build periods; quality (99.9% reliability); after sales support; and, lastly, price. Thus, the quality of the product and service are the key selling points, not price, so there is little threat of cheaper substitute products.

Radstone provides free engineers during the design phase at the customer's premises, enhancing personal contact and effectively selling new products. Demand is product driven and thus is not very dependent on the economic cycle so the company is recession resistant. Design wins over the last few years are now entering volume production. Initially, the sale of non-rugged computers is followed by 10-30 months when the customer writes software. Radstone then supplies a rugged version and goes into production. This glues the customer because this commits them from the start, since the intricate project makes changing to a competitor impractical. The average length of a contract is five years and there will be various programmes in different production cycles with good repeat orders. Strong cash flow enables a high level of research and development, driving growth, which in turn drives more research and development and so on in a virtuous circle. Conservatively, research and development is expensed, not capitalised.

Radstone has global reach for its global customers. Customers are blue chip, which is a strong endorsement. They are multinational defence contractors with an average order of £700,000. The top customers are BAE Systems, Lockheed Martin, Northrop Grumman and Raytheon. The largest order was $50 million for upgrading the multi-launch-rocket-system (MLRS). Other orders include Eurofighter, at $30 million; Firefinder radar, at $28 million; helicopter upgrade, at $20 million; and Abrams tank, at $40 million. There was also a $3 million order for a processor in a space shuttle crew return vehicle. Radstone is not overly dependent on a few customers, as the largest 20 of them provide half of sales with none representing more than 10%.

There is foreign exchange risk, primarily against the dollar, and the net exposure is hedged. Foreign exchange losses were 8% of 2003 profit, though they were nil in 2004. The US defence department can terminate projects, although this is unusual and recompense is paid. The research and development expenditure could be wasted if there is a shift away from current technology, although this is improbable. A previous shortage of first-rate design engineers has been alleviated by the demise of the TMT sector, freeing up such talent.

b) Electronic manufacturing

The electronic manufacturing division makes Radstone's own boards, which facilitates control and reliability. It also undertakes third party work, which provides a contribution to overhead costs. Competition has increased in the lower complexity market and this has adversely affected margins, to some extent, even for high-end specialist providers, such as Radstone. Electronic manufacturing is a depressed market and Radstone has embarked on a cost reduction programme.

Robust defence industry

Radstone enjoys several tailwinds that drive demand for its products. Eighty per cent of sales stem from upgrades, so the substantial installed base provides steady growth and it is not overly dependent on new systems which could be cancelled in a cut-back. Asset lives are increased thanks to re-fits. This is important, as the average US military aircraft is 22 years old and needs such work. The maximum safe operating age can reach 60 years. Upgrades are cheaper than new systems and have kept the B-52 bomber in service for 40 years, for example.

The demand for more 'smart' weapons has increased dramatically. Only 8% of bombs were smart in the 1991 Gulf War. This leapt to 66% in the 2003 Iraq war. Radstone's computers were used in the latter in various systems including radar, MLRS, F-18 advanced targeting, and patriot and cruise missiles.

Defence spending is a massive, global industry and growing strongly. It will increase in the US from $400 billion in 2004 to $500 billion by 2011. The UK defence budget will increase by 1% each year and reach £33 billion in 2006. NATO is likely to review its previous cuts and Asian annual growth is forecast to be 4%, reaching $158 billion by 2006. The amount spent on technology will increase at a faster rate than this: 5% per year compound to 2012 in the US. By then, 20% of the budget will be on electronics, compared to 18% now. The 'war on terrorism' is an attractive sound bite but is as unlikely to be won as the 'war on drugs', 'poverty' and 'crime', so the pressure for increased security and modern armed forces can be expected to be a multi-year tailwind. However, there have been some cut-backs in peripheral areas, given the sluggish economies, and more can be expected in a recession.

Major growth areas

Future defence will need fewer main battle tanks, heavy artillery and long-range, heavy bombers that were important in the Cold War. The demand will be for rapid deployment of smaller, better armed, more mobile forces, relying heavily on technology to fight rogue states and the elusive terrorist. The latter is unlikely to fade away.

There are some megatrends underway which are in Radstone's favour, given the long wish list by military forces and the public's support. It must be stressed that these are opportunities, not certainties, but they include the following. If there was a complete upgrade of the MK-48 torpedo then this could be worth up to $500 million to Radstone, although any starting contract should be under $2 million. The Abrams tank upgrade is worth $40 million to Radstone, with potential for $100 million.

There are 163 unmanned airborne vehicles (UAV) in service, which are mainly reconnaissance but the next generation will carry missiles. UAV spending will be $10 billion by 2010. There will be unmanned helicopters and planes. A third of US deep strike aircraft by 2011 will be unmanned and, astonishingly, the new F-35 fighter is expected by many to be the last manned combat aircraft. There will be resistance to the programme on logic grounds and vested interests. UAVs are very much cheaper, risk no lives, are lighter, need less armour and have increased performance with longer flights. They have an accident rate 100 times that of manned flights but the US is determined to improve this. UAVs are stuffed with technology and ideal for Radstone's computers in sensors, controls and communications.

The future combat system is a momentous programme already under development, with delivery due in 2012 to 2025. This would transform the US army by having a co-ordinated group of vehicles, UAVs and robots that would make the tank and armoured fighting vehicle largely obsolete. Highly advanced command, control, communications, computer intelligence, surveillance and reconnaissance are crucial to this system and such modern warfare and will continue to be well funded.

There is renewed interest in the 'direct attack, munition affordable seeker' that enhances the accuracy of smart weapons. Radstone's systems were used in its development phase and should benefit enormously, given the huge number of unguided weapons that could be upgraded. Significant naval forces were crucial in the Iraq war and both the UK and US have major ship building programmes. Identification of friend or foe is a real issue after numerous 'friendly fire' incidents and progress is being made on sensor tagging to improve detection.

Bolt-on acquisitions

In 2003, Radstone bought ICS, a Canadian specialist in digital signal processing (DSP) that sells mainly to the sonar and radar military markets. DSP processes analogue voice, sound and data traffic into a digital format for speed, efficiency and accuracy. This is used for infrared sighting in the Abrams tank and in radar, electronic warfare, smart weapons, sensors, radio and information displays. Radstone had some DSP products already before it bought ICS but it enhances Radstone's skills and it, in turn, can introduce rugged products to ICS. It is a high growth area and ICS made operating profits of £1 million in its interims.

Radstone bought Octec in 2004, a supplier of off-the-shelf video tracking and image processing systems to the aerospace market worldwide. This widens the range of system solutions and is highly complementary to Radstone's computer subsystem expertise. Octec's pre-tax profit was £1.1 million.

Competition

The main competitor is the Canadian DY4, which was taken over at double Radstone's PER rating. It has struggled in the larger group and has been sold again for the third time in four years. There is a considerable amount of consolidation in the industry with Curtiss-Wright, who acquired DY-4, being the most active at present. Radstone is outdistancing the other competition, such as SBS Technologies, Thales Computer and Vista Controls, since it has the broadest range of leading-edge rugged systems in the defence sector. These companies are unquoted or part of groups which do not have the rugged computers as their core business. There are four non-rugged quoted manufacturers, including Concurrent Technologies, and they are on similar or higher valuations to Radstone. Non-rugged computers are more of a commodity product, since they lack differentiation, and thus have poor pricing power. That these second division companies have a similar or higher rating implies Radstone is undervalued. The competitors for Radstone's manufacturing division are minor players and weak.

Strong management

The non-executive chairman, Rhys Williams, was an executive director of GEC and managing director of what is now BAE Systems. Directors' remuneration is generous at £784,000, or 26% of 2004 pre-tax profit. This included share option gains of £233,000. Outstanding share options and directors' service contracts are reasonable.

Fine track record

Forbes Global selected Radstone for its 2003 list of the world's 200 most successful companies outside the US, drawn from 19,000 candidates with sales below $1 billion. The criteria were rewarding shareholders and other financial performance measures. This is quite an achievement for a small company like Radstone.

EPS have trebled in the last five years. The record order book is £79 million, up from £20 million in 1998. It represents 1.8 years of 2004 sales and is deliverable over the next six years. This book continues to grow and the quality of earnings is thus high. Sales are very second half weighted and fulfilment of orders can be lumpy. The profit margin is good at 18%. The return on capital employed is a solid 23% and comfortably supports the gearing of 40%. Goodwill is now £21 million, being amortised at £0.8 million a year, and compares to equity of £33 million. The share has substantially outperformed its index since 1999, which is impressive as it is in the deeply unloved IT hardware sector. This strength confirms the market's assessment of the soundness of the business model. There is solid institutional support with a 53% holding and the directors own 2%, worth £1.5 million.

Business model table

The competitive advantage of the business model in the first column is the same as that at the start of chapter 2. This is added to Radstone's score in the second column to produce a weighted average in the third column. Thus, the competitive advantage of having a moat is rated 1 and Radstone's score for this category is 2, so the weighted average is 1.5.

	Competitive advantage	Radstone score	Radstone weighted average
	(1 highest, 5 lowest)		
1. Competitors			
1a. Barriers to entry and exit	2	2	2.0
1b. Being number one or two in the sector	2	1	1.5
1c. First and late mover advantage	2		
1d. Lack of competition	2	2	2.0
1e. Moats	1	2	1.5
1f. Threat of substitute products	2	1	1.5
2. Customers			
2a. Choosing customers	2	2	2.0
2b. Cross-selling	2	1	1.5
2c. Global reach	3	1	2.0
2d. Long-term contracts	1	1	1.0
2e. Niche player	2	2	2.0
2f. Not dependent on a few customers	2	2	2.0
2g. Owning the customer	2	1	1.5
2h. Payments in advance	4		
2i. Recurring contacts	3	2	2.5
2j. Recurring revenues	1	2	1.5
2k. Selling directly	3		
2l. Stature of customers	3	2	2.5
3. Economics of the company			
3a. Appropriate gearing	4	2	3.0
3b. Asset-backed shares	4		
3c. Bolt-on acquisitions	3	2	2.5
3d. Bull market acquisitions	4	2	3.0
3e. Changing sector and FTSE index	5		
3f. Economies of scale	2	2	2.0
3g. Feed off another's growth	2	2	2.0
3h. Good institutional and directors' shareholdings	4	2	3.0
3i. Headroom to grow	2	2	2.0
3j. High dividends	2		
3k. KISS principle	3		
3l. Low break-even point	2		
3m. One-off action provides revenue for years	2		
3n. Public perception	4		
3o. Recreate the company	2	1	1.5

3p. Strong cash flow	3	2	2.5
4. Management			
4a. Auditors, opinions and policies	3	2	2.5
4b. Changes in professional advisors	4		
4c. Conflicts of interest	2	2	2.0
4d. Corporate governance	2	2	2.0
4e. Excellent, honest, well-motivated management	2	2	2.0
4f. Follow the man when a talented director moves on	4		
4g. Modest head office	4		
4h. Past success	3	2	2.5
4i. Shareholder values	2		
4j. Something new	2	2	2.0
5. Products			
5a. Brand loyalty rather than a well-known name	2		
5b. Dumbing down of products creates niche market	4		
5c. Focus on competitive advantage	1	1	1.0
5d. Growth in profits for a decade or more	3		
5e. Launching new products	2	2	2.0
5f. Lean manufacturing	3		
5g. Like-for-like sales growth	3	2	2.5
5h. Low depreciation and amortisation	3	3	3.0
5i. Maximising profit from different revenue streams	2	3	2.5
5j. Moving up the value chain	2		
5k. Owning the standard	1	2	1.5
5l. Product differentiation	1	1	1.0
5m. Rolling out a consumer chain	3		
5n. Secondary profit zones	3		
5o. Superior product or service	2	2	2.0
5p. Supported by a famous personality	5		
5q. Unique selling point	2	2	2.0
6. Suppliers			
6a. Bargaining power over suppliers	1	2	1.5
6b. Buying opportunistically	4		
6c. Not dependent on a few suppliers	2	2	2.0
Company score average		**2**	**2.0**

Conclusion

As mentioned above, the weighted average score for Radstone is two out of five, which is very good. Note that if a business model is not applicable to Radstone then the score is left blank. In no category does Radstone score lower than a three. Readers can make use of the blank table at the start of chapter 2 to score companies in a like manner.

Appendix 2. How Microsoft triumphed because of its business model

'There are only two ways to rise in this world, either by one's one industry or the stupidity of others.'
Jean de la Bruyere, author.

Microsoft is the best example

There are many examples of how a company's business model has been the cornerstone of its success but, arguably, the best is Microsoft. It had the largest market capitalisation in the world when it exceeded $400,000,000,000 in 1999, making Bill Gates the richest man in the world, with £53 billion, and the fourth richest American of all time. Not bad, when you consider that critics joke that the only thing it invented was the scrolling wheel on the mouse. Clearly, it was doing something right and that was to concentrate on having a business model that enabled it to own the computer operating and application standards. In addition, it built a very wide and deep moat to protect its business and then scorched the earth around it. Any competitor that strayed into its profit zone was roasted and served as a lesson to others. This was hugely successful but resulted in a long, damaging and famous court case. Microsoft's strategy was very shrewd and often counter-intuitive. It did not lose the bigger picture about how to gain competitive advantage, unlike the competition.

The early years

Bill Gates and Paul Allen, the founders of Microsoft, were very lucky pioneers, being in the right place at the right time. They were young and talented in the mid-1970s when personal computers and operating standards had not been invented. They would not be so fortunate if they were starting now. There were some microcomputers but they were rudimentary since they had no disk drive, keyboard or simple programming language. Gates and Allen knew if they could format the code then they might have a computer which would be useful. However, they were not alone in this race. They realised that grabbing a customer was paramount and producing the goods was a secondary consideration. The laurels would go to the company with first mover advantage and is a common business model. The Japanese do the same and rush out a rudimentary product, like an automatic camera or video, and worry about refining it later.

Microsoft did not invent the computer language but used one that already existed, called Basic. The result was PC Basic. The competition was increasing but Microsoft could not shut them out, as it did not own the language and therefore it could not become the industry standard. However, their business model was to encourage wide adoption because it could be used on any hardware and this flexibility strengthened its position. Programmers would only have to learn one language to write software for different hardware. This is an overwhelming, unique selling point because software is complicated to use and one learning curve is enough for anyone. That was true then and is true today. However, the language was 'one size fits all', since it had to work on different machines, so it was unwieldy and had bugs.

The next step in the business model was to charge a modest, flat price that did not increase with the number of computers produced by the manufacturer. This gave them an incentive to install the language. Microsoft soon had agreements with 50 manufacturers and an army of outside programmers was writing software at no cost to itself. This success fed on itself in a virtuous circle and a critical mass was reached. Although turnover was miniscule initially, this grew to $1m by the end of the 1970s.

The turning point: thank you IBM, you fool

The personal computer market was now growing and IBM decided to become involved. This added credibility to the product, so was good news, but Microsoft did not want to be crushed, which was the fate of many competitors. IBM's next step was to invent an operating system that would make tasks much more user friendly. IBM's goal in 1980 was to do this in one year. This short time frame had far reaching consequences and is known as the '$100 billion mistake', referring to how much this was to cost IBM. It had to seek outside help to develop the operating system and this secured Microsoft's success for decades. It wanted a language from Microsoft and an operating system from Digital, which was in a position to deliver but not in the timeframe. Microsoft seized the opportunity and promised both, effectively using IBM as a distributor of its products, and crucially it wanted to own both standards.

The snag was that Microsoft did not possess an operating system but it did want first mover advantage. It acquired a 'quick and dirty' operating system, improved it somewhat, and called it MS-DOS. Foolishly, IBM let Microsoft retain ownership and the ability to license it to others, since IBM's pre-eminence made it over-confident. Within a few years, most manufacturers were installing Microsoft's systems and paying a very profitable royalty that grew inexorably with the widespread adoption of personal computers then underway. With its near monopoly, it could now increase its previous low price and charge for every installation. It seemed to have reached an unassailable position.

The first gold mine: Windows

Owning the standard for the language and operating systems was most of the battle but, to be victorious, Microsoft had to provide the application programmes, such as Word and Excel, which customers would actually use. Hence, it was dismayed in 1982 to discover that a competitor, VisiCorp, had a prototype mouse and various applications. This was the beginning of the Windows operating system and application programmes, which would make MS-DOS obsolete. Windows is easy to use by pointing with a mouse and choosing menu options. MS-DOS had an unhelpful C:> as a prompt and the user had to know what instruction to type in, which was hard and frustrating. Microsoft's response was the same as it had been with IBM earlier and promised that it had a Windows product, which it did not. This was a spoiler action aimed at buying time and stopping VisiCorp from gaining market share.

This was a successful strategy and customers held off and waited for Microsoft's product, which incredibly was not available for another eight years. Arguably, its business model thus considerably held back the development of the personal computer. VisiCorp had the better product but not a sound business model, whereas Microsoft had the reverse. VisiCorp's product was not pre-installed with new personal computers and cost an exorbitant $1,000 so locked out the mass market. It was not a universal system either, as it was designed to run on IBM personal computers, and needed expensive modification to run on others. It hindered, instead of fostered, an army of outside programmers to develop applications, as it wanted these applications for itself. Demand was thus still born, sealing VisiCorps' fate and it was taken over.

The second gold mine: applications

Microsoft eventually launched its Windows 3.0 operating system in 1990 in a fanfare of publicity, since it was crucial to let the public know it had a superior product. Its business model was to pre-install it on all personal computers. In fact, the Macintosh computer had a mouse driven, graphical user interface like Windows and applications similar to Word and Excel back in 1984 but this was incompatible with personal computers. Microsoft imitated these applications which were easy to use. The main players in applications were Lotus and Word Perfect and they chose IBM's operating system rather than Windows to try to tame Microsoft. This inadvertently played right into Microsoft's hands, as it left the field open for it to corner the applications market in personal computers with Office in 1991. Not only that, Microsoft's product used a mouse rather than the opposition's old fashioned and cumbersome keyboard. Microsoft made the switching costs inexpensive and easy. Once customers were locked in, new versions would continue to lock out the competition. If a customer could get all he wanted from Microsoft and learn just one system, then why go elsewhere? There was no other killer application or incentive to do so.

How Microsoft must have laughed at the ineptitude of competitors. It wanted its software to become the standard and so co-operated with thousands of software developers and applications that would expand the market at no cost to itself. This was the opposite strategy to that which had proved so unsuccessful at VisiCorp. Thus, users could run a vast array of programmes on Windows which was not feasible with other operating systems, such as Macintosh, IBM or Linux, which did not achieve critical mass. Windows' installed base quickly exceeded 100 million customers and Windows 95 cemented its position with sales of $1 billion a year, with huge gross profit margins. This low cost and a differentiated product produced an immensely strong business model and competitive advantage. It quickly became obvious that it would be impossible to work in an office unless the employee could use Microsoft software so was a 'must-have' skill and product. Also, once it had been learnt, this facilitated blossoming home use, aided by the growth of the internet. Microsoft has continued its stranglehold on the operating systems and applications for personal computers.

Mainframe computers

Microsoft turned its attention to capturing some of the mainframe computer market. This was achieved by networking personal computers together with a server using Windows NT, which was launched in 1991. It was a poor product compared to the market leader, Novell. Microsoft used its familiar strategy of persuading people that they should use its product. NT was upgraded in 1994 and Microsoft concentrated on what the customer wanted, such as low cost, speed, ease of use with a mouse-driven interface and being straightforward to switch. NT quickly gained market share.

The internet

Microsoft is at the fulcrum of home internet applications with communications, such as Hotmail and Messenger, small business, advertising, and selling goods and services. This is a crowded market with direct competitors such as AOL and Yahoo, as well as a myriad of secondary competitors which offer similar services, such as information. Nevertheless, Microsoft is in a key position with its software dominance, including its Internet Explorer browser. It was slow off the mark, as its focus was the personal computer operating system and applications, rather than the internet. It thought, for instance, that e-mail would not be significant, although it quickly revised its opinion.

The court case

Microsoft's defeat of Netscape resulted in a US court case, some details of which are included below. The judge concluded in 2000 that its strategy was built upon maintaining its monopoly with applications that were a barrier to entry, the key being the applications programming interface. The initial judgement was to break Microsoft in two, namely an operating system and a software company, with strict procedures. However, the decision has since been watered down with the advent of Republican power and Microsoft remains intact.

a) What are application programming interfaces and why are they important to Microsoft's strategy?

All applications need to interface with the Windows operating system and programmers need a considerable knowledge of the interface to write software. Microsoft deliberately made its operating system big and complex by developing a large number of these interfaces. This consumed a great deal of programmer expertise and time, making it difficult for them to develop versions of their applications to run on competitors' operating systems. As a result, fewer applications were developed for them and this enhanced Microsoft's dominance in operating systems.

In addition, Windows has undocumented interfaces, which are features of the operating system not made generally available to the software community. This knowledge was available to Microsoft's own applications programmers and made it easier for them to develop applications that work well with Windows in comparison to their competitors. This was one of the factors which enabled Microsoft to achieve a technical dominance and a near monopoly in not just the operating system but also in key areas of applications software.

b) Why did Microsoft start the browser war?

Internet browsers, such as Microsoft's Internet Explorer, Netscape Navigator and Opera, are not just programs to see internet documents. Like operating systems above, they also have interfaces. Therefore, it was possible to develop an application, such as an accounting system, to run on top of the Netscape browser. What is more, Netscape could run on several operating systems. Therefore, Windows would no longer be essential. Microsoft recognised this at a very early stage in the development of the internet and was determined that it must own the interfaces available to software developers. It decided to kill off the Netscape browser by using all means at its disposal.

The battle followed the usual tactics with extensive publicity and Microsoft bundling its browser with Windows 95. It then spent hundreds of millions of dollars developing its Internet Explorer browser, which was bundled with Windows 98. It was also involved in extensive manipulation of the personal computer hardware and software market using a combination of payments, inducements, favours, threats and other chicanery, many of which were determined to be illegal by the judge. This manipulation covered, inter alia, computer manufacturers, such as Apple Computer and Intel, internet access and content providers, independent software and middleware vendors.

Netscape was the clear market leader at the start but fell by the wayside. Microsoft's success in removing Netscape as a force in the browser market probably slowed down the development of internet applications, such as browser-based accounting systems which appeared several years later than otherwise might have been the case.

c) When Windows 95 first appeared, there was a button on the desktop to go to MSN, a site owned by Microsoft. Most computers supplied in 1998 had a button for AOL instead. Why did Microsoft allow a rival to take over this important market?

Microsoft granted a favour to AOL to allow its button on the desktop in 1998. This was a quid pro quo for AOL migrating its subscribers from the Netscape browser to Microsoft's Internet Explorer as part of the effort to kill off Netscape. This has largely changed now and MSN is starting to overtake AOL.

d) Why did Windows 98 need much more memory and why was it more sluggish than Windows 95?

Microsoft re-engineered the heart of Windows 95 before releasing Windows 98. This was primarily to try to prove in court that the browser could not be separated from Windows 98, when in fact it could. It rebuilt the software to intimately combine the browsing and operating system capabilities. Much of this rebuilding was for legal not technical reasons and it goes against normal software design methodology, which is to build in major new features as add-ons to save large scale software development or re-engineering. The result was that dynamic link library files were created for Windows 98 which were larger than needed, took a long time to load and required more memory than Windows 95, thereby making it slower. Consumer satisfaction thus arguably came second to maintaining a monopoly.

e) Why were personal computers poor at displaying video until recently when Intel Pentium chips had excellent video for many years?

Intel designed Pentium multimedia extensions chips with excellent video capabilities many years ago. It was trying to diversify away from chips by forming a software division, which had created video software to work with their chipset and was to be sold to several operating system vendors. Microsoft realised this was a threat to their operating system and they forced Intel to close down their software division under threat of migration of Windows to Intel's competitors' chips. Microsoft would develop all the video software and, in return, Windows would remain on the Intel chipset. In fact, Microsoft was considerably behind in video software development and its focus was elsewhere. It was not until several years later that Microsoft produced acceptable video performance in Windows.

f) Why was Java widely hailed in the mid-1990s and why do we not hear much about it now?

'You don't know how good it feels to have Microsoft come crawling on its knees to buy something from you instead of the other way around.'
Scott McNealy, CEO of Sun Microsystems.

The goal of Java was to enable people to develop programs that could run on many kinds of computers and operating systems. This was a threat to Microsoft's interface monopoly in an analogous manner to a competing browser, like Netscape. Again, Windows would not be an essential item. Microsoft countered by making subtle changes to Windows to prevent it working with standard Java and issuing their own version of Java for Windows. The effect was to remove completely the main advantage of Java, which was its portability to other operating systems. Programs developed with Microsoft's Java were confined to working only with Microsoft's operating system. This has been the subject to a long and bitter court case.

Business model table

We now score Microsoft's business model using the table in chapter 1, in the same manner as for Radstone Technology in appendix 1. Microsoft scores 2.2 out of five, which is very good. Its outstanding business model is held back because it has been so successful and resulted in serious court cases and damaging publicity. At one point, it was ordered to be split in two, threatening the whole structure of the company. Such threats may re-occur. Other negatives included non-amortisation of goodwill and hugely excessive share options.

	Competitive advantage (1 highest, 5 lowest)	Microsoft score	Microsoft weighted average
1. Competitors			
1a. Barriers to entry and exit	2	2	2.0
1b. Being number one or two in the sector	2	1	1.5
1c. First and late mover advantage	2	1	1.5
1d. Lack of competition	2	2	2.0
1.e Moats	1	1	1.0
1f. Threat of substitute products	2	3	2.5

2.	**Customers**			
2a.	Choosing customers	2	2	2.0
2b.	Cross-selling	2	2	2.0
2c.	Global reach	3	1	2.0
2d.	Long-term contracts	1	2	1.5
2e.	Niche player	2		
2f.	Not dependent on a few customers	2	2	2.0
2g.	Owning the customer	2	1	1.5
2h.	Payments in advance	4	3	3.5
2i.	Recurring contacts	3	1	2.0
2j.	Recurring revenues	1	2	1.5
2k.	Selling directly	3	3	3.0
2l.	Stature of customers	3	2	2.5
3.	**Economics of the company**			
3a.	Appropriate gearing	4		
3b.	Asset-backed shares	4	3	3.5
3c.	Bolt-on acquisitions	3	3	3.0
3d.	Bull market acquisitions	4	3	3.5
3e.	Changing sector and FTSE index	5		
3f.	Economies of scale	2	1	1.5
3g.	Feed off another's growth	2	1	1.5
3h.	Good institutional and directors' shareholdings	4	1	2.5
3i.	Headroom to grow	2	2	2.0
3j.	High dividends	2	3	2.5
3k.	KISS principle	3	4	3.5
3l.	Low break-even point	2	2	2.0
3m.	One-off action provides revenue for years	2	1	1.5
3n.	Public perception	4	4	4.0
3o.	Recreate the company	2	2	2.0
3p.	Strong cash flow	3	2	2.5
4.	**Management**			
4a.	Auditors, opinions and policies	3	3	3.0
4b.	Changes in professional advisors	4		
4c.	Conflicts of interest	2	3	2.5
4d.	Corporate governance	2	4	3.0
4e.	Excellent, honest, well-motivated management	2	2	2.0
4f.	Follow the man when a talented director moves on	4		

4g.	Modest head office	4	3	3.5
4h.	Past success	3	1	2.0
4i.	Shareholder values	2	2	2.0
4j.	Something new	2	1	1.5
5.	**Products**			
5a.	Brand loyalty rather than a well-known name	2	2	2.0
5b.	Dumbing down of products creates niche market	4		
5c.	Focus on competitive advantage	1	1	1.0
5d.	Growth in profits for a decade or more	3		
5e.	Launching new products	2	1	1.5
5f.	Lean manufacturing	3		
5g.	Like-for-like sales growth	3	2	2.5
5h.	Low depreciation and amortisation	3	2	2.5
5i.	Maximising profit from different revenue streams	2	2	2.0
5j.	Moving up the value chain	2	2	2.0
5k.	Owning the standard	1	1	1.0
5l.	Product differentiation	1	1	1.0
5m.	Rolling out a consumer chain	3		
5n.	Secondary profit zones	3	2	2.5
5o.	Superior product or service	2	1	1.5
5p.	Supported by a famous personality	5	3	4.0
5q.	Unique selling point	2	1	1.5
6.	**Suppliers**			
6a.	Bargaining power over suppliers	1		
6b.	Buying opportunistically	4		
6c.	Not dependent on a few suppliers	2		
	Company score average		**2**	**2.2**

Further information

'To write it took three months; to conceive it – three minutes; to collect the data in it – all my life.'
F Scott Fitzgerald, author of *The Great Gatsby*.

Books

Essential reading

Many of the gurus in chapter 9 on investment axioms have said what books most influenced them. The following two classics feature repeatedly.

Reminiscences of a Stock Operator, Edwin Lefevre
The Intelligent Investor, Benjamin Graham

Recommended reading

Accounting for Growth, Terry Smith
Beyond the Zulu Principle, Jim Slater
Common Stocks & Uncommon Profits, Philip Fisher
Competitive Advantage, Michael Porter
Contrarian Investment Strategies, David Dreman
Extraordinary Popular Delusions and the Madness of Crowds, Charles Mackay
Investing With The Grand Masters, James Morton
Letters to shareholders by Warren Buffett, at www.berkshirehathaway.com
Manias, Panics and Crashes, Charles Kindleberger
Market Wizards; New Market Wizards, Jack Schwager
One Up On Wall Street, Peter Lynch
The Alchemy of Finance, George Soros
The Art of War, Sun Tzu
The FT Global Guide to Investing, James Morton
The Great Crash, John Galbraith
The Money Masters; The New Money Masters, John Train
The Prince, Machiavelli
The Profit Zone, Adrian Slywotzky and David Morrison
The Templeton Touch, William Proctor
The Zurich Axioms, Max Gunther
What Works on Wall Street, James O'Shaughnessy

Broker research notes

reuters.co.uk/research

Databases

Investorease (www.investorease.com) for narrative on companies.

REFS (Really Essential Financial Statistics) (www.companyrefs.com)
for company and sector sieving.
Sharescope software (www.sharescope.co.uk) for charting.

Investor organisations

The Serious Investor Groups network (www.signet.org.uk).

John Lander, Chairman, Waterdale House, Chequers Lane, Waterdale, Watford,
WD25 0GP.
Telephone: 01923 671031, Fax: 01923 682698, E-mail: signet@btinternet.com

United Kingdom Shareholders' Association Limited (www.uksa.org.uk)

Toby Keynes, National Secretary, BM UKSA, London WC1N 3XX
Telephone: 020 8249 5923

Proshare (www.proshare.org)

Centurion House, 24 Monument Street, London, EC3R 8AQ.
Telephone: 020 7220 1730

Newspapers

The Economist, The Financial Times, Investors Chronicle.

Websites

There is a bewildering choice of websites to aid the investor. The following
selection is worth noting.

Charting

www.investtech.com

Comprehensive share information

www.advfn.com
uk.finance.yahoo.com

Company analysis

www.investorschronicle.co.uk

E-mail daily newsletter on the markets and economy:

www.dailyreckoning.com

Stock exchange announcements

www.uk-wire.com

Index

A

T

U

V

The Serious Investor Groups network

Objective

The objective of The Serious Investor Groups network (SIGNet) is to enable members to improve their investment performance from organised discussion with other investors of similar interest and experience at local meetings, specialist groups and via the web.

Membership of a group helps an investor to increase confidence in their investment decisions. An open mind and an ability to listen to others are assets. The emphasis is on investment techniques and knowledge rather than tips.

Key features

- Local groups across the country, usually meeting monthly. Small enough to allow everyone to contribute.
- Specialist groups for Buffettology, technical analysis, options, etc.
- No group investment portfolio so no financial commitment. A member's investments are their own private concern.
- Newsletter reporting on activities, research and topics relevant to private investors.
- Web site with information, research, links and bookshop.
- Discounts on products and services - software, training, exhibitions and publications.

Independent

SIGnet is an independent association of serious private investors and it is not a pressure group. Members' details are treated as confidential.

Membership

There is a free trial membership period. The annual subscription is £25. For more details or trial membership please complete and despatch the slip below or apply on the website signet.org.uk. Alternatively, call The Chairman, John Lander, on 01923 671031; fax 01923 682698, e-mail signet@btinternet.com.

I am interested in more details/trial membership of SIGnet

Name . . . .

Address . . . .

. . . .

. . . .

. . . .

. . . .

Telephone . . . . e-mail . . . .

Please send to SIGnet, Waterdale House, Chequers Lane, Watford, WD25 0GP.